APPLICATIONS OF QUANTUM COMPUTING IN A VARIETY OF DOMAINS

APPLICATIONS OF QUANTUM COMPUTING IN A VARIETY OF DOMAINS

Gunjan Mukherjee, PhD
Biswadip Basu Mallik, PhD
Rahul Kar
Özen Özer, PhD
Digvijay Pandey, PhD
Binay Kumar Pandey, PhD
Editors

AAP | APPLE ACADEMIC PRESS

First edition published 2026

Apple Academic Press Inc.
1265 Goldenrod Circle, NE,
Palm Bay, FL 32905 USA

760 Laurentian Drive, Unit 19,
Burlington, ON L7N 0A4, Canada

CRC Press
2385 NW Executive Center Drive,
Suite 320, Boca Raton FL 33431

4 Park Square, Milton Park,
Abingdon, Oxon, OX14 4RN, UK

Apple Academic Press exclusively co-publishes with CRC Press, an imprint of Taylor & Francis Group, LLC

Library and Archives Canada Cataloguing in Publication

CIP data on file with Canada Library and Archives

Library of Congress Cataloging-in-Publication Data

CIP data on file with US Library of Congress

ISBN: 978-1-998511-04-4 (hbk)
ISBN: 978-1-998511-05-1 (ebk)
DOI: 10.1201/9781998511051

About the Editors

Dr. Gunjan Mukherjee
Associate Professor in the Department of Computational Sciences, Brainware University, Kolkata, India

Dr. Gunjan Mukherjee is currently working as an Associate Professor in the Department of Computational Sciences, Brainware University, Kolkata, India. He completed his BSc in physics from Calcutta University, MCA from IGNOU, MTech from Calcutta University, and PhD degree in engineering from Jadavpur University, West Bengal. His research interests include computer vision, machine learning, soft computing, image processing, etc. He is a life member of the Computer Society of India (CSI), the Internet Society (ISOC), and the International Association of Engineers (IAENG). He has published a number of papers in different journals and international conferences of repute. Dr. Mukherjee has also guided many BTech and MCA students in their projects and research works. He also authored the school computer book series (class 3 to 10) under his sole authorship, a textbook on IT systems theory for engineering students, and is presently writing a book on python technology (in press). He is currently attached to a reputed publishing house for publication of question-and-answer-based books for diploma and engineering level students. He has also acted as a reviewer for many technical books. He worked as an assistant teacher at the Sree Aurobindo Institute of Education, as an education officer at CSI, Kolkata chapter, as a senior faculty in NIT Ltd, and as a lecturer at the Calcutta Institute of Technology, respectively. He also served as a visiting faculty at Aliah University, Techno India College and JIS College.

Dr. Biswadip Basu Mallik
Professor,
Department of Basic Science and Humanities,
Institute of Engineering & Management, University of Engineering and Management, Kolkata, India.

Dr. Biswadip Basu Mallik is currently a Professor of Mathematics in the Department of Basic Science & Humanities at the Institute of Engineering & Management, University of Engineering and Management, Kolkata, India. With more than 23 years of experience in teaching and research, he has published numerous research papers and book chapters in scientific journals from esteemed international publishers, including CRC Press, Wiley, Springer, IGI Global, Nova Science, and IEEE. Dr. Basu Mallik has authored five undergraduate-level books on Engineering Mathematics, Quantitative Methods, and Computational Intelligence. He has also published five Indian patents and edited twenty-two books. His research interests include Computational Fluid Dynamics, Mathematical Modeling, Optimization, and Machine Learning. He serves as the Series Editor for the book series titled *Mathematics and Computer Science*, published by Wiley-Scrivener, USA. He is the Managing Editor of the *Journal of Mathematical Sciences & Computational Mathematics* (JMSCM), USA. Additionally, Dr. Basu Mallik is an Editorial Board member and reviewer for several scientific journals. He holds senior life membership in the Operational Research Society of India (ORSI) and life membership in the Calcutta Mathematical Society (CMS), Indian Statistical Institute (ISI), Indian Science Congress Association (ISCA), and the International Association of Engineers (IAENG).

Rahul Kar
Faculty of Mathematics, Kalyani Mahavidyalaya, Kalyani, Nadia, West Bengal, India

Rahul Kar is currently working as a faculty of Mathematics at Kalyani Mahavidyalaya, Kalyani, Nadia, West Bengal, India. He completed his MSc in Pure Mathematics and pursuing a PhD in Mathematics from Bankura University. He worked as a guest faculty at the Gurunanak Institute of Technology and other two colleges. In total, he has eight years of teaching experience. He has published many research papers indexed by Scopus. He is also working as an editor of four national and international journals and reviewer for five international journals. He is working as an editor of 15 mathematics/computer books. He is an annual member of the Indian Mathematical Society as well as an honorary member of the Carmels Research Institute, Dakar, Senegal.

Prof. Dr. Özen Özer
Full Professor, Department of Mathematics, Faculty of Science and Arts, Kırklareli University, Turkey

Prof. Dr. Özen ÖZER completed her bachelor's and master's degrees in Mathematics at Trakya University in Edirne, Turkey and earned her PhD in Mathematics (Number Theory) from Süleyman Demirel University in Isparta, Turkey. She has been serving as a full Professor of Mathematics at Kırklareli University, Faculty of Science and Arts, Kırklareli Province, Turkey. for more than two years.

Her research spans a broad spectrum of mathematical and computational fields, including real quadratic number fields, diophantine equations and diophantine sets, arithmetic functions, matrix theory, fixed point theory, p-adic and q-analysis, C*-algebras, Nonlinear analysis, optimization and approximation theory, cryptography, artificial intelligence, machine learning, mathematical modeling, differential equations, statistics, fuzzy systems, engineering mathematics, etc.

Prof. Özer has authored over 100 peer-reviewed research articles published in reputable international journals, contributed to or authored more than 20 books and book chapters, and participated in multiple national and international scientific projects. She has presented over 120 papers and has been invited as a keynote or plenary speaker at numerous international conferences.

She serves as a reviewer for more than 85 journals and publishing houses, and she actively contributes as an editor, guest editor, and editorial board member for academic books, journals, and conference proceedings. Her scientific work reflects a strong commitment to interdisciplinary collaboration, and she continues to engage in research activities that bridge mathematics, computation, and emerging technologies.

Dr. (h.c) Digvijay Pandey
Senior Lecturer, Department of Technical Education Kanpur, Government of Uttar Pradesh, India

Dr. Digvijay Pandey is a distinguished academic and researcher in the field of Electronics Engineering, currently serving as a Senior Lecturer under the Department of Technical Education . Recognized among the world's top 2% scientists by Stanford University for both 2024 and 2025, Dr. Pandey brings a wealth of expertise and dedication to technical education and research. He holds a PhD in Electronics Engineering from Dr. A.P.J. Abdul Kalam Technical University, Lucknow, and a Master of Technology in Digital Systems and Design from Kamla Nehru Institute of Technology (KNIT), Sultanpur. His foundational engineering education was completed with a Bachelor of Technology in Electronics Engineering from the Institute of Engineering and Rural Technology (IERT), Allahabad. Dr. Pandey has made significant contributions across both academic and industry domains. His early academic career included teaching at his alma mater, IERT Allahabad. He also brought his technical expertise to the corporate sector through his role as an IT Analyst and Technical Expert at Tata Consultancy Services, where he was actively involved in campus recruitment and talent development initiatives.A passionate educator and mentor, Dr. Pandey is deeply committed to student development, research excellence, and academic innovation. His active involvement in a range of social, academic, and research endeavors highlights his multifaceted contributions to the field and underscores his status as a valuable asset to the technical education ecosystem.

Dr. Binay Kumar Pandey
Department of Information Technology, College of Technology, Govind Ballabh Pant University of Agriculture and Technology Pantnagar, Udham Singh Nagar, Uttarakhand, India

Prof. Binay Kumar Pandey is an Assistant Professor (Selection Grade) in the Department of Information Technology at Govind Ballabh Pant University of Agriculture and Technology, Pantnagar, Udham Sing Nagar, Uttarakhand, India. He is a life member of the Indian Society for Technical Education (ID-LM 90463), a life member of the Institution of Engineers (India) (Id. No. 1685295), and a member of the ACM Association for Computing Machinery (9809629). He has six book chapters and more than 90 research papers published in UGC/SCI/Scopus indexed journals. He has presented several research papers at national and international conferences. He is currently guiding one MTech student and has previously guided 12 MTech students. He served as a session chair at the *IEEE International Conference on Advent Trends in Multidisciplinary Research and Innovation* (ICATMRI-2020). He has three patents that have been published in *The Patent Office Journal*, and one that is currently being processed in the *Australian Patent Office Journal*. He serves as a reviewer for several prestigious Springer Publication journals, including *Environmental Monitoring and Assessment, Regenerative Engineering and Translational Medicine,* sleep and vigilance. Image processing, text extraction, biomedical image processing, and information security are among his research interests.

Contents

Contributors

Sudipta Adhikary
Department of Law, Brainware University, Kolkata, West Bengal, India

Shirley Chellathurai Pon Anna Bai
Department of Computer Science and Engineering, Karunya Institute of Technology and Sciences, Coimbatore, Tamil Nadu, India

Sundaravadivazhagan Balasubramanian
Department of Information Technology, University of Technology and Applied Sciences, Al Mussanah, Oman

Kaushik Banerjee
Department of Law, Brainware University, Kolkata, West Bengal, India

Mohamed Imran Kareem Basha
Department of Computer Application, Merit Haji Ismail Sahib, Arts and Science College, Pernambut, Vellore, Tamil Nadu, India

Romit S. Beed
Department of Computer Science, St. Xavier's College (Autonomous), Kolkata, West Bengal, India

Tamal Chakraborty
Department of Computer Science, Mrinalini Datta Mahavidyapith, Kolkata, West Bengal, India

Kaushik Chanda
Department of Computational Sciences, Brainware University, Kolkata, West Bengal, India

Yongqing Chang
College of Marxism, Xingtai Polytechnic College, Xingtai, Hebei, China

Panem Charanarur
Department of Cyber Security & Digital Forensics, National Forensic Sciences University, Goa Campus, Goa

Subha Shree C. V.
Department of Bio-Engineering, Vels Institute of Science, Technology & Advanced Studies, Chennai, Tamil Nadu, India

K. Dhanalakshmi
Department of Computer Science and Engineering, PSNA College of Engineering and Technology, Dindigul, Tamil Nadu, India

Elakkiya Elango
Department of Computer Science, Government Arts and Science College for Women, Sivaganga, Tamil Nadu, India

Debosree Ghosh
Department of Computer Science and Engineering, Swami Vivekananda Institute of Science and Technology, West Bengal, India

Rakesh Gnanasekaran
Department of Computer Science, Thiagarajar College, Madurai, Tamil Nadu, India

Partha Sarathi Goswami
Department of Cyber Forensics and Information Security, Behala Government Polytechnic, Kolkata, West Bengal, India

Srinivasa Rao Gundu
Department of Computer Sciences, School of Sciences, Malla Reddy University, Hyderabad, India

Ahamed Lebbe Hanees
Department of Computer Science, South Eastern University of Sri Lanka, Sammanthurai, Sri Lanka

Manikandan J.
Department of Information Technology, St. Joseph's College of Engineering, OMR, Chennai, Tamil Nadu, India

Biswadip Basu Mallik
Department of Basic Science and Humanities, Institute of Engineering & Management, University of Engineering and Management, Kolkata, India

Marc Maußner
Business Unit Industry, infoteam Software AG, Bubenreuth, Germany

Gnanasankaran Natarajan
Department of Computer Science, Thiagarajar College, Madurai, Tamil Nadu, India

K. Jayashree
Department of Artificial Intelligence and Data Science, Panimalar Engineering College, Chennai, Tamil Nadu, India

Balasubramanian Shanmuganathan
DDE, Alagappa University, Karaikudi, Tamil Nadu, India

Rupali Mitra
Department of Computer Science, Mrinalini Datta Mahavidyapith, Kolkata, West Bengal, India

Gunjan Mukherjee
Department of Computational Sciences, Brainware University, Kolkata, West Bengal, India

Hemalatha P.
Vel Tech Rangarajan Dr.Sagunthala R&D Institute of Science and Technology, Chennai, Tamil Nadu, India

Suman Patra
Department of Physics, Netaji Nagar Day College, Kolkata, West Bengal, India

S. Ivo Romauld
Department of Bio-Engineering, Vels Institute of Science, Technology & Advanced Studies, Chennai, Tamil Nadu, India

Jayasuryan S.
Department of Bio-Engineering, Vels Institute of Science, Technology & Advanced Studies, Chennai, Tamil Nadu, India

Meenambiga S. S.
Department of Bio-Engineering, Vels Institute of Science, Technology & Advanced Studies, Chennai, Tamil Nadu, India

Gurpreet Singh
Computer Science & Engineering, Guru Kashi University, Talwandi Sabo, Punjab, India

Sukhpreet Singh
Department of Computer Applications, Guru Kashi University, Talwandi Sabo, Punjab, India

P. Vivek
Department of Bio-Engineering, Vels Institute of Science, Technology & Advanced Studies, Chennai, Tamil Nadu, India

Abbreviations

AI	artificial intelligence
APN	absolute pulse number
AQCs	annealing-based quantum computers
a-VQE	accelerated VQE
BNS	beam splitting attack
CGA	conventional genetic algorithms
CL	channel loss
CNN	convolution neural networking
CNOT	controlled NOT
DAC	direct air capture
DE	differential evolution
EAC	environment apperceive coefficient
ECC	elliptic curve cryptography
EDA	exploratory data analysis
EDA	estimation of distribution algorithms
EER	equal error rate
EPR	Einstein–Podolsky–Rosen
GA	genetic algorithms
GANs	generative adversarial networks
GCA	general collective attack (GCA)
GLCM	gray level co-occurrence matrix
GPUs	graphical processing units
GRASP	greedy randomized adaptive search procedure
HHL	Harrow–Hassidim–Lloyd
IoT	Internet of Things
IQP	instantaneous quantum polynomial-time
KDM	key distribution mechanism
ML	machine learning
MOFs	metal–organic frameworks
MPC	multivariate polynomial cryptography
NERC	North American Electric Reliability Council
NISQ	noisy intermediate-scale quantum computer
NWP	numerical weather prediction
OPF	optimal power flow
PES	potential energy surfaces
PLM	product lifecycle management

PNS	photon number splitters
PQC	parameterized quantum circuit
PSO	particle swarm optimization
PSP	partner selection problem
PV	photovoltaic
QA	quantum annealing
QAgents	quantum agents
QAOA	quantum adiabatic optimization algorithms
QAOA	quantum approximation optimization algorithm
QBMs	quantum Boltzmann machines
QC	quantum computing
QCA	quantum dot cellular automata
QEA	quantum-inspired evolutionary algorithm
QGA	quantum-inspired genetic algorithm
QGANs	quantum generative adversarial networks
QKD	quantum key distribution
QKP	quadratic knapsack problem
QML	quantum machine learning
QNLP	quantum natural language processing
QNNs	quantum neural networks
QPCA	quantum principal component analysis
QPE	quantum phase estimation
QRAM	quantum random access memory
QRL	quantum reinforcement learning
QSVD	quantum singular value decomposition
QSVM	quantum support vector machines
Qubits	quantum bits
QUBO	quadratic unconstrained binary optimization
RBF	radial basis function
RSA	Rivest–Shamir–Adleman
SAN	system area networks
SCA	specific collective attack
SHA-3	secure hash algorithm
SVM	support vector machine
TSP	traveling salesman problem
UAVs	unmanned aerial vehicles
USD	unambiguous state discrimination
VE	virtual enterprise
VGE	variational quantum eigensolver
vQEA	versatile quantum-inspired evolutionary algorithm
WRF	weather research and forecasting

Preface

The book *Applications of Quantum Computing in a Variety of Domains* aims to provide a comprehensive overview of the rapidly evolving field of quantum computing and its diverse applications across various domains. The triumph of such computing field over the traditional and conventional classical computing has been the marked achievement which will certainly bring about some new direction of research to the forefront. Quantum computing has emerged as one of the most promising frontiers in computer science, promising to revolutionize computation by leveraging the principles of quantum mechanics to perform complex calculations at speeds unattainable by classical computers. As this technology progresses, it has the potential to tackle some of the most challenging problems in science, engineering, finance, healthcare, and beyond. The attainment of intermediate levels of computations has become the backbone of future research works.

In this book, we have gathered insights from leading experts and researchers to explore the fundamental concepts of quantum computing, delve into the latest advancements in quantum algorithms and hardware, and examine the practical applications of quantum computing across a range of industries and social media. We begin by laying the groundwork with an introduction to the principles of quantum mechanics and quantum computation, providing readers with a solid understanding of the theoretical underpinnings of quantum computing. From there, we delve into the various quantum computing models, architectures, and algorithms, highlighting their unique advantages and challenges.

Since the diversification of quantum field is very huge and challenging to some extent, the scope of discussion of such a subject can be broadened up by including some significant application scopes which has been the major subject of this book. The salient parts of the quantum computing which we have covered in this book are applications of quantum computing in the field of *computer security, manufacturing and industrial design, application in financial sectors, cyber security, drug manufacturing,* etc. The potentiality of research works in the field of quantum computing has proved to pave a promising field and has been discussed elaborately in this book. The practical consideration of the scenarios and some important aspects of quantum computing fields with some aberrations like error corrections and cubit coherence have been discussed in this book in detail. Overall, the book caters to readers of different categories with a good insight on the subject in an easy approach so that the entire subject can be grasped very lucidly. Students pursuing higher degrees or research works will find the book extremely useful. Moreover, the book will cater hugely to professionals in different quantum fields the book must cater hugely to the professionals in quantum fields.

CHAPTER 1

Practical Quantum Cryptographic Architecture: A Perspective Approach

SRINIVASA RAO GUNDU[1*], PANEM CHARANARUR[2], and BISWADIP BASU MALLIK[3]

[1]*Department of Computer Sciences, School of Sciences, Malla Reddy University, Hyderabad, India*

[2]*Department of Cyber Security & Digital Forensics, National Forensic Sciences University, Goa Campus, Goa*

[3]*Department of Basic Science and Humanities, Institute of Engineering & Management, University of Engineering and Management, Kolkata, India*

*Corresponding author

ABSTRACT

We now have a safe way to communicate, thanks to quantum key distribution (QKD). In recent years there have been the emergence of brand-new challenges in the realm of QKD. Let us take a look at the analysis of the study on the topic of QKD. This research informs us that protected keys cannot be created when a weaker laser is used as the source of the photons, so let us look at that. The sequential unambiguous state discrimination (USD) attack, a variation of the photon number splitting (PNS) attack, is at fault for this issue. The mechanism used to generate keys must have a higher security level. An experiment based on superconducting single photon detector (SSPD) was reported, in which a differential phase shift of 10 GHz was applied to a clock utilized for QKD. We can produce protected keys using a 10-GHz clock system due to the minimal timing jitter and low

Applications of Quantum Computing in a Variety of Domains. Gunjan Mukherjee, Biswadip Basu Mallik, Rahul Kar Özen ÖZER, Digvijay Pandey, and Binay Kumar Pandey (Eds.)

DOI: 10.1201/9781998511051-1

dark count rate provided by the SSPD. For us to scatter protected keys against sequential USD attacks across 200 km of fiber with a channel loss of 42.1 dB and general collective attacks for single photons, we needed to use thread. In addition, the protected key rate that we accomplished at 105 km was 17 kilobits per second, far greater than the previous record by two orders of magnitude. If we could do this, it would be a significant step forward in our capacity to understand the interrelationships of cities in real time. Installation of a QKD system and a worldwide QKD system using geostationary satellites. It is essential to consider that the 30–35 dB channel loss is enough for most geo-synchronized satellites.

1.1 INTRODUCTION

Let us pick two different persons who are essential for us to talk about, the first one is Alice (the Sender), the second one is Bob (the Receiver), and the third one is Eve (the intruder).

1. For the time being, let us pretend that "Alice" (The Sender) sends a message to Bob (The Receiver), a secret decryption key based on the concept of "polarized photons" that have been entwined.
2. If so, "Bob" (who exactly is the recipient) then receives them and, using the computations provided by, verifies the key polarization.
3. At the moment, once the Bob (Receiver) transmits back the signal, the polarization is measured. The computed key determines how the polarization values are set.
4. Alice after that, (the Sender) will deliver the concept to every recipient.
5. The recipient transmits the premise based on the fact that the photon was polarized. The polarization of each photon was determined in the experiment.
6. With Alice verifies the values of these individual photons, of which there are many, for each Alice. Both Bob and I formed the polarization using the same foundation, and we both lived it.

Any violation of these ideals should warn them that a covert infiltration operation will be carried out by "Eve" (The Intruder) for the technique to be abandoned and the beginning of the new procedure to be made. This method uses "photons" to transmit as a communication key in this period instance. Because the keys were sent, communication between the parties, the Alice and Bob, is now possible, respectively. In this situation, the no-cloning principle ensures Eve lives with the key in the wrong place [1].

This could be because of Eve's implication, which results in a shift in the direction of polarity photons. Because of the polarization of the photon, we will only be able to do 1, the smallest unit of data that may be sent. Therefore, the rate of crucial generation is then tightened the reins on. Photon number splitting (PNS) attacks are especially likely to be successful against it. The QKD protocol creates a secure channel for our communications [2].

When it comes to the distribution of quantum keys in the modern world, there are several new problems that need to be overcome. The most current one will be able to obtain QKD by using a channel loss of 40 dB. Let us look at the research that has been done on the distribution of quantum keys, as well as the analysis that has been done on it. When it comes to the distribution of keys in quantum, we often make use of something that is referred to as "protected keys." Distribution is based on a channel loss of 42 dB and an optical distance of 200 km of fiber [3, 4].

In order to carry out the operation with the assistance of a clock frequency of 10 GHz, in addition to the assistance of superconducting single photon detector (SSPDs), it is required to make use of a technique of QKD that is based on a differential phase shift protocol (DPS-QKD). This method of QKD is referred to as DPS-QKD, which is the name given to this approach, which is carried out using NbN nanowire. The SSPD offers a significantly reduced dark count rate in a small number of hertz (Hz) of frequency as well as a small amount of fluctuation in the length of a full width of 60 ps when measured at half the maximum. Because of these features, it is conceivable to create a QKD environment capable of working at 10 GHz. As a result of this, it is possible to disseminate keys that are safe within the channel while experiencing a loss of 42 dB in signal strength. In addition, the protected key rate (PKR) will be 17 kbits per second. A total of 105 km of fiber optical cable, which is comparable to two orders of magnitude more than the previous record, as well as a secure key with a bit rate of 12.1 bits per second rate over 200 kilometers of optical fiber, have not been accomplished as of yet and have not been proved [5]. This particular terrestrial QKD is the longest one that can be obtained at the moment.

The secrets of the keys that are generated via the use of this program are safely kept. Because of this, a general collective attack (GCA) and a specific collective attack (SCA) were launched against both the unique and multiple photons. GCA and SCA are both abbreviations for "collective attack." The sequential USD attack is the name given to this technique when it is discussed in technical contexts. Even if the first quantum research on key distribution was to be carried out with the assistance of just one meter, it was claimed that a free space transmission line would still be built. In BB84, they are used on a consistent basis in various ways. It is required to cut down on the overall amount of laser light that is utilized in the production of the protocols, which may be found at protected keys, which could not be created for reasons that are now unclear. It is vulnerable to an attack that makes use of photon number splitting, often known as PNS. The Sniffer or eavesdropper, also known as Eve, is now taking into consideration the quantum nondemolition measurement, which is carried out on each feeble simultaneous pulse that is produced [6].

Eavesdropper is going to provide you with a notice in the event that it finds anything that has more than one occurrence. Despite its small size, a photon can be broken down into its component parts using the eavesdropper in a single operation. Photon in her quantum memory, and after that, she transfers the other photons to the Bob, functioning as the Receiver, which assured that she experienced no data loss during the whole of the transfer across the transmission line. This was accomplished by moving the photons to the Bob. As soon as eavesdropper realized what was taking on, he immediately set up a measurement basis communication channel between the individual who was giving the message and the individual who was receiving it. This was accomplished with the help of members of the general public. The receiver, also known as the snoop, would be able to construct a "prospective" photon moment of measurement for a photon that has been stored, and as a result, they would get a comprehensive understanding of the rhythm [7].

The eavesdropper does not have any effect on the polarization of photons and does not change the polarization of photons in any manner when this procedure is taking place. The BB84 protocol, which may also be reduced to the "Bennet and armour plate Protocol" of the QKD environment, has not totally gained what it needed as a result of the fact that this is the case. This is because of the "Bennet and armor plate Protocol." This is the situation that has arisen because the BB84 protocol has not fully achieved what it needs, successful, but they did discover a means to get through a handful of the security system's weak points and exploit the issues. In order to protect ourselves against attacks of this kind, we have no choice but to make use of the PNS as a defensive mechanism; only we have access to a single source of photons in their arsenal. As a direct consequence of this, everyone was forced to reassess the merits of their stance. QKD when it comes to the question of where individual photons come from, BB84 makes an effort that is comparable to the one that came before it. The technique was used, but the PKR ended up being much lower than expected [8, 9].

One such method for finding potential new processes that may be Decoy State is to look for a method that enables powerful attacks to be carried out on the side of PNS. Protocol-BB84 or DSP-BB84 as it is more often known, is a name that is sometimes also used. Decoy Pulses, often known as DPs for short, are being shown in this section. A rate (BR) of approximately 0.1 bit/s has been presented after being randomly positioned within the boundaries of whose average photon the absolute pulse number (APN) is higher than the total number of signal pulses in the latest protected key distribution distance of 107 km with a little bit of time in our research. The most recent findings by scientists were made possible through research using sensors that employ superconducting transition-edge technology (superconducting transition edge sensors). If the method of differential phase shift QKD is used, then it is possible to use many levels to represent the quantum state of a single photon. This is one of the advantages of using this method, pulses emitted by a continuously operating laser source [10].

The changes that Alice made are in no way connected to one another. The specific pulse phases for each signal that were created by the accountable party using the notation 0 in each case. As a consequence of the adjustment that is made to the pulse's strength, the standard deviation of the number of photons that are included inside each pulse has the potential to change from one to either one or zero. Bob is prepared to begin using a one-bit delayed Mach–Zehnder interferometer that currently has two output ports that are being sought after now that everything has been set up properly by using two distinct photon detectors working in conjunction with one another. The detector will provide 0 (1) clicks to signal that there is no phase difference between two subsequent pulses when there is no phase difference between them. In contrast to the past, when Bob's detectors only clicked one at a time, they are now capable of clicking many times in rapid succession. This is because the specific number of photons that are included inside each pulse is now lower than it was before. Bob provided precise time periods during which he saw the clicks to Alice by employing the public communication channel, and Alice spoke with Bob at the same time, keeping the information that was received by the detector. Since Alice applied the data about the initial modulation and transmission about the time instance, she is aware of which sensor was active at those specific moments of time. Bob's webpage [11].

Because of this, Alice and Bob are both able to make contributions to a similar bit string, which has the ability to act as a key for a one-time pad. As a result of this, both of their contributions will be valid. When a PNS attack is carried out, it is the responsibility of the QND to communicate any bit defects that have occurred to the eavesdropper. This is because a measurement of QND carried out on two consecutive multiple pulses may be used to divide the consistency of a multiple-pulse quantum. Eve has the ability to lessen the possibility that a mistake will be made. (Explanation is supplied between brackets) Even though time was measured using a QND, it is possible to keep the element of chance by increasing the number of pulses that are given at the same instant [12].

When Eve clicks on the detector more than once, the likelihood that she will get the essential information decreases, which in turn leads the wave function to collapse right then and there. When it does happen to Bob, it does so in a way that is not just arbitrary, but also in a way that cannot be predicted with certainty. In addition to the wave packets that Eve had already despatched. Let us assume, just for the purpose of the argument, that evesdropper has access to some kind of apparatus that can determine the possibility that the PNS will come under assault. During the course of this time period, the "information" will appear on the screen for an undetermined number of times at various intervals. Chunk that Eve may obtain by using a PNS assault may be represented by the symbol 2M, where M stands for the APN, which is also known as pulse. Chunk' may also be referred to as a "chunk." Chunk is an abbreviation for "chunk," which is an acronym that stands for "photon number." In this circumstance, Eve may also try to carry out an optimal quantum measurement attack, on the proportion of photons that are directed toward Bob. Let us call it pc0, which is an abbreviation for the likelihood that there will be a collision [13].

$$Pc0 <= 1-e2 - (1-6e2)/2 \tag{1.1}$$

where every bit is bounded. Where the e- is the system's innocent bit error rate. At that moment, considering a twofold attack consisting of a PNS attack and an optimal quantum measurement attack, the upper bound of the collision probability of n-bit shifted key Pc could be written as

$$Pc<=(Pc0)n(1-2T)=(1-e2-1-6e2/2)n(1-2\ T) \tag{1.2}$$

$$T=-(1-2\ T)\log 2(1-e2-1-6e2/2) \tag{1.3}$$

Then the PKR R pro will be decreased from the shifted key rate R shift as per the equation,

$$Rpro=Rshift(T+f(e)h(e)) \tag{1.4}$$

Here h(e)=–e log 2 e– (1–e)log2 (1–e) will be a binary entropy function, and f(e) characterizes the performance of the error correction algorithm.

Calculating the PKRs may be done with the help of the graph that is located at the very top of the page (Figure 1.1). PKR vs channel loss (CL) in connection to DPS-QKD with the assistance of well known and consistent lasers and BB84, which utilized single photon sources with a range of properties. This was done with the aid of well known and consistent lasers. Let us make the assumption that the identical detector is being used in this specific investigation as a part of an inquiry that is now being carried out by our analysts inside the scope of an experiment. Let us consider the following: It is required that the quantum efficiency be 1.4%, the dark count rate be 50 Hz, the duration be a window width of 50 ps, and the time be sufficient to induce a decline of 36% in the effective quantum effectiveness. Because an error-free implementation of the BB84 protocol environment is a method of active demodulation that does not result in any additional loss, Bob could only use two single-photon detectors in his experiment [14]. This was because Bob's experiment was designed to investigate whether or not it is possible to detect a single photon.

PROTECTED KEY PULSE	CHANNEL LOSS
10	0
10	50
100	100
100	150
10000	200
100000	250
10000000	300
10000000	350

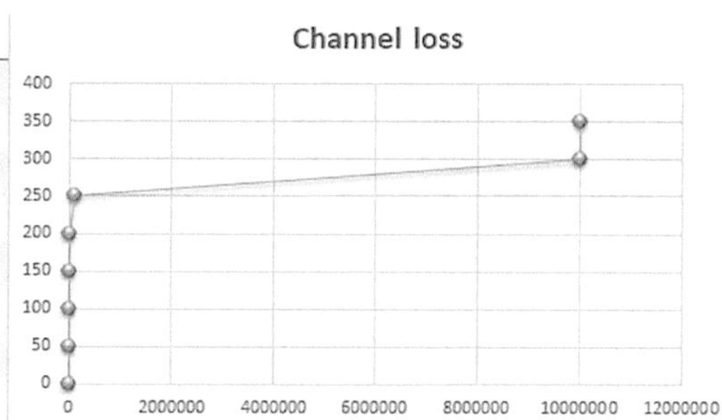

FIGURE 1.1 Protected key rates (PKR) vs channel loss.

Even in its most degraded form, the DPS-QKD method is superior to the BB84 technique in terms of the CL it causes. The study that is now available and is based on trials has shown that the efficacy of employing a single photon source with a g(2) (0) value of 10-5 and an efficiency of equal to one is far higher than what has been shown by the trial-based research. As a direct consequence of the findings acquired from our earlier scientific investigation, the system configuration for the 10-GHz clock has been given the term DPS-QKD as the name given to it by the scientific community. A laser's output may produce a continuous wave and a clock pulse with a frequency of 10 GHz. The frequency of the clock pulse is measured in gigahertz. Exercise with an InGaAsP electroabsorption modulator can help you hone your existing abilities. We successfully produced pulses with a width of just 15% of their most considerable extent at their highest degree. The phase of each vibration is altered in some way by a device known as a phase modulator. A pattern generator able to create pulses at a high rate controls the operation of a modulator controlled by a pseudo-random bit pattern of 10 GHz. The pattern generator produces this pattern. A decrease in the overall quantity of photons that are produced by each pulse is brought about by an optical attenuator's value on average [15].

A unique dispersion-shifted fiber or a single attenuator may serve as the quantum channel. Bob has a screwdriver. However, it only comes with a single bit for use. The delayed interferometer is a technology that is built using planar light-wave interference as the foundation for the circuit-based technology that makes it up. According to the specs, the interferometer has a sensitivity loss of more than 2.5 dB. Each interferometer has its unique SSPD attached to the output port of that particular interferometer. The hermetically sealed detector may be housed inside a closed-cycle housing. A refrigerator that does not utilize any cryogens and has an operating temperature of 3 K, so its usage may be simplified in research that uses quantum information [16]; this refrigerator's temperature working range is likewise 3 K. The temperature working range of this refrigerator is also 3 K.

The following is a more in-depth explanation of how the detector functions: The current that is being carried by the superconducting wire is far lower than the current that may be considered to be the carrying capacity of the wire. A resistive hot spot is formed in a wire due to a photon colliding with the wire. This occurs because the collision causes the photon and the wire to come into contact. After that, the current finally reaches a level greater than the critical threshold because the current density continues to grow in the area surrounding the spot. This happens after the required entry has been crossed. A voltage pulse is formed as a direct result of a barrier not enabling superconductivity to cover the whole width of the wire, which results in the barrier preventing superconducting from covering the entire width of the wire. As a consequence, a voltage pulse is produced. We can proceed with our inquiry by distinguishing between detecting the photon at the leading edge of the voltage pulses and the moment of arrival with absolute timing accuracy [17]. This allows us to continue our research.

The SSPD's quantum efficiency and dark count rate are subject to change, whenever there is a change in the bias current. Counting individual photons, the mechanism of an avalanche photodiode, also known as an APD, is somewhat complicated (which includes absorption, diffusion, and avalanche), which causes an increase in the number of dark counts and non-Gaussian timing jitter characteristics. However, the SSPD operates on the idea of relatively straightforward, as was discussed before, which contributes to the low count. Compared to different types of detectors, the SSPD has greater rate and timing resolution properties in comparison to those of an APD. We measured the jitter in the timing of the SSPD by sending out pulses of 10 ps. The comparison may be seen in Figure 1.2c. Compared to the newly acquired histogram of the photon arrival time to one for a single photon detector based on an upconverter for higher frequencies next was a Si APD, used in our earlier DPS-QKD studies. This entails that the blue squares and the line may identify the histogram for the SSPD [18].

Additionally, the up-conversion detector is shown by the red line. Even though the jitter has a full width at half maximum value of roughly 60 ps, which is longer than the up-conversion single-photon detectors; hence, the histogram matches quite well, nicely with Gaussian, and contrary to popular belief, it does not have a long tail. Measurements were taken similarly for the up-conversion detectors. As a result, we can lower the likelihood of errors being caused by interference between symbols achieved by using SSPD. In addition to this, it was determined that the count rate of the SSPD was less than 10 Hz (usually a few Hz) at a time when the quantum efficiency was set at 0.7%, which has a very significantly reduced size in comparison to one of the up-conversion detectors performed in the same manner in terms of quantum efficiency (350 Hz at 0.4%). Based on the findings of our prior scientific studies [19], it is expected that there will be,

1. SSPD close-up picture observations made using a scanning electron microscope.

2. Fiber alignment under an optical microscope.
3. Histograms showing the arrival time of photons in SSPD, which may be seen as squares, a blue line, and a red up-conversion detector line when a pulse of 10 ps is input.

In addition, there was a relatively short time window to the data of the obtained time instances to reduce the contributions made by the dark counts and the inter-symbol interference brought on by signals from nearby sources. To demonstrate the efficiency of this method, which we have here, the quantum of both the SSPD's efficiency and dark count rate were determined to be 0.7%. The frequency that is less than 10 Hz individually and collectively, and there was a 31.7 dB loss in the channel. We were able to see that there was a signal. Because of the jitter in the detector's timing, there was some overlap in the pulses.

However, when we used 10 ps, the peaks were differentiated by time frame or window. Our study on QKD involves rearranging the quantum efficiency, dark count rate, and time width of the window at 1.4%, frequency of 50 Hz, and duration of 50 ps, respectively. The decline may be attributed to the use of the time frame approximately 36% in terms of the effective quantum efficiency. The protection that gained significance is shown in the following tables and graphs. This most recent result will significantly influence the previous quantum study of key distribution conducted in protected key, and the generation rate and the distribution distance are essential to consider.

At 105 miles, we successfully created protected keys at a distance rate of 17 kilobits per second, two times that of the standard rate of greater by orders of magnitude than any of our previous records, which were 166 bits each second while traveling at 100 km. If we transmit signals through a 200 km long fiber optic cable and analyze them, we may be able to generate protected keys at a rate of 12 bits per second. for the bit rate. The most significant channel loss for producing protected keys was 42.1 dB, a more excellent value, a level other than 20 dB louder than the previous long-distance studies on QKD are being conducted. Now that we have some time, with the assistance of GCA, we will analyze the protection. in the case of singular photons.

Let us think about how we might defend ourselves against an assault carried out in sequence and using USD as we go along in this conversation. Let us pause here for a minute and consider the following: The predicament brought on by the erroneous idea that the evesdropper had a local oscillator that is "phase-locked" to the constant light source. Alice is the one who is responsible for providing the authorization to access the source. Given the fact that there is a chance of 0.5, eavesdropper is now in a position to establish which of the two is the pulse regulated by either 0 or 1, as the case may be. When Eve reaches m (>M) with the support of the positive findings from a series of measurements, the evesdropper generates a large number of stable pulses while maintaining phase modifications determined by the results of the measurements, which are then sent to Bob. When Eve achieves m (>M), the helpful discoveries from the sequence of measurements help her achieve this milestone. When Eve has accomplished her mission, which is represented by the symbol m (=M), the results of subsequent measurements along with the probability *p*, then the evesdropper will resend "m" number of consistent pulses with associated phase modulations, and doing so with a probability of one over *p*, and evesdropper resends a "vacuum." The condition is met if evesdropper can obtain m (M) due to a successful sequential attempt. After receiving the results of the measures to be taken, she resends another Hoover cleaner.

There is no instance of inaccuracy that takes place within the pulses because of the nature of this assault; nevertheless, the boundary of the combination of the vibration and the vacuum does result in an arbitrary mistake. This is because of the nature of the attack. The evesdropper has a distinct advantage in situations when there is a substantial level of channel loss. In fact, the total number of successful USD assaults in rapid succession does not necessarily need to be highly significant. As a direct result, the coordinated assault on the USD may provide a more substantial danger when there is considerable channel loss.

As part of our investigation on the probability of a sequential assault using USD, we are also accountable for determining the error level that will apply to this assault. As a result of the miscalculation, the condition that required a gearbox that used SSPDs to travel more than 200 km at a quantum efficiency of 1.4% was exceeded. Still, the effective quantum efficiency was decreased by 36%. There was a 4.74 percentage point boost in the quantum efficiency when the time window was used. Suppose we assume that an error threshold of = 0.2 is acceptable for creating protected keys. In that case, the value estimated from GCA for individual photons is about 4.1%. This statement enlightens us to the fact that this is pertinent to our DPS-quantum research on the key distribution utilizing SSPDs and GCA on individual photons, which gives us what we may refer to as "complete protection," in contrast to the constant barrage of money that is denominated in USD. Therefore, the data presented in the form of facts and graphs protects us against GCA attacks that use SCA on individual photons and are followed by sequential attacks employing USD. The PKR as a function of fiber optical length with a loss of 0.2 dB/km and the PKRs calculated, tells us through 10- and 1-GHz clock systems with SSPDs.

Fibre optical length in KM	Protected key rate
0	10
50	10
100	100
150	100
200	10000
250	100000
300	10000000
350	10000000

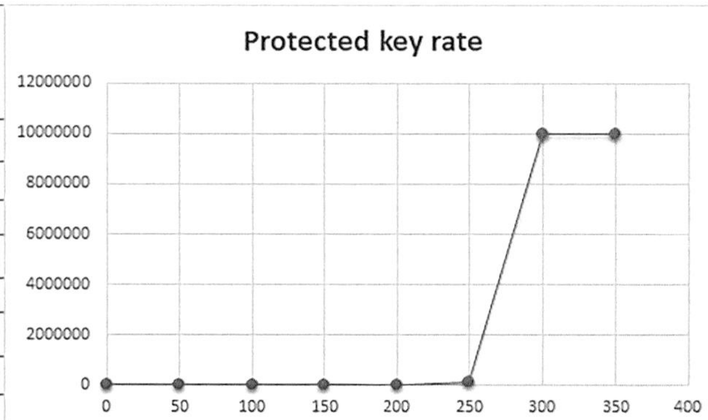

CHANNEL LOSS (IN DBS)	FIBRE OPTICAL CABLE LENGTH (IN KM)
10	0
10	50
20	100
30	150
50	200
60	250
70	300
80	350

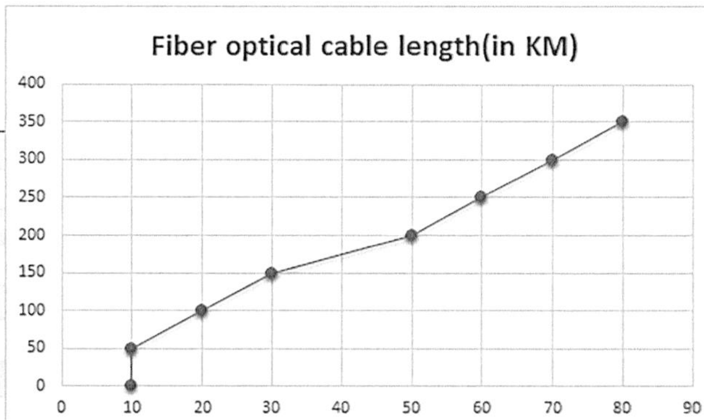

FIGURE 1.2 Protected key rate as a function of fiber optical length.

1.2 CONCLUSION

We discussed how SSPDs might generate a 10-GHz differential phase shift (DPS) between two clocks for use in a quantum key distribution experiment. The SSPDs low dark count rate and little timing jitter allow us to generate safe keys using a 10-GHz clock setup. With a channel loss of 42.1 dB in the direction of GCA for individual photons, this is essential for deploying protected keys across 200 km of fiber. Additionally, we surpassed the previous record by order of magnitude, sending 17 kilobits per second across a distance of 105 km using a PKR. This will be a big step toward our goal of creating a future where geostationary satellites keep tabs on a global network of dispersed QKD nodes connecting cities worldwide. The value of geo-synchronized satellites is highlighted as an important lesson.

KEYWORDS

- **quantum key distribution**
- **Bennet and armor plate protocol**
- **photon number splitting**
- **unambiguous state discrimination**
- **differential phase shift quantum key distribution**

REFERENCES

1. Aguado, A., et al. (2017). Secure NFV orchestration over an SDN-controlled optical network with time-shared quantum key distribution resources. *Journal of Lightwave Technology*, *35*(8), 1357–1362, https://doi.org/10.1109/JLT.2016.2646921./
2. Cintas-Canto, A., Kermani, M. M., & Azarderakhsh, R. (2023). Reliable architectures for finite field multipliers using cyclic codes on FPGA utilized in classic and post-quantum cryptography. *IEEE Transactions on Very Large Scale Integration (VLSI) Systems*, *31*(1), 157–161, https://doi.org/10.1109/TVLSI.2022.3224357.
3. Martínez, J. C., de Haro, L., & González, A. (2010). Simulation model applied to IP protocols and satellite communications. *2010 Second International Conference on Advances in Satellite and Space Communications,* Athens, Greece, pp. 122–127, https://doi.org/10.1109/SPACOMM.2010.34.
4. Kim, J. et al. (2022). ARK: Fully homomorphic encryption accelerator with runtime data generation and inter-operation key reuse. In *2022 55th IEEE/ACM International Symposium on Microarchitecture (MICRO),* Chicago, IL, USA, pp. 1237–1254, https://doi.org/10.1109/MICRO56248.2022.00086.
5. Prateek, K., Maity, S., & Saxena, N. (2022). A quantum communication based secure road condition monitoring application in intelligent internet of vehicular things. In

2022 IEEE 19th India Council International Conference (INDICON), Kochi, India, pp. 1–6, https://doi.org/10.1109/INDICON56171.2022.10040136.

6. Mailloux, L. O., et al. (2015). A modeling framework for studying quantum key distribution system implementation nonidealities. *IEEE Access*, *3*, 110–130, https://doi.org/10.1109/ACCESS.2015.2399101.
7. Alshowkan, M. et al. (2022). Advanced architectures for high-performance quantum networking. *Journal of Optical Communications and Networking*, *14*(6), 493–499, https://doi.org/10.1364/JOCN.450201.
8. Anastasova, M., Azarderakhsh, R., & Kermani, M. M. (2021). Fast strategies for the implementation of SIKE round 3 on ARM Cortex-M4. *IEEE Transactions on Circuits and Systems I: Regular Papers*, *68*(10), 4129–4141, https://doi.org/10.1109/TCSI.2021.3096916.
9. Yan, R., Wang, Y., Dai, J., Xu, Y., & Liu, A. Q. (2022). Quantum-key-distribution-based microgrid control for cybersecurity enhancement. *IEEE Transactions on Industry Applications*, *58*(3), 3076–3086, https://doi.org/10.1109/TIA.2022.3159314.
10. Ebrahimi, S., & Bayat-Sarmadi, S. (2020). Lightweight and DPA-resistant post-quantum cryptoprocessor based on binary ring-LWE. In *2020 20th International Symposium on Computer Architecture and Digital Systems (CADS),* Rasht, Iran, pp. 1–6, https://doi.org/10.1109/CADS50570.2020.9211858.
11. Shen, S. et al. (2022). A hierarchical parallel discrete gaussian sampler for lattice-based cryptography. In *2022 IEEE International Symposium on Circuits and Systems (ISCAS),* Austin, TX, USA, pp. 1729–1733, https://doi.org/10.1109/ISCAS48785.2022.9937989.
12. Faraj, S. T. (2008). A novel extension of SSL/TLS based on quantum key distribution. In *2008 International Conference on Computer and Communication Engineering,* Kuala Lumpur, Malaysia, pp. 919–922, https://doi.org/10.1109/ICCCE.2008.4580740.
13. Thangavel, T. S., & Krishnan, A. (2010). Performance of integrated quantum and classical cryptographic model for password authentication. In *2010 Second International Conference on Computing, Communication and Networking Technologies,* Karur, India, pp. 1–8, https://doi.org/10.1109/ICCCNT.2010.5591718.
14. Tan, W., Wang, A., Lao, Y., Zhang, X., & Parhi, K. K. (2021). Pipelined high-throughput NTT architecture for lattice-based cryptography. In *2021 Asian Hardware Oriented Security and Trust Symposium (AsianHOST),* Shanghai, China, pp. 1–4, https://doi.org/10.1109/AsianHOST53231.2021.9699608.
15. Tan, W., Case, B. M., Wang, A., Gao, S., & Lao, Y. (2021). High-speed modular multiplier for lattice-based cryptosystems. *IEEE Transactions on Circuits and Systems II: Express Briefs*, *68*(8), 2927–2931, https://doi.org/10.1109/TCSII.2021.3064232.
16. Cao, Y., Zhao, Y., Zhang, J., & Wang, Q. (2022). Software-defined heterogeneous quantum key distribution chaining: An enabler for multi-protocol quantum networks. *IEEE Communications Magazine*, *60*(9), 38–44, https://doi.org/10.1109/MCOM.001.2101006.
17. Cao, Y., Zhao, Y., Zhang, J., Wang, Q., Niyato, D., & Hanzo, L. (2022). From single-protocol to large-scale multi-protocol quantum networks. *IEEE Network*, *36*(5), 14–22, https://doi.org/10.1109/MNET.001.2200144.

18. Song, Y., Hu, X., Tian, J., & Wang, Z. (2023). A high-speed FPGA-based hardware implementation for leighton-micali signature. *IEEE Transactions on Circuits and Systems I: Regular Papers*, *70*(1), 241–252, https://doi.org/10.1109/TCSI.2022.3210016.
19. Song, Y., Hu, X., Wang, W., Tian, J., & Wang, Z. (2021). High-speed and scalable FPGA implementation of the key generation for the leighton-micali signature protocol. In *2021 IEEE International Symposium on Circuits and Systems (ISCAS)*, Daegu, Korea, pp. 1–5.

CHAPTER 2

Applications of Quantum Computing in the Field of Chemistry

MARC MAUSSNER*

Business Unit Industry, infoteam Software AG, Bubenreuth, Germany

*Corresponding author

ABSTRACT

Using quantum computers to tackle problems in chemistry is one of the first and most promising fields of application for near-term available quantum computers in the noisy intermediate-scale quantum computer (NISQ) era. To present applications, we start from small examples well known in classical computing and move to open questions we—all of humanity—face in solving issues like reducing the amount of energy needed to produce fertilizers and optimizing the underlying chemical reaction. We begin with the general process of simulating chemical molecules with quantum computers. Our first goal is to use potential energy surface calculation to determine the bonding energy of H_2. We then adapt the example to CO_2 and the metal–organic frameworks used in direct air capture. We show the adaptions and restrictions for current quantum computer hardware with a limited number of qubits during the NISQ era. We present the Haber–Bosch process and its importance for all humanity and investigate how and in which areas quantum computing can be applied in future research. We conclude the chapter by outlining what still needs to be done in research to constructively apply quantum computing in chemistry.

2.1 INTRODUCTION

As one of its most promising fields for application, quantum computing is expected to be used for simulating chemical molecules and materials. This

Applications of Quantum Computing in a Variety of Domains. Gunjan Mukherjee, Biswadip Basu Mallik, Rahul Kar Özen ÖZER, Digvijay Pandey, and Binay Kumar Pandey (Eds.)

DOI: 10.1201/9781998511051-2

is especially important for the search for more sustainable processes and chemical reactions and improving processing and simulation speed.

This chapter will present the theory and application for calculating the ground-state energies of molecules, starting from H_2 and moving to some more complex examples. We present the workflow to be used and show current difficulties we face for the noisy intermediate-scale quantum computer (NISQ) era.

Afterward, we present current thoughts on applying quantum computing to optimize the Haber–Bosch [1, 21] process.

The end of the chapter presents the conclusion of everything presented, the current limitations, and the expected date when quantum computing for applications in chemistry will be considered for real-world examples.

2.2 POTENTIAL ENERGY SURFACE (PES)

2.2.1 GENERAL OVERVIEW OF PES

According to Ref. [23], a PES is defined as the description of the energy of a system, especially a collection of atoms, for certain parameters, usually the positions of the atoms.

We can construct a molecule with atoms arranged in 3D, with parameters for transformation. For a linear molecule, like hydrogen, we then get a plot of the ground-state energy by distance. This is shown in Figure 2.1.

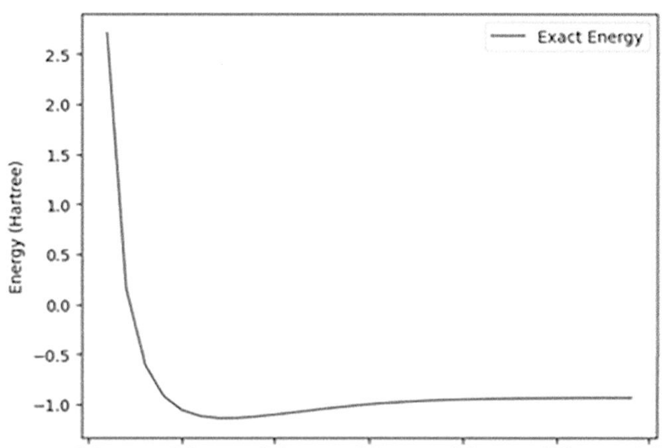

FIGURE 2.1 The exact Hartree energies in relation to the atomic distance of the two H–H atoms.

For simulating the electronic energies of chemical molecules, Refs. [9] and [15] list the steps to be done. First, we must define the problem as an electronic structure Hamiltonian H_{el} [15, 22]. We apply the Born–Oppenheimer approximation [20] and use the time-independent Schrödinger equation [24] to get the following formula:

$$H_{el} = -\Sigma_i \frac{\nabla_{ri}^2}{m_e} - \sum_I \Sigma_i \frac{Z_I e^2}{|R_I - r_i|} + \sum_i \Sigma_{j>i} \frac{e^2}{|r_i - r_j|} \tag{2.1}$$

Then, we can calculate the ground energy of the system with given ground state Ψ_0 with:

$$E_0 = \frac{\langle \Psi_0 | H_{el} | \Psi_0 \rangle}{\langle \Psi_0 | \Psi_0 \rangle} \tag{2.2}$$

Afterward, we can apply the Hartree–Fock method, which approximates the N-body problem to N one-body problems.

To map our problem to a quantum computer, we transfer the fermionic Hamiltonian to the qubit Hamiltonian—by using, for example, the Jordan–Wigner transformation [7]—which then can be transferred to Pauli spin matrices to be used directly on a quantum computer.

We can then solve the ground-state problem with the variational quantum eigensolver (VQE). The VQE tries to find the minimal eigenvalue corresponding to the minimum ground state of the system. The algorithm consists of a quantum ansatz with parameters that represent the energy of the system. These parameters are classically optimized in an iterative process. Using this approximative approach may lead to the minimal eigenvalue of the system—or to other values when stuck in a barren plateau. For small examples, this solution can be compared to the classically calculated exact solution.

To estimate the PES, the above steps must be done for each distance or molecule geometry adaption used.

2.2.2 *PES FOR* H_2

To calculate the PES of H_2 in Qiskit, we have to create the electronic structure problem, find the second quantized form, apply the Hartree–Fock method, map from fermionic Hamiltonian to qubit Hamiltonian, and receive the ground-state energy with the VQE [14–16]. The program flow is depicted in Figure 2.2. The results shown in Figure 2.3 prove that, for this small problem with only two qubits, the exact solution determined by NumPyMinimumEigensolver and the VQE do not differ.

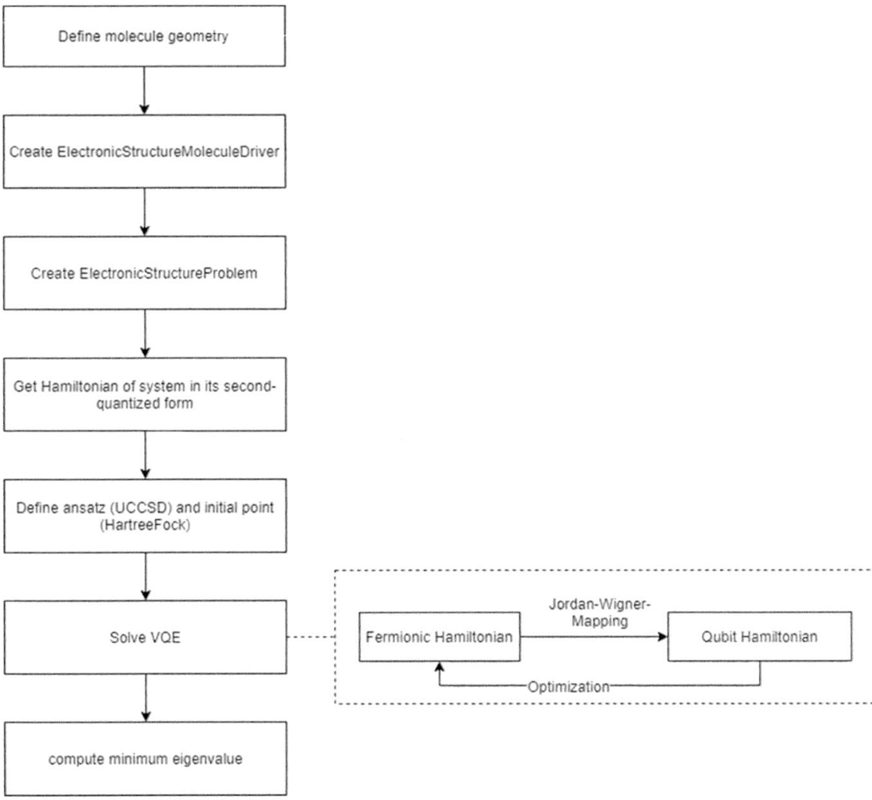

FIGURE 2.2 Algorithm design for estimating the ground-state energy of electronic structure problems, especially for H_2.

A proof-of-concept implementation in Qiskit can be found in the GitHub repository created for this chapter [10].

2.2.3 PES FOR CO_2 AND METAL–ORGANIC FRAMEWORKS (MOFS)

In Section 2.2.2, we created a solution to calculate the PES for a small problem. In this section, we adapt this solution to determine the PES for CO_2 and MOFs. As CO_2 in the air has a huge impact on change to

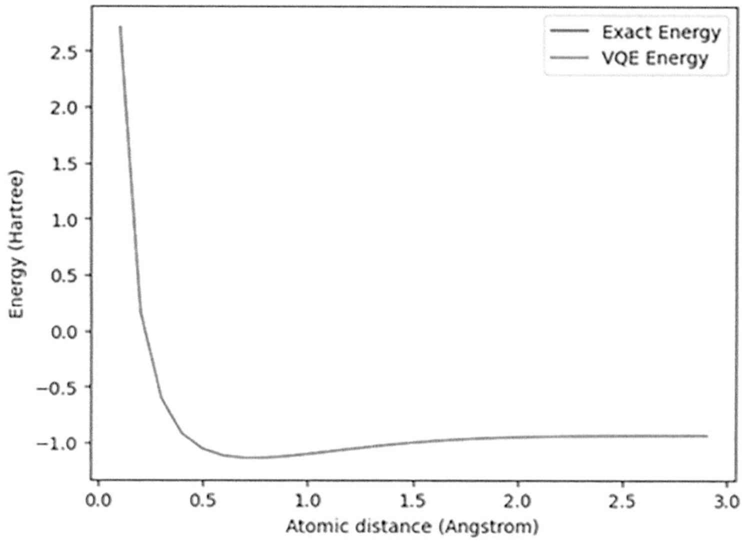

FIGURE 2.3 PES of H_2 with exact energy calculation using NumPyMinimumEigensolver in blue and with VQE in orange. We can see that for this simple problem the exact and the VQE solution do not differ.

the Earth's climate, the simulation of the bonding of CO_2 to MOFs is important for the application of direct air capture (DAC). The process is well described and was investigated during Deloitte's Quantum Climate Challenge in 2023 [3].

When first trying our solution, by changing just the underlying molecule, we can see that 40 qubits are needed to perform the calculation. However, currently only 32 qubits are freely accessible from IBM's cloud services. Therefore, we need to adapt our solution.

We first try to optimize the needed resources by freezing the core and removing the inner orbitals. This can be done because the binding only takes place locally between the valence electrons of the Mn and O atoms. Doing this reduces the number of qubits used to express our problem to 26. This even fits on the underlying simulators or hardware provided by IBM. However, the runtime is very large. So, we must further reduce the precision of the solution.

The next thing that can be done is to reduce the active space simulated by our algorithm. This then leads to the use of five qubits. We further adapt the ansatz to a more hardware-efficient variant "EfficientSU2." The example layout for four qubits is shown in Figure 2.4.

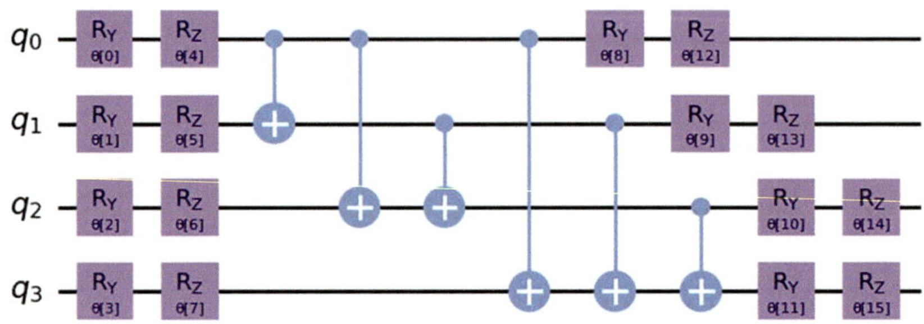

FIGURE 2.4 Example layout of EfficientSU2 quantum circuit for four qubits with parameters reps = 1 and entanglement = "full."

We then obtain the result for the PES of $CMnO_2$ as shown in Figure 2.5. The overall algorithm including all steps for optimization is shown in Figure 2.6.

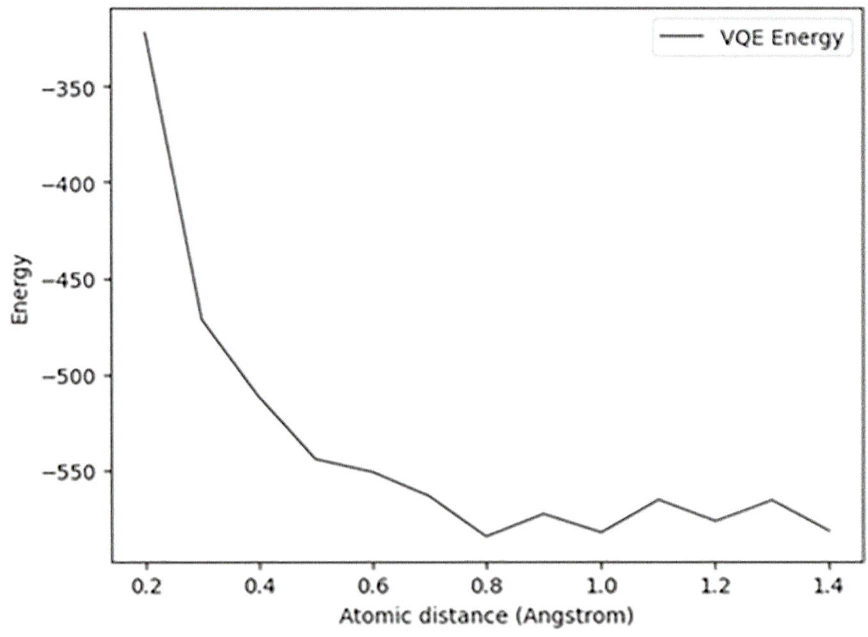

FIGURE 2.5 PES of $CMnO_2$ with VQE in blue. One can see that this estimation—having been steeply optimized from 40 to 5 qubits—does not really meet the expected curve.

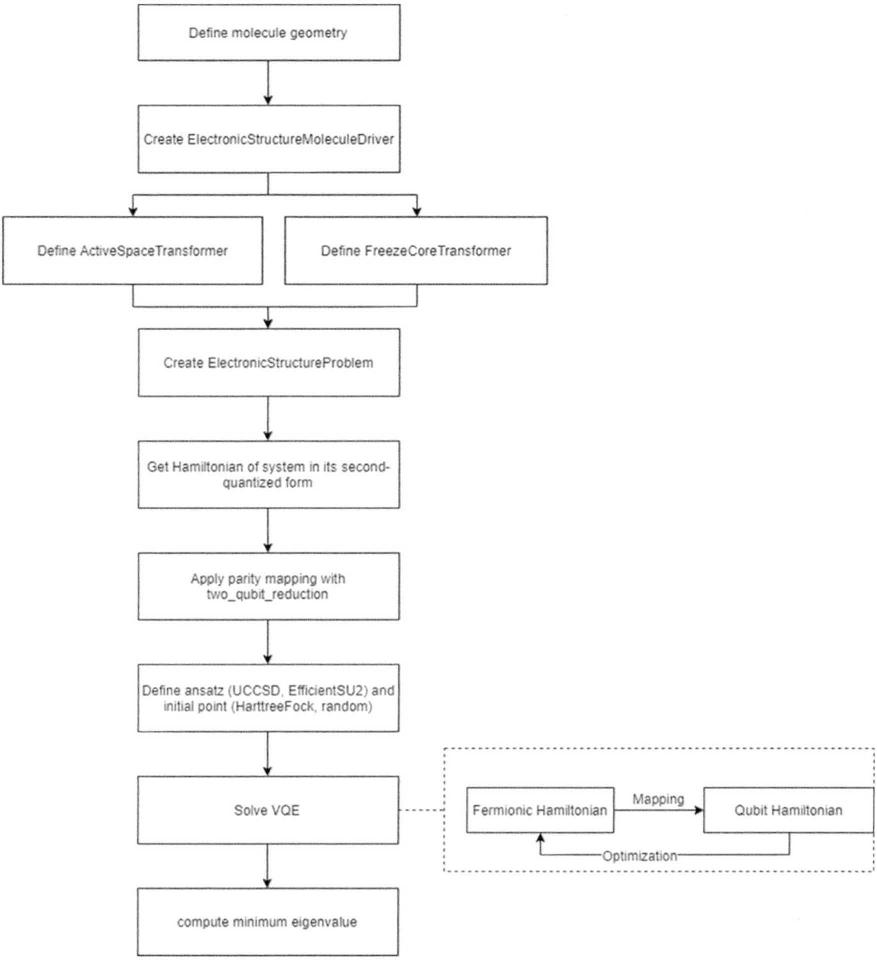

FIGURE 2.6 Optimized algorithm design for estimating the ground-state energy of electronic structure problems, especially for $CMnO_2$

A proof-of-concept implementation in Qiskit can be found in the GitHub repository for this chapter [10]. There is also an example included of the use of the tool "Atomic Simulation Environment" [4] to visualize the defined module geometries.

As we saw, many reductions are currently necessary in the NISQ era to simulate molecules with quantum computing. Following these reductions and simplifications, the results are no longer useful. According to

IBM's roadmap [6], starting in 2026, it might be possible for us to simulate $CMnO_2$ to precisely obtain the PES.

Nevertheless, we can think about further possible adaptions of our algorithm that might yield better results—maybe by switching from 1D bonding to 2D. This can be done in the phase of defining the molecule geometry so that it not only variates in distance but also in a 2D landscape, as shown in Figure 2.7.

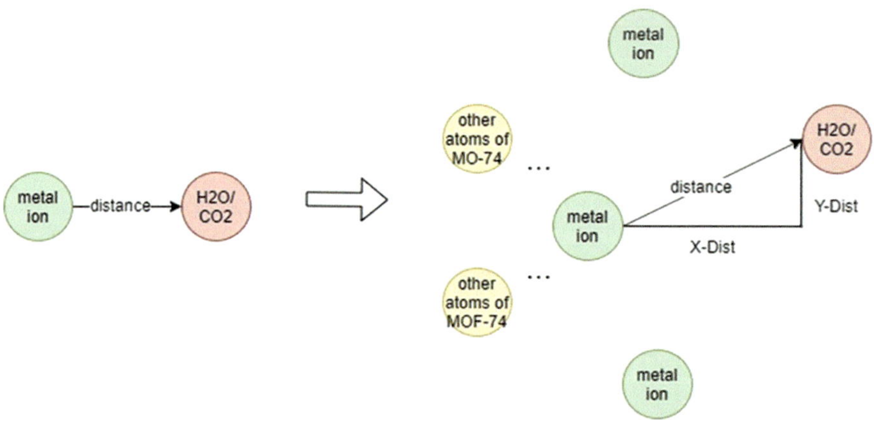

FIGURE 2.7 2D landscape for CO_2 binding to MOF-74.

The metal ion needs to be extended to the 2D structure of MOF-74 in the molecule geometry. This leads to an increase in spins/electrons, leading to an increase in the number of qubits needed (e.g., for Mn-MOF-74 = Mn2 (dobdc) [2, 5] for absorbing CO_2 from 43 to 397).

Further improvements in the level of detail are needed to get a solution for just a 2D slice of the MOF. Therefore, one must consider a full hexagon consisting of 3×Mn-MOF-74 for CO_2 (e.g.,$3C_{25}H_6MnMg_5O_{20}$), which would consist of 3×57 = 171 molecules and 3×399 electrons. This leads our ansatz to consist of 3(399) – 2 = 1195 qubits, with 4780 parameters, consisting of 5976 (2×barrier, 2390×ry, 2390×rx, 1194×cx) operations (extrapolated from Figure 2.4) and with a depth of 1198.

Considering the median gate time of "ibm_perth" at 398.222 ns and the layout of our ansatz circuit, this leads to an estimated execution time of:

$$(2\times ry) + (2\times rz) + (1194\times cx) + (2\times barrier) = 1200\times \text{gate time}$$
$$= 477{,}866 \text{ ns} = 477\ \mu s$$

This means the circuit needs 477 μs for one shot. Usually, we use at least 1024 shots, which gives us 477 μs×1024 = 488 ms. This is the time needed for just the quantum part of the calculation, for one optimization iteration, without any error suppression or error mitigation means.

It was shown in Ref. [13] that an iteration value for the optimizer greater than 100 is needed.

From 2024, IBM wants to have noise-free observables for 100 qubit circuits [12]. Unfortunately, we do not currently know when this will be applicable for around 1200 qubits. Also, the coherence time will be a big problem. According to Ref. [17], IBM currently has a coherence time greater than 1 ms, which is insufficient even if we have the necessary number of qubits ready with IBM's Flamingo [6] and error suppression and mitigation for it in 2024.

So, as an outline result, it might be possible to run our algorithm after 2026 when, according to the road map in [6], we will have enough qubits and error suppression and error mitigation will be integrated into the different quantum frameworks.

2.3.1 APPLICATION TO HABER–BOSCH

2.3.1 GENERAL OVERVIEW OF HABER–BOSCH

The population of the world will continue to grow. This means more food will be needed, and the key element of efficiently producing it is the efficiency of producing fertilizers, as nitrogen fertilizers help to feed half of the global population [11].

Fertilizers mainly consist of ammonia, produced through the well-known Haber–Bosch process [1, 19, 21]. The process was invented in the first decade of the 20th century and is resource-intensive. The temperatures needed are in the range of 350–550°C and pressures lie in the range of 150–300 bar [19]. Bacteria found in nature [8, 18] produce ammonia in normal environments (around 37°C and 1 bar), which brought scientists to the idea of better understanding the process to make it more sustainable and optimize the resource requirements.

Although the general chemical reaction (2.3) seems quite simple, the Haber–Bosch process consists of several steps (2.4)–(2.6) with specific surrounding temperatures and pressures to produce hydrogen, which then, together with nitrogen out of the air, can be used to produce ammonia. For better understanding, the industrial process, and the general workflow are shown in Figure 2.8.

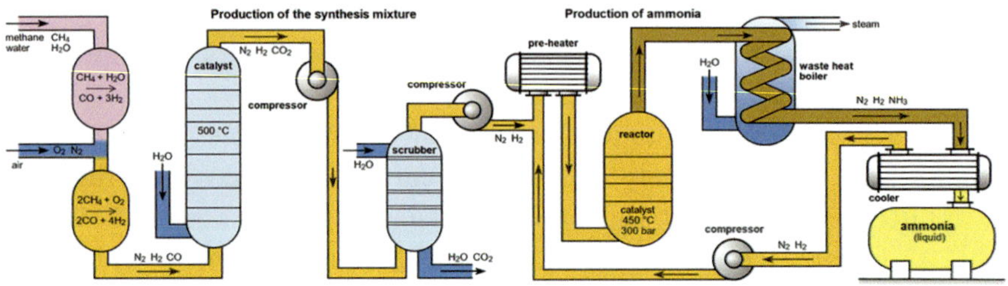

FIGURE 2.8 Industrial overview of applied Haber–Bosch.

Source: Reprinted with permission from Ref. [21]. https://creativecommons.org/licenses/by/4.0/

$$N_2 + 3H_2 \rightleftharpoons 2NH_2 \quad (2.3)$$

$$CH_4 + H_2O \rightarrow CO + 3H_2 \quad (2.4)$$

$$2CH_4 + O_2 \rightarrow 2CO + 4H_2 \quad (2.5)$$

$$CO + H_2O \rightarrow CO + H_2 \quad (2.6)$$

2.3.2 APPLICATIONS OF QUANTUM CHEMISTRY

According to Ref. [19], "the current international ammonia market [...] is responsible for 1.3% of global CO_2 emissions." Quantum chemistry is considered one of the most promising tools to optimize the reaction and the required resources. This will be achieved by faster simulation of the chemical reactions, with greater exactness than that offered by the classical computed results.

Tables 2.1 and 2.2 give an overview of the number of qubits needed to completely estimate the ground states, and thus, the energies consumed or produced by each formula. We can see that at maximum, 22 qubits are needed. This number is currently provided by the NISQ devices available, but we have to consider that noise and error mitigation techniques to reduce the error in energy estimation also need some resources. We have to adjust and recalculate the exact energies when changing module geometry and environmental parameters like temperature and pressure, too. Alternatively, we may change the reactions comprising the reaction molecules themselves if we come to understand the chemical reactions of ammonia-producing bacteria [18]. This would mean investigating the bacteria and determining the chemical reaction, which is under the umbrella of quantum computing for biology and not considered here.

TABLE 2.1 Resources/Qubits Needed for Estimating Ground State of Reaction Molecules, Sorted by Appearance in Reaction Formulas 2.3–2.6

Reaction Molecule	Number of Qubits
N_2	14
H_2	2
NH_3	10
CH_4	10
H_2O	10
CO	14
O_2	16
CO_2	22

TABLE 2.2 Maximum Resources/Qubits Needed for Simulating Reaction Formulas 2.3–2.6

Reaction Formula	Maximum Number of Qubits
2.3	14
2.4	14
2.5	16
2.6	22

One of the benefits of quantum chemistry is that there is no need to prepare the reactions and environments in the laboratory. This reduces the time preparing the laboratory, the chemicals, and the environmental conditions. It also reduces the energy needed to produce the exact environment and reduces waste, because unwanted chemical products will only be simulated and not produced in real space. Furthermore, an increase in exactness over that offered by classical simulations is expected for real-world chemical reactions and simulations starting in 2026 [6].

To outline our result, our algorithm might be able to run after 2026, when, according to the road map of Ref. [6], we will have enough qubits and error suppression and error mitigation will be integrated into the different quantum frameworks.

2.4 CONCLUSION

In this chapter, we saw that the use of quantum computing for chemical simulations is quite handy but limited with the currently available resources. As the number of qubits increases, quantum circuits get deeper and the reduction techniques for noise and errors improve, it is estimated that around 2026 [6] we will be able to simulate real-world examples of the reaction chains and molecules needed for to produce ammonia.

In the meantime, researchers in academia and industry are working on other sustainable ways to produce H_2 with renewable energy sources [11, 19]—like wind farms and photovoltaic sites—leading to reduction of CO_2 emitted.

Maybe the reduction of CO_2 in combination with DAC will lead to more benefits in the near future. Moreover, we as quantum enthusiasts play a very important part in helping to accelerate and optimize this progress to build a more sustainable future.

KEYWORDS

- **chemistry**
- **potential energy surface**
- **CO2 emissions**
- **direct air capture**
- **metal-organic frameworks**
- **Haber–Bosch**
- **bacteria**
- **ammonia production**

REFERENCES

1. chemie.de. (2024, 01 12). *Haber-Bosch-Verfahren.* Retrieved from https://www.chemie.de/lexikon/Haber-Bosch-Verfahren.html#:~:text=Beim%20Haber%2DBosch%2DVerfahren%20wird,der%20eigentliche%20Katalysator%20alpha%2DFe
2. de Oliveira, A., de Lima, G. F., & De Abreu, H. A. (2018). Structural and electronic properties of M-MOF-74 (M = Mg, Co or Mn). *Chemical Physics Letters*, *691*, 283–290.
3. Deloitte Quantum.Link. (2024, 01 12). Deloitte's quantum climate challenge. Retrieved from https://www2.deloitte.com/de/de/pages/innovation/contents/deloitte-quantum-climate-challenge.html
4. GitLab. (2024, 01 12). Atomic simulation environment. Retrieved from https://gitlab.com/ase/ase/-/tree/master
5. Henkelis, S., Rademacher, D., Vogel, D. J., Valdez, N. R., Rodriguez, M. A., Rohwer, L. E. S., & Nenoff, T. M. (2020). Luminescent properties of DOBDC containing MOFs: The role of free hydroxyls. *ACS Applied Materials & Interfaces, 12*(20), 22845–22852.
6. IBM. (2024, 01 12). IBM quantum roadmap 2025. Retrieved from https://research.ibm.com/blog/ibm-quantum-roadmap-2025
7. Jordan, P., & Wigner, E. (1928). Über das paulische äquivalenzverbot. *Zeitschrift für Physik*, *47*, 631–651.
8. Kaku, M. (2023). *Quantum Supremacy: How the Quantum Computer Revolution Will Change Everything.* Knopf Doubleday Publishing Group.
9. Keeper, L., & Sharkey, A. C. (2022). *Quantum Chemistry and Computing for the Curious.* Packt.
10. Maußner, M. (2024, 01 12). 2023_application_quantum_chemistry. Retrieved from https://github.com/MarcMaussner/2023_application_quantum_chemistry
11. McCormick, A., Cussler, E., Dauenhauer, P., Daoutidis, P., & Reese, M. (2023, 09 07). Small scale ammonia synthesis using stranded wind energy. Retrieved from https://www.ammoniaenergy.org/wp-content/uploads/2021/11/AEA-November-2021-v11Nov.pdf
12. Qiskit. (2024, 01 12). Error suppression and error mitigation with qiskit runtime. Retrieved from https://qiskit.org/ecosystem/ibm-runtime/tutorials/Error-Suppression-and-Error-Mitigation.html
13. Qiskit. (2024, 01 12). Leveraging Qiskit runtime. Retrieved from https://qiskit.org/ecosystem/nature/tutorials/07_leveraging_qiskit_runtime.html
14. Qiskit Nature. (2024, 01 12). An introduction to Qiskit Nature. Retrieved from https://github.com/qiskit-community/qiskit-application-modules-demo-sessions/blob/main/qiskit-nature/Qiskit_Nature_YouTube_Tutorial.ipynb
15. Qiskit Nature. (2024, 01 12). Tutorial on electronic structure calculations. Retrieved from https://qiskit.org/documentation/nature/tutorials/01_electronic_structure.html
16. Quantaggle. (2024, 01 12). Calculating potential energy surface of ground states of small molecules (GS-PES). Retrieved from https://quantaggle.com/competitions/gs-pes/
17. Techcrunch. (2024, 01 12). IBM hopes a new error mitigation technique will help it get to quantum advantage. Retrieved from https://techcrunch.com/2022/07/19/

ibm-hopes-a-new-error-mitigation-technique-will-help-it-get-to-quantum-advantage/?guce_referrer=aHR0cHM6Ly93d3cuZ29vZ2xlLmNvbS8&guce_referrer_sig=AQAAAF9OKwP9XElKCV-7o5MsOXtgnfRxbnWjqiOBC5fuuVNN3ZOaSEOtVZzsQzytyDgjHmR0Izd

18. Vince, A., & Burridge, S. (1980). Ammonia production by intestinal bacteria: The effects of lactose, lactulose and glucose. *Journal of Medical Microbiology*, *13*(2), 177–191.
19. Wang, C., Walsh, S., Longden, T., Palmer, G., Lutalo, I., & Dargaville, R. (2023). Optimising renewable generation configurations of off-grid green ammonia production systems considering Haber–Bosch flexibility. *Energy Conversion and Management*, *280*, 116790.
20. Wikipedia. (2024, 01 12). Born–oppenheimer approximation. Retrieved from https://en.wikipedia.org/wiki/Born%E2%80%93Oppenheimer_approximation
21. Wikipedia. (2024, 01 12). Haber process. Retrieved from https://en.wikipedia.org/wiki/Haber_process
22. Wikipedia. (2024, 01 12). Hamiltonian (Quantum Mechanics). Retrieved from https://en.wikipedia.org/wiki/Hamiltonian_(quantum_mechanics)
23. Wikipedia. (2024, 01 12). Potential energy surface. Retrieved from https://en.wikipedia.org/wiki/Potential_energy_surface
24. [24] Wikipedia. (2024, 01 12). Schrödinger equation. Retrieved from https://en.wikipedia.org/wiki/Schr%C3%B6dinger_equation

CHAPTER 3

Quantum Computing Applications in Data Science: A Comprehensive Survey

GNANASANKARAN NATARAJAN [1],
SHIRLEY CHELLATHURAI PON ANNA BAI [2],
AHAMED LEBBE HANEES[3], ELAKKIYA ELANGO[4], and
RAKESH GNANASEKARAN[1]

[1]Department of Computer Science, Thiagarajar College, Madurai, Tamil Nadu, India

[2]Department of Computer Science and Engineering, Karunya Institute of Technology and Sciences, Coimbatore, Tamil Nadu, India

[3]Department of Computer Science, South Eastern University of Sri Lanka, Sammanthurai, Sri Lanka

[4]Department of Computer Science, Government Arts and Science College for Women, Sivaganga, Tamil Nadu, India

*Corresponding author

ABSTRACT

Quantum computing is an upcoming paradigm that has been in the transformation process in data science in the light of quantum physics. On that account, the present chapter delivers in-depth details on how quantum phenomena like superposition and entanglement could be brought to bear on data-intensive problems that are beyond classical computational means. Basic concepts such as qubits, gates, and circuits are studied with an emphasis on parallelism and interference to speed up computations. They look at the major applications for data science with a focus on

Applications of Quantum Computing in a Variety of Domains. Gunjan Mukherjee, Biswadip Basu Mallik, Rahul Kar Özen ÖZER, Digvijay Pandey, and Binay Kumar Pandey (Eds.)

DOI: 10.1201/9781998511051-3

promising quantum machine-learning techniques: quantum support vector machines and quantum neural networks that promise a quantum speed-up in classifying and regressing data sets. It also looks at quantum methods for clustering, dimensionality reduction, and combinatorial optimization, including quantum annealing and the quantum approximate optimization algorithm, to name just a few, with respect to speed and accuracy. Therefore, quantum simulation is strongly promoted for the simulation of complicated systems, which are of interest, for example, in chemistry, materials science, and drug discovery. Besides, some shelves are kept for an overview of the interdisciplinary approaches of quantum computing with big data analytics and also with cryptography, including quantum-safe encryption. The hardware scalability stands as the main challenge, while the prime concern is error correction. Other than these issues, advances in investigating and developing are schema concepts for unleashing the power of quantum computing to change data science.

3.1 INTRODUCTION TO QUANTUM COMPUTERS

Quantum computers are a paradigm-shifting development in the fields of cutting-edge technology and scientific inquiry that have the potential to completely alter the way that computation is done today. In contrast to classical computers, which use bits as the basic building block of information processing, quantum computers use quantum bits, or qubits, which operate according to the laws of quantum mechanics. This radical departure from conventional computer principles has the ability to solve difficult problems at rates previously thought unthinkable, opening up new research directions in a wide range of areas including artificial intelligence (AI), materials science, drug development, and cryptography. Richard Feynman, a physicist, originally proposed the idea of quantum computing in 1981. He realized that it was impossible to simulate the behavior of quantum systems using classical computers due to the rapid increase in computational specifications as the number of quantum elements increased. This realization served as the impetus for the creation of quantum computers, which use the special properties of quantum mechanics to carry out calculations for some problems with enormously higher efficiency.

The foundation of quantum computing is the idea of superposition, which allows qubits to exist in several states concurrently as opposed to classical bits, which can only have one of two possible states. Another essential idea is entanglement, which enables qubits to be coupled in ways that classical bits cannot, leading to previously unimaginable information-sharing and processing capacities. Due to these characteristics, quantum computers are uniquely able to investigate several answers and may be able to solve complicated problems much more quickly compared to their classical equivalents. They are actual gadgets that have been created by top technology companies, research institutions, and governments all around the world. They are not just abstract concepts. Despite having a finite number of qubits and high error rates, companies like IBM, Google, and Rigetti have created working quantum processors. Nevertheless, we are getting closer to the implementation of practical quantum computing, thanks to the quick developments in quantum hardware and software [1].

There is a plethora of different ways that quantum computers might be used. They propose to revolutionize cryptography by breaking existing encryption algorithms and, in turn, developing untraceable quantum-safe encryption techniques, upending entire industries. Additionally, quantum computing has the potential to streamline complex supply chains, speed up the development of novel materials with unique features, and alter the healthcare industry by advancing molecular modeling and drug discovery. Additionally, it is anticipated that quantum computing will unleash the full potential of AI, enabling more advanced machine learning techniques and advancing fields like quantum machine learning and optimization. Quantum computers have incredible potential, but they also face some difficulties. There are still significant challenges dealing with the stability of qubits, cutting error rates, and scaling up quantum processors. In addition, as these innovations advance, considerable thought must be given to the ethical aspects of quantum computing, including its effects on security and privacy.

With the potential to change industries, find solutions to previously unsolvable issues, and unleash previously unheard-of computational power, quantum computers represent a paradigm-shifting advance in computing technology. The opportunities are only restricted by our creativity and capacity to harness the mysterious yet fascinating laws of quantum physics as we proceed to explore the limits of quantum computing research and development. This foray into the quantum world brings in a new phase in the development of computing and has an opportunity to alter what is known and what is possible for humans [2].

3.1.1 BASIC PRINCIPLES BEHIND QUANTUM COMPUTING

In contrast to conventional computing, quantum computing functions on an entirely distinct set of principles. Quantum computers utilize quantum bits, or qubits, as opposed to classical computers, which utilize bits as the fundamental unit of information that can be either 0 or 1. Quantum computing's breakthrough computational capacity is made possible by the special quantum mechanical concepts that form its foundation. Let us examine the fundamentals of quantum computing in more depth:

3.1.1.1 SUPERPOSITION

Superposition is one of the fundamental ideas behind quantum computing. In traditional computing, a bit can only be in one of the two states—0 or 1—at once. A qubit, on the other hand, can concurrently be in both the 0 and 1 state. This significantly expands the range of possible computations because a qubit can, up until it is measured, represent any combination of 0 and 1.

- ***Mathematical Representation:*** A qubit in a superposition state can be represented as $|\Psi\rangle = \alpha|0\rangle + \beta|1\rangle$, where α and β are complex numbers that determine the probability of measuring the qubit in the $|0\rangle$ or $|1\rangle$ state.

3.1.1.2 ENTANGLEMENT

Another quantum principle that distinguishes qubits from conventional bits is entanglement. Despite the physical distance separating them, qubits become associated with one another's states when they become entangled. Qubits may communicate information and carry out operations in ways that conventional bits cannot because of this phenomenon. For quantum computer techniques and quantum communication, entanglement is a vital resource.

- ***Bell States:*** Famous entangled qubit pairs known as bell states show strong association even when they are separated by great distances. The most well-known Bell state is the maximally entangled $|\Phi^+\rangle = (|00\rangle + |11\rangle) / \sqrt{2}$, where the states of both qubits are linked.

3.1.1.3 MEASUREMENT

A distinct measurement component is included in quantum computing. A qubit collapses out of its superposition of states into a distinct 0 or 1 state when it is measured. The measurement's result, however, is probabilistic and is based on the square of the amplitudes (α and β) connected to every basis state.

- ***Probabilistic Outcomes:*** The probabilities of measuring a qubit in its $|0\rangle$ or $|1\rangle$ state are $|\alpha|^2$ and $|\beta|^2$, respectively. A key characteristic of quantum computing is its probabilistic nature, which frequently necessitates the development of algorithms that make use of it.

3.1.1.4 QUANTUM INTERFERENCE

To increase their computing power, quantum computers take advantage of interference events. In order to increase the chance of the desired event and decrease the probability of the undesirable consequence, it is necessary to manipulate the amplitudes of qubit states. Quantum algorithms are created to increase the probability of proper responses and decrease errors via interference [3].

3.1.1.5 NO-CLONING THEOREM

It is difficult to create a perfect replica of any given unknown quantum state in quantum computing. Contrasting with conventional bits that are simple to replicate is the no-cloning theorem. This idea has ramifications for quantum cryptography and information security.

3.1.1.6 QUANTUM GATES

Quantum gates, which are used to manipulate qubits, serve as classical logic gates' quantum equivalents. The Hadamard gate, the CNOT gate (controlled-X gate), and the Toffoli gate are examples of typical quantum gates. In order to execute quantum calculations, these gates control qubits using techniques that benefit from superposition, entanglement, and interference.

The principles of quantum computing, including superposition, entanglement, measurement, quantum interference, and the no-cloning theorem, are rooted in the fundamental principles of quantum mechanics. These principles enable quantum computers to perform certain types of computations exponentially faster than classical computers and hold the potential to revolutionize fields ranging from cryptography to materials science and AI. While quantum computing is still in its infancy, ongoing research and development aim to harness these principles for practical applications in the near future [4].

3.1.2 IMPORTANCE OF QUANTUM PARALLELISM AND ITS ADVANTAGES

The foundational ideas of quantum physics serve as the basis for the fundamental concepts of quantum computing, such as superposition, entanglement, measurement, quantum interference, and the no-cloning theorem. These concepts have the potential to transform a variety of industries, including encryption, materials science, and artificial intelligence. They allow quantum computers to do some sorts of computations tenfold faster than conventional computers. Even though quantum computing is still in its early stages, continued advancements are being made to eventually apply these concepts in real-world settings.

3.1.2.1 SUPERPOSITION AND QUANTUM STATES

In classical computing, bits can exist in one of two states, 0 or 1. However, in quantum computing, qubits can exist in a superposition of both 0 and 1 states simultaneously. This means that a quantum computer can represent multiple possible outcomes or solutions in a single quantum state.

3.1.2.2 SIMULTANEOUS COMPUTATIONS

A basic idea in quantum computing that results using the superposition principle is quantum parallelism. It alludes to quantum computers' capacity to carry out several calculations or investigate several possibilities at once. One of the main benefits of quantum computing over classical computing is its built-in parallelism. Let us explore deeper into quantum parallelism and its benefits.

3.1.2.3 QUANTUM ALGORITHMS

Quantum algorithms use quantum parallelism in order to resolve particular problems more rapidly than classical algorithms. Grover's algorithm, which speeds up unstructured search, and Shor's algorithm, which effectively factors big numbers—a process that serves as the foundation for many encryption schemes—are two well-known quantum algorithms that make use of parallelism.

3.1.2.4 SPEEDUP FOR CERTAIN PROBLEMS

When dealing with issues, quantum parallelism's benefit compared to classical approaches is shown as an exponential speedup. Shor's algorithm, for instance, can factor huge numbers in polynomial time on a quantum computer, posing a possible challenge to conventional encryption techniques, whereas classical approaches for factoring large numbers take exponential time.

3.1.2.5 QUANTUM SIMULATION

When simulating complicated quantum systems, such as molecules or materials, where the number of potential states increases exponentially with system size, quantum parallelism is especially helpful. The fast parallel exploration of these states by quantum computers makes it possible for simulations to be more accurate and may even result in new insights into fields like chemistry and materials research.

3.1.2.6 OPTIMIZATION

When trying to choose the optimal option from a huge pool of options, optimization issues benefit from the use of quantum parallelism. For problems like supply chain or financial portfolio optimization, quantum algorithms including the quantum approximate optimization algorithm (QAOA) can continuously investigate multiple solutions.

3.1.2.7 REDUCED COMPUTATION TIME

Quantum parallelism holds out the possibility of a reduction in processing time for problems the computational complexity of which makes it unfeasible to tackle them with classical computers. This can have important ramifications in areas like drug research, where finding novel molecules with particular features requires a lot of computing.

3.1.2.8 POTENTIAL FOR QUANTUM MACHINE LEARNING

The parallel examination of several hypotheses or model parameters is made possible by the application of quantum parallelism to machine learning methods. This might result in more effective training and better performance for applications involving quantum machine learning.

The ability of quantum computing to investigate and process several possibilities is known as quantum parallelism. When compared to traditional computers, this feature offers a substantial advantage in the efficient solution of specific types of issues. The potential for quantum parallelism to revolutionize areas like cryptography, optimization, simulation, and machine learning makes this a fascinating field of study and advancement with broad ramifications for different sectors, even though quantum computing technology is still developing and faces difficulties [5, 6].

3.1.3 QUANTUM INTERFERENCE

A key component of quantum computing and quantum information processing is quantum interference, a fundamental quantum mechanical phenomenon. It is caused by the wave-like properties of quantum particles like electrons, photons, and qubits (quantum bits), and it has both positive and negative effects. When working with quantum systems, it is essential to comprehend the idea of quantum interference. Here is a thorough introduction to quantum interference:

3.1.3.1 WAVE-PARTICLE DUALITY

Particles like electrons and photons display both particle-like and wave-like features in quantum physics. This wave-particle duality indicates that these particles have related wave functions that characterize their probability of being in various states or locations instead of possessing well-defined positions (like particles).

3.1.3.2 INTERFERENCE OF PROBABILITY WAVES

When two or more probability waves (expressed by quantum wave functions) overlap or interfere with one another, quantum interference results. Waves that overlap can reinforce or cancel each other out depending on whether their amplitudes are positive or negative (constructive interference).

3.1.3.3 SUPERPOSITION PRINCIPLE

The superposition principle, which enables quantum particles to exist in several states concurrently, and quantum interference are closely linked concepts. According to this principle, we can create a superposition state, which is a linear combination of two or more quantum states, when we have two or more of them. In mathematical terms, it appears as follows: $|\Psi\rangle = \alpha|A\rangle + \beta|B\rangle$, where $|\Psi\rangle$ is the superposition state, $|A\rangle$ and $|B\rangle$ are the individual states, and α and β are complex numbers that determine the probabilities of finding the particle in state $|A\rangle$ or $|B\rangle$.

3.1.3.4 CONSTRUCTIVE INTERFERENCE

Positive interference occurs when two quantum states are in phase, or when their peaks and troughs line up. As a result, there is a better chance of locating the particle in particular areas or states since the amplitudes add up. Specific measurement results are more likely to occur when there is constructive interference.

3.1.3.5 DESTRUCTIVE INTERFERENCE

In contrast, destructive interference occurs when two quantum states are out of phase, meaning that their peaks do not line up with their troughs. As a result, amplitudes cancel out, decreasing the likelihood of discovering the particle in particular areas or states. Some measurement results are suppressed by destructive interference [7].

3.1.3.6 QUANTUM GATES AND QUANTUM CIRCUITS

A crucial component of quantum algorithms is quantum interference. Qubits are manipulated using quantum gates, which are the quantum equivalents of classical logic gates, by creating carefully regulated interference between various quantum states. For instance, depending on the input states and gate operations, the Hadamard gate generates superposition states and can result in either constructive or destructive interference.

3.1.3.7 QUANTUM ALGORITHMS

Quantum algorithms use quantum interference to increase the likelihood of getting the right answer while decreasing the likelihood of getting it wrong. Examples include Grover's algorithm for unstructured search and Shor's algorithm for factoring huge numbers. Quantum computers are able to solve some problems tenfold quicker than classical computers, thanks to this interference-based amplification.

- ***Quantum Interference Applications:*** Quantum cryptography, quantum key distribution, and quantum simulations are just a few of the many uses for quantum interference. The privacy of quantum key distribution procedures, for example, is ensured by the interference of quantum states in quantum cryptography, making eavesdropping more challenging to detect.

  Of course, the wave-like properties of quantum particles and the superposition principle lead to quantum interference, a fundamental quantum mechanical event. It is essential to quantum computing because it enables qubit manipulation and computations that are impossible for classical computers. Quantum interference is a fundamental idea in the study of quantum information science because it has both beneficial and harmful consequences that can be used to produce quantum speedup in a variety of applications [8].

3.2 DATA SCIENCE AND ITS APPLICATIONS—AN OVERVIEW

Data science is an interrelated discipline that integrates methods from domain expertise, statistics, computer science, and data engineering to glean useful information from massive and complicated databases. It has become a potent instrument for problem-solving, prediction, and decision-making in a variety of fields and sectors. This comprehensive explanation of data science will go over its essential elements, procedures, applications, benefits, and difficulties.

3.2.1 KEY COMPONENTS OF DATA SCIENCE

3.2.1.1 DATA COLLECTION

The first step in the process of data science is data collection, which involves gathering unprocessed data from a variety of sources, such as databases, sensors, social media, and more. Data might be unstructured (like text, photos, and videos) or structured (like databases and spreadsheets).

3.2.1.2 DATA CLEANING AND PREPROCESSING

Raw data are frequently erratic, insufficient, or inconsistent. In order to prepare the data for analysis, data scientists clean and preprocess it, which includes activities like missing value imputation, outlier detection, and data normalization.

3.2.1.3 EXPLORATORY DATA ANALYSIS (EDA)

In order to obtain preliminary insights, EDA uses data visualization and summarization. To comprehend the distribution, connections, and patterns in the data, data scientists utilize statistical and graphical techniques.

3.2.1.4 FEATURE ENGINEERING

The process of adding novel characteristics to data that already exist or of altering data to make it more suitable for modeling is known as feature engineering. It is needed for both innovation and domain knowledge.

3.2.1.5 MODELING

This forms the basis of data science, where methods based on math and statistics are utilized to evaluate the data and create predictions. Techniques including regression, clustering, classification, and machine learning algorithms are frequently used.

3.2.1.6 MODEL EVALUATION

Based on the scope of the problem, models are assessed using a variety of measures, including accuracy, precision, recall, F1-score, and more. To enhance model performance, cross-validation and hyperparameter adjustment are performed.

3.2.1.7 DEPLOYMENT

The model can be used in real-world applications like recommendation systems, detecting fraud, and autonomous vehicles after it has been trained and evaluated [9].

3.2.2 DATA SCIENCE PROCESS

The iterative techniques of data science often go as follows:

- Problem Clarification: Clearly state the issue at hand and the objectives of the data analysis. It is essential to comprehend the industry and the business environment.
- Data Gathering: Compile pertinent data from a variety of sources.
- ata Preprocessing: Cleansing, transforming, and preparing the data for analysis.
- Exploratory Data Analysis: Examine the data to learn about its features and any connections.
- Feature Engineering: To enhance model performance, add new features or modify current ones.
- Model Development: Create, refine, and test machine learning models.
- Model Evaluation: Use the right metrics to gauge the model's effectiveness.

- Model Deployment: Set up the model for application in real situations.
- Monitoring and Upkeep: Constantly keep an eye on the performance of the model and update it as necessary.

3.2.3 APPLICATIONS OF DATA SCIENCE

Data science is used in many different industries, including:

- Business and finance: fraud detection, customer segmentation, portfolio optimization, and predictive analytics.
- Healthcare: Medical imaging analysis, drug discovery, disease prognosis, and patient outcome forecasting.
- Marketing: A/B testing, recommendation systems, and customer behavior analysis.
- E-commerce: Demand forecasts, supply chain optimization, and customized product suggestions.
- Social sciences: Social network analysis, sentiment analysis, and opinion mining.
- Manufacturing: Process optimization, quality assurance, and predictive maintenance.
- Environmental science: Resource management, pollution monitoring, and climate prediction.

3.2.4 ADVANTAGES OF DATA SCIENCE

3.2.4.1 INFORMED DECISION-MAKING

Data science gives businesses data-driven insights that help them make wise decisions. Data-driven judgments are frequently more precise and trustworthy, whether they are made in business, medicine, finance, or any other industry.

3.2.4.2 PREDICTIVE ANALYTICS

Businesses can predict future developments, find potential opportunities, and foresee difficulties, thanks to data science. Risk management and proactive decision-making are made easier using predictive analytics.

3.2.4.3 COST REDUCTION

Organizations can find inefficiencies, improve procedures, and cut costs by exploring data. This may result in major operational expense savings.

3.2.4.4 PERSONALIZATION

In order to provide clients with individualized experiences, data science is essential. Personalized recommendations, for instance, increased customer engagement and happiness in e-commerce and digital marketing.

3.2.4.5 AUTOMATION

Using chatbots, data science may automate repetitive and time-consuming operations such as data entry, data cleansing, and even customer service. This improves efficiency while freeing up human resources for more strategic duties.

3.2.4.6 COMPETITIVE ADVANTAGE

Organizations that successfully apply data science acquire a competitive advantage. They are able to adjust swiftly to market developments, tailor products and services to consumer requirements, and surpass competition.

3.2.4.7 HEALTHCARE AND MEDICINE

By enhancing patient outcomes, anticipating disease outbreaks, and optimizing treatment approaches, data science has transformed healthcare. Early detection and personalized medication have the potential to save lives.

3.2.4.8 SCIENTIFIC DISCOVERY

Data science allows scientists to explore huge databases and generate new findings in domains such as astronomy, genetics, and particle physics. Data analysis approaches, for example, enabled the detection of gravitational waves.

3.2.4.9 SOCIAL IMPACT

Data science has the potential to address significant societal issues such as climate change, poverty, and the health of the public. It assists governments and organizations in developing data-driven policies and activities.

3.2.4.10 CONTINUOUS IMPROVEMENT

Data science is an evolving field. As new data sources and technologies emerge, organizations can continuously improve their processes and decision-making through ongoing data analysis [10].

3.2.5 CHALLENGES IN DATA SCIENCE

Although data science has many benefits it additionally comes with several drawbacks, including data protection, ethical problems, model interpretability, and a shortage of experienced specialists. Overcoming these obstacles is critical to generating ethical and successful data-driven decisions.

Numerous challenges facing data science:

- Data Quality: Ensuring that data is accurate, full, and representative can be difficult.
- Privacy and Ethics: It is critical to handle sensitive data while respecting privacy. Ethical issues in AI and data usage are becoming increasingly important.
- Model Interpretability: Complex machine learning models may lack transparency, make understanding how they make decisions challenging.
- Scalability: To analyze massive datasets and construct scalable models, efficient algorithms and infrastructure are required.
- Bias and Fairness: Models may acquire biases from data, resulting in inaccurate predictions. Fairness in algorithms is becoming a serious topic.
- Continuous Learning: Because the area of data science is always growing, practitioners must keep up with new approaches and technology.

Data science is a dynamic discipline that uses data to solve complicated issues, make educated decisions, and create value in a variety of businesses. Data science's applications are expanding, and as it tackles the problems, it will continue to be a major engine of innovation and advancement in the digital era [11].

3.3 APPLICATIONS OF QUANTUM COMPUTING IN DATA SCIENCE

Quantum computing has the potential to transform data science by tackling complicated problems quicker and more effectively than traditional computers. Its distinct features, such as quantum parallelism and quantum interference, have the potential to profoundly affect different elements of data science. We may explore exploring the potential uses of quantum computing in data science in the part below:

3.3.1 OPTIMIZATION PROBLEMS

Quantum computers are very good at addressing optimization issues, which are common in data science. Here are a few examples:

- Portfolio Optimization: Quantum algorithms can effectively optimize investment portfolios by determining the ideal asset combinations to maximize returns while controlling risk.
- Supply Chain Management: Quantum computing can optimize supply chain logistics by calculating the most effective routes and inventory levels to satisfy demand while minimizing expenses.
- Resource Allocation: In settings such as cloud computing, energy distribution, and traffic management, quantum algorithms can best distribute resources.

3.3.2 MACHINE LEARNING AND AI

Quantum computing has the potential to improve several elements of machine learning and AI:

- Quantum Machine Learning (QML): Quantum computers can accelerate specific machine learning activities, such as training complicated models or addressing optimization issues that are at the heart of machine learning algorithms.
- Quantum Neural Networks: Quantum computing may be utilized to create quantum neural networks, which may outperform traditional neural networks in certain applications, such as quantum data processing.
- Chemoinformatics: Quantum computers are capable of effectively simulating molecular structures and interactions, which can help in drug development and materials research.

3.3.3 DATA ANALYTICS

Quantum computing has the potential to speed data analytics processes:

- Big Data Analysis: Quantum algorithms are able to more effectively handle and analyze enormous datasets, lowering processing times for applications such as data mining and pattern identification.
- Clustering and classification: Quantum algorithms can enhance clustering and classification jobs, making it simpler to glean insights from large amounts of data [12].

3.3.4 CRYPTOGRAPHY

The implications of quantum computing for the safety of data are significant:

- Quantum Cryptanalysis: Quantum computers have the ability to break commonly utilized encryption algorithms like RSA and ECC. As a result, quantum-resistant encryption algorithms must be developed.
- Quantum Key Distribution (QKD): Via QKD, by offering evidently secure communication channels, quantum computing can improve data security.

3.3.5 SIMULATION AND MODELING

Quantum computers are very helpful in modeling complicated systems:

- Quantum Simulations: Quantum computers are more effective than conventional computers in simulating quantum processes, which benefits fields such as quantum chemistry, physics, and materials research.
- Climate Modeling: Quantum computing can assist expedite climate modeling and more precisely anticipate the impacts of climate changes.

3.3.6 DATA COMPRESSION

Quantum algorithms may be utilized to provide more efficient data compression solutions for massive datasets, lowering storage and transmission costs.

3.3.7 ANOMALY DETECTION

Anomaly detection techniques can be improved by quantum computing, which makes it simpler to find strange patterns or outliers in data, which is critical for detecting fraud and network security.

3.3.8 NATURAL LANGUAGE PROCESSING

Quantum computers have the potential to increase the efficiency of natural language processing activities such as machine translation, sentiment analysis, and chatbots.

3.3.9 GRAPH THEORY

Quantum computing speeds up the solution of graph theory problems, which benefits the analysis of networks, analysis of social networks, and recommendation systems. It is critical to highlight that quantum computing continues to be in its early stages, with real, large-scale quantum computers not yet readily available. However, as quantum technology advances, its applications in data science are projected to expand, allowing data scientists to effectively solve more complicated issues and extract important insights from enormous databases [13].

3.4 A DETAILED OVERVIEW OF IMPORTANT QUANTUM COMPUTING ALGORITHMS

Now, we will study more about Quantum Support Vector Machines (QSVMs), Quantum Neural Networks, and the Quantum Approximate Optimization Algorithm in this section.

3.4.1 QUANTUM SUPPORT VECTOR MACHINE

A QSVM is a quantum computing-based technique for tackling SVM issues. To comprehend QSVM, you must first be acquainted with SVM, a traditional machine-learning technique used for classification and regression applications. SVM searches the feature space for a hyperplane that optimally divides two classes of data points whilst maximizing the margin among them. Quantum computing, on the other hand, uses quantum physics concepts to accomplish tasks that conventional computers find difficult or impossible. QSVM combines components of both quantum computing and classical SVM to potentially provide advantages for some sorts of issues, particularly those involving high-dimensional data.

Let us take a look more closely at how QSVM works in detail:

3.4.1.1 QUANTUM BITS (QUBITS)

Bits (0 and 1) are the basic units for data in traditional computing. We employ qubits in quantum computing because they can be present in several states at the same time due to superposition principles. This characteristic enables quantum computers to handle massive amounts of data simultaneously.

3.4.1.2 QUANTUM STATES

Qubits can exist in a state denoted by a superposition of 0 and 1 ($\alpha|0\rangle + \beta|1\rangle$), where α and β are complex integers. This enables quantum computers to represent and modify information in ways that classical computers cannot.

3.4.1.3 QUANTUM GATES

Quantum gates are used to execute quantum processes. These gates change the state of the qubits. The Hadamard gate (which generates superpositions), the Pauli-X gate (bit-flip), the Pauli-Y gate (bit-flip and phase-flip), and the Pauli-Z gate (phase-flip) are all notable quantum gates.

3.4.1.4 QUANTUM ENTANGLEMENT

Qubits can also be entangled, which means that the state of one is reliant on the state of another, regardless of how far apart they are. Certain quantum algorithms can benefit from this characteristic [14].

3.4.2 WORKING PROCEDURE OF QSVM

3.4.2.1 QUANTUM DATA ENCODING

Data points are encoded into quantum states in order to employ a quantum computer for SVM tasks. This is often accomplished through the use of quantum feature maps, which convert classical data into quantum states. Quantum feature maps can be used to generate complicated data representations in high-dimensional quantum space.

3.4.2.2 QUANTUM KERNEL

The quantum kernel is at the heart of QSVM. There are different kernel functions in traditional SVM, such as linear, polynomial, and radial basis function. A quantum kernel is used in QSVM, which is frequently designed using quantum circuits. The quantum kernel compares the likeness of quantum-encoded data points.

3.4.2.3 QUANTUM SVM ALGORITHM

QSVM combines a quantum kernel with a traditional SVM algorithm. The quantum kernel assesses similarities of quantum-encoded data points, while the conventional SVM algorithm optimizes the hyperplane for separating the data while maximizing the margin. This method is comparable to conventional SVM, except that it uses quantum parallelism and possibly higher-dimensional feature spaces.

3.4.2.4 QUANTUM ADVANTAGE

The quantum benefit of QSVM is its capacity to do particular computations tenfold quicker than conventional computers. This benefit is especially noticeable when working with high-dimensional data or when the quantum kernel is able to effectively capture the fundamental layout of the data.

3.4.2.5 QUANTUM HARDWARE

To operate QSVM, we must have a connection to quantum hardware, including quantum processors and quantum gates, which continue to be in the initial stages of development and may be limited in the way of qubit count, error rates, and coherence durations.

QSVM is a quantum computing-based solution to addressing SVM issues that takes advantage of quantum mechanics' unique qualities like as superposition, entanglement, and quantum gates. QSVM offers the ability to provide benefits for specific kinds of issues; however its actual implementation is dependent on quantum hardware maturity and scalability [15].

3.4.3 QUANTUM NEURAL NETWORK

Quantum neural networks (QNNs) represent a kind of quantum machine learning model with the goal of utilizing quantum computing abilities to accomplish certain tasks more effectively or to handle specific kinds of data more efficiently than conventional neural networks. To handle information in a fundamentally novel way, they mix components of quantum computing with traditional neural networks. Let us get into more information about quantum neural networks:

QNNs work using quantum bits, also known as qubits, which vary from classical bits. A conventional bit may be either 0 or 1, but a qubit can exist in a superposition of the two states, denoted as |0 + |1, where and are complex integers. Qubits can execute concurrent calculations because to this characteristic. Quantum operations in QNNs are carried out with the help of quantum gates. Such gates, like classical logic gates (AND, OR, NOT), modify the states of qubits. The Hadamard gate (which causes superpositions), the Pauli-X gate (bit-flip), the Pauli-Y gate (bit-flip and phase-flip), and the Pauli-Z gate (phase-flip) are all common quantum gates.

Qubits can also be entangled, which means that the state of one relies on the state of another, regardless of their distance. Entanglement is a valuable resource for quantum algorithms such as QNNs. A parameterized quantum circuit (PQC) is at the heart of a QNN. A PQC is a series of quantum gates with programmable parameters that may be taught using conventional optimization approaches. The quantum circuit's behavior is determined by these parameters. In QNNs, input data is often encoded into the quantum states of qubits. This encoding is accomplished by the use of quantum feature maps, which convert classical data into a quantum state representation. Quantum feature maps can be used to generate sophisticated quantum states capable of capturing detailed data patterns. A quantum layer in a QNN is generally made up of a PQC. The quantum layer processes input data in a quantum state, changing it into another quantum state according to the parameters of the PQC. This modified state encodes features which are relevant to the job at hand.

Following the quantum layer, there is normally a classical layer composed of classical neurons. To generate an output, these neurons use quantum-encoded input and perform conventional operations such as linear combinations and activation functions. Training a QNN entails utilizing classical optimization techniques to optimize the parameters of the quantum circuit (PQC). During the training phase, the goal is to minimize a loss function that measures the difference between the QNN's predictions and the ground truth labels. This is frequently accomplished through the use of gradient-based optimization algorithms. QNNs are projected to give advantages in a variety of circumstances, including quantum-enhanced feature extraction, optimization issues, and quantum system simulation. When run on a suitably powerful quantum computer, they may provide an exponential speedup for some quantum algorithms. Access to quantum gear, such as quantum processors and quantum gates, is required to operate QNNs. The current level of quantum computing technology has restrictions in terms of qubit count, error rates, and coherence durations, limiting QNNs' practical application [16].

QNNs are a type of quantum machine learning model that combines quantum computing principles such as superposition and entanglement with classical neural networks. They may have the ability to excel at some jobs, especially those involving high-dimensional data or quantum processes. Their practical value, however, is dependent on the evolution of quantum hardware and algorithms.

3.4.4 QUANTUM APPROXIMATE OPTIMIZATION ALGORITHM

The QAOA is a quantum algorithm developed to handle optimization issues, which entails choosing the optimum answer from a list of feasible options. QAOA excels in combinatorial optimization issues such as finding the greatest clique in a graph, solving the traveling salesman problem, and optimizing the architecture of qubits in a quantum circuit.

The QAOA is explained in full below:

3.4.4.1 PROBLEM REPRESENTATION

QAOA starts with an optimization problem that we wish to address. We should have a well-defined goal function that we aim to maximize or minimize in the challenge. This function is sometimes referred to as the cost function, and its value is determined by the specific restrictions and objectives of the task.

3.4.4.2 QUANTUM CIRCUIT LAYERS

QAOA runs on quantum circuits with alternating layers of quantum gates, exactly like how neural networks use layers. Each layer is made up of two kinds of quantum gates:

- Cost Hamiltonian Operator (U_C): This gate encodes the cost function of the issue into the quantum state. The cost function indicates the goal you wish to achieve. The U_C gate is built around the problem's Hamiltonian, which is a mathematical operator that describes the energy of the problem.

- Mixer Hamiltonian Operator (U_B): This gate functions as a "mixer" to investigate various quantum states. It is usually intended to encourage state transitions that aid in the optimization process.
- For a fixed number of layers, indicated as p, the quantum circuit alternates between U_C and U_B gates. These gates' settings are optimized in order to discover the optimum answer to the optimization issue [17].

3.4.4.3 INITIAL STATE PREPARATION

The quantum circuit begins with an initial state, which is frequently selected to be a uniform superposition of all conceivable states. This is represented as a quantum state with amplitudes that are equal for all conceivable bit strings.

3.4.4.4 QUANTUM STATE EVOLUTION

The U_C and U_B gates are applied consecutively in each layer of the quantum circuit. This procedure brings the quantum state closer to solving the optimization issue. In each layer, the characteristics of these gates are modified to increase the state's quality.

3.4.4.5 MEASUREMENT

The final quantum state is determined after applying the quantum circuit layers to yield a conventional result. This measurement approximates the ideal solution to the optimization issue.

3.4.4.6 CLASSICAL POSTPROCESSING

Classical postprocessing techniques are used to the quantum circuit measurement data, which may involve refining the solution, assessing the solution quality, and perhaps running the procedure numerous times to boost confidence in the achieved solution.

3.4.4.7 OPTIMIZATION OF PARAMETERS

The optimization of the parameters in the quantum circuit is a critical component of QAOA. Classical optimization approaches, such as gradient-based methods, are often used to discover the values that maximize the objective function.

3.4.4.8 PERFORMANCE AND ITERATION

The number of layers (*p*) in the quantum circuit and the optimization of gate parameters influence the quality of the solution provided by QAOA. It may take several iterations to increase the quality of the answer.

3.4.4.9 QUANTUM ADVANTAGE

The capacity of QAOA to explore a superposition of states gives it the potential benefit over classical algorithms in finding better solutions for specific optimization issues faster than classical counterparts.

A quantum method developed to handle optimization issues is the QAOA. It evolves a quantum state toward the ideal solution using alternating layers of quantum gates while optimizing gate settings to increase solution quality. Although it has a chance to provide benefits for particular optimization issues, the practical implementation and performance of QAOA are dependent on the problem instance and accessible quantum hardware [18].

3.5 CONVERGENCE OF QUANTUM COMPUTING WITH BIG DATA

The confluence of quantum computing with big data signifies a meeting of two transformational technologies having a chance to revolutionize a variety of areas. In this extensive discussion, we will look at how quantum computing and big data collide, as well as the potential consequences of this convergence:

Quantum computing uses quantum physics concepts to accomplish tasks that traditional computers cannot. Quantum computers employ qubits, which may exist in superpositions and entangled states, rather than classical bits (0s and 1s). This trait enables them to handle massive volumes of data in parallel, making them potentially useful for dealing with big data. The term "big data" refers to the vast volume of organized and unstructured data created by numerous sources such as sensors, social media, scientific investigations, and others. Big data is defined by the "3Vs": volume (huge data size), velocity (real-time data generation), and variety (data in many forms). Big data analysis frequently necessitates advanced algorithms and large processing resources [19].

3.5.1 INTERSECTION POINTS

3.5.1.1 DATA PROCESSING AND ANALYSIS

Quantum computing has the ability to speed up data processing and analysis activities including cleaning, filtering, and feature extraction. Quantum techniques, such as Grover's algorithm, have the potential to accelerate search and pattern identification jobs in huge data.

3.5.1.2 MACHINE LEARNING AND OPTIMIZATION

Machine learning and optimization projects frequently make use of big data. Quantum computers offer an opportunity to improve these fields by accelerating machine learning model training (e.g., QSVMs) and solving complicated optimization problems (e.g., the traveling salesman problem) more effectively.

3.5.1.3 SIMULATIONS AND MODELING

Quantum computing can accurately and rapidly mimic quantum systems and physical events than conventional computers. This is critical for scientific research, drug development, and materials science, all of which produce large amounts of data via simulations and experiments.

3.5.1.4 CRYPTOGRAPHY AND SECURITY

Big data frequently contains confidential data. Due to Shor's algorithm, quantum computing provides a danger to classical encryption approaches (e.g., RSA), but it additionally offers the opportunity for quantum-resistant cryptography, safeguarding massive data in the quantum era.

3.5.1.5 QUANTUM DATABASES

Quantum databases may develop as a novel approach to effectively store and retrieve data in a quantum-computing environment. Quantum databases might manage enormous amounts of data more efficiently, benefiting big data applications.

3.5.2 CHALLENGES AND CONSIDERATIONS

- Limitations of Quantum Hardware: Quantum computers are still in their infancy, with restricted qubits, error rates, and coherence times. Handling genuinely massive amounts of data necessitates substantially more powerful quantum gear.
- Hybrid Approaches: Practical solutions may include hybrid quantum-classical algorithms, in which quantum computers help with certain jobs inside a traditional big data pipeline.
- Data Preprocessing: The capabilities of quantum computing in data analysis may need preprocessed data being encoded into quantum states, which may provide obstacles and overheads.
- Scalability: A continuing research problem is for quantum algorithms to scale efficiently with the amount and complexity of big data.
- Impact: The convergence of quantum computing and big data has the potential to:
    - Accelerate scientific research ideas and findings
    - Increase the efficiency and precision of machine learning and optimization processes
    - Improve data security in the quantum computing age
    - Enable new sorts of apps and services that use quantum capabilities to handle and analyze large amounts of data

The convergence of quantum computing with big data offers intriguing possibilities for speeding up processing, analyzing, and scientific discovery. However, it is filled with difficulties due to hardware limits and algorithm scalability. We may expect quantum computing to play a growing part in the area of big data as quantum technology improves [20].

3.6 CONVERGENCE OF QUANTUM COMPUTING WITH CRYPTOGRAPHY

Because quantum computers possess the ability to undermine commonly utilized conventional encryption techniques, the confluence of quantum computing and cryptography is a vital and challenging field of study. This intersection centers on quantum computing's weaknesses and prospects in the realm of cryptography.

We will look at how quantum computing overlaps with encryption in more depth below: Shor's algorithm, which can effectively factor enormous numbers, has become one of the most well-known quantum algorithms having cryptography implications. Large number factoring is an essential procedure in cracking many traditional encryption methods.

3.6.1 VULNERABILITIES

Classical cryptography techniques are significantly vulnerable to quantum computing:

3.6.1.1 FACTORING AND RSA

Shor's method can effectively factor big numbers, putting the security of the commonly used RSA encryption scheme at risk. The complexity of scaling the product of two big prime integers is used by RSA.

3.6.1.2 DISCRETE LOGARITHM AND ECC

Quantum computers are also capable of solving the discrete logarithm issue, which is at the heart of the security of elliptic curve cryptography (ECC). Modern encryption systems, such as ECC-based public-key cryptography, make extensive use of ECC.

3.6.1.3 SYMMETRIC KEY CRYPTOGRAPHY

Grover's approach can halve the efficient key length needed for security by speeding up the brute force look for symmetric encryption keys [21].

3.6.2 QUANTUM-RESISTANT CRYPTOGRAPHY

To solve these flaws, academics are working on quantum-resistant encryption methods. These algorithms are intended to be resistant against quantum computer assaults. Lattice-based cryptography, hash-based cryptography, code-based cryptography, and multivariate polynomial cryptography are among the examples. These techniques are based on mathematical issues that are thought to be difficult to solve effectively even with quantum computers.

3.6.3 QUANTUM KEY DISTRIBUTION (QKD)

Quantum computing also provides chances to improve cryptographic security. QKD is a secure key exchange mechanism based on quantum mechanics concepts. QKD enables two parties to produce a shared secret key that is theoretically resistant to any computational attack, including quantum computer assaults. BB84 and E91 are two well-known QKD methods.

3.6.4 POSTQUANTUM CRYPTOGRAPHY TRANSITION

With the advancement of quantum computing, there will be an urgent need to move to postquantum cryptography. Government organizations, standards organizations, and businesses are all working hard to create and standardize quantum-resistant cryptographic algorithms that will replace susceptible classical methods. The idea is to keep encryption safe even when quantum computers become capable of cracking present techniques.

3.6.5 QUANTUM CRYPTANALYSIS CHALLENGES

While quantum computing threatens traditional cryptography, it also offers certain difficulties for quantum cryptanalysis. Quantum error correction, qubit stability, and scaling up quantum computers are all key challenges that can be addressed before practical quantum computers designed for splitting strong cryptographic systems can be built.

3.6.6 HYBRID APPROACHES

Hybrid cryptographic solutions are anticipated to develop in the near to medium future. To give a layered approach to security, these systems mix conventional and quantum-resistant algorithms. For example, a traditional public-key infrastructure might be utilized for authentication, while quantum-resistant symmetric encryption protects data.

3.6.7 CONTINUOUS RESEARCH

The interaction of quantum computing and encryption is a fluid and ever-changing field. In order to prepare toward the era of quantum computing, researchers are currently investigating novel cryptographic primitives, postquantum cryptographic systems, and quantum-resistant technology.

The area of quantum computing and cryptography is sophisticated and varied. While quantum computing exposes traditional cryptographic systems to flaws, it also provides prospects for quantum-resistant cryptography and safe quantum key distribution. To assure the future security of digital communication and data protection, preparing for the quantum era entails defining new cryptographic standards and migrating to postquantum encryption.

3.7 POTENTIAL THREATS OF QUANTUM COMPUTING WITH CLASSICAL CRYPTOGRAPHIC SYSTEMS

In the field of cybersecurity, the potential danger of quantum computing to traditional cryptography systems is the key worry. Many widely used classical encryption techniques can be effectively broken by quantum computers, which has substantial consequences for data security, privacy, and trust in digital communication. Let us investigate this threat in depth:

3.7.1 SHOR'S ALGORITHM

One of the most well-known quantum algorithms, Shor's algorithm, poses a substantial danger to traditional cryptography systems. It factors big numbers quickly and determines discrete logarithms in polynomial time.

These two procedures serve as the foundation for various widely used traditional encryption methods.

3.7.2 RSA ENCRYPTION

The difficult task of factoring the product of two big prime integers underpins RSA encryption. Shor's method is considerably quicker than the most widely utilized classical algorithms for factoring huge numbers, thereby defeating RSA encryption.

- ***Diffie-Hellman Key Exchange:*** Several key exchange protocols, notably Diffie-Hellman, rely on the discrete logarithm issue for security. Shor's method will fix this problem quickly, jeopardizing the secrecy of shared keys.

3.7.3 IMPACT ON DATA SECURITY

Quantum computing has the ability to have a significant influence on data security:

- *Confidentiality:* Because quantum computers may decode previously encrypted data, sensitive data including financial transactions, personal conversations, and confidential government material could be exposed.
- *Integrity:* Quantum attacks have the potential to threaten the integrity of digital signatures and certificates, rendering it difficult to authenticate the validity of digital documents and software upgrades.
- *Breach of Privacy:* Privacy in communications may be jeopardized if eavesdroppers overcome encryption and intercept sensitive information.

3.7.4 TRANSITION TO POSTQUANTUM CRYPTOGRAPHY

To mitigate the danger of quantum computing to traditional cryptographic systems, the cryptographic community is actively creating and standardizing postquantum cryptographic methods. These algorithms are intended to be resistant to quantum assaults. Following are a few instances of postquantum cryptography approaches:

- *Lattice-Based Cryptography:* Lattice-based cryptography represents one of the greatest exciting possibilities for postquantum security since it is based on the strength of particular lattice issues.
- *Code-Based Cryptography:* This technique is being investigated for secure key exchange and digital signatures because of the difficulties of decoding linear codes.
- *Multivariate Polynomial Cryptography:* This technique is based on multivariate polynomial problems with no effective solution algorithm for quantum computers.

3.7.5 QUANTUM-RESISTANT ALGORITHMS

While these postquantum cryptographic systems are thought to be safe against quantum assaults, careful design, analysis, and standardization are required before they can be widely implemented.

3.7.6 QUANTUM KEY DISTRIBUTION (QKD)

QKD is a safe communication method that makes use of quantum physics. It enables two parties to produce a shared secret key that is very secure. QKD is thought to be resistant to quantum assaults and offers a viable solution for secure key exchange during the quantum era.

3.7.7 TRANSITION PERIOD

Making the transition to postquantum encryption and quantum-safe protocols will be difficult and possibly require years, if not decades. Throughout this shift, certain systems could become vulnerable because they still use traditional encryption.

3.7.8 CYBERSECURITY PREPAREDNESS

Organizations, governments, and enterprises must brace themselves for the implications of quantum computing on data security. This involves examining their cryptographic infrastructure, comprehending the dangers, and planning for the eventual deployment of quantum-resistant encryption.

The capacity of quantum computers to effectively deal with issues that underpin current encryption methods poses a possible threat to classical cryptography systems. Transitioning to postquantum encryption and developing quantum-resistant algorithms are critical stages in dealing with this danger and assuring the privacy of digital communication and data protection in the quantum era [22].

3.8 CONCLUSION

In the area of data science, quantum computing offers enormous promise, with the ability to revolutionize several elements of data analysis, machine learning, and optimization challenges. Quantum computing can undeniably accelerate difficult computations on massive datasets. It has the potential to enhance machine learning algorithms by allowing for improved optimization procedures. Quantum-enhanced algorithms have the potential to improve solutions to issues such as feature selection, grouping, and classification. Quantum computers possess the capability of breaking commonly utilized encryption techniques, posing a risk to data security. They can, however, be utilized to create quantum-resistant encryption systems to protect sensitive data. Quantum computing may be used simply on quantum datasets produced by quantum sensors or quantum simulations. Quantum algorithms are intended to analyze such data effectively, opening up novel fields of study. QML seeks to use quantum qualities to more effectively process and analyze data, perhaps leading to advances in pattern recognition and optimization tasks.

Quantum computers excel at tackling combinatorial optimization issues, allowing for more optimum resource allocation and scheduling solutions. This algorithm can aid enhance clustering and dimensionality reduction approaches in high-dimensional datasets. This can result in more accurate data analysis and improved data visualization. Quantum computing has the ability to change data science by making data analysis, machine learning, and optimization quicker and more efficient. While actual quantum computers remain in their infancy, continued research and development in the subject promises to unleash new capabilities and handle difficult data-related issues. As quantum technologies advance, data scientists and researchers will rapidly investigate and exploit their potential for a wide range of applications.

KEYWORDS

- **quantum computers**
- **qubits**
- **quantum gates**
- **quantum algorithms**
- **quantum approximate optimization algorithm**

REFERENCES

1. Hevia, J. L., Peterssen, G., Ebert, C., & Piattini, M. (2021). Quantum computing. *IEEE Software*, *38*(5), 7–15, https://doi.org/10.1109/MS.2021.3087755.
2. Preskill, J. (1998). Reliable quantum computers. *Royal Society*, *454*(1969), https://doi.org/10.1098/rspa.1998.0167.
3. Vedral, V., & Plenio, M. B. (1998). Basics of quantum computation. *Progress in Quantum Electronics*, *22*(1), 1–39, https://doi.org/10.1016/S0079-6727(98)00004-4.
4. Rietsche, R., Dremel, C., Bosch, S., Steinacker, L., Meckel, M., & Leimeister, J.-M. (2022). Quantum computing. *Electronic Markets, Springer*, *32*, 2525–2536, https://doi.org/10.1007/s12525-022-00570-y.
5. Austin, J. (2015). A case for quantum parallelism. *Physics World*, *27*, 03, http://doi.org/10.1088/2058-7058/27/03/27.
6. Nagy, M., & Akl, S. G. (2005). On the importance of parallelism for quantum computation and the concept of a universal computer. *International Conference on Unconventional Computation, Unconventional Computation*, *3699*, 176–190.
7. Hornberger, K., Gerlich, S., Haslinger, P., Nimmrichter, S., & Arndt, M. (2012). Colloquium: Quantum interference of clusters and molecules. *Reviews of Modern Physics*, *84*, 157, https://doi.org/10.1103/RevModPhys.84.157
8. Kleiner, R., Koelle, D., Ludwig, F., & Clarke, J. (2004). Superconducting quantum interference devices: State of the art and applications. *Proceedings in IEEE*, *92*(10), 1534–1548, https://doi.org/10.1109/JPROC.2004.833655.
9. Donoho, D. (2017). 50 years of data science. *Journal of Computational and Graphical Statistics*, *26*(4), 745–766, https://doi.org/10.1080/10618600.2017.1384734.
10. Van der Aalst, W. (2016). *Data Science in Action, Process Mining.* Springer, pp. 3–23, https://doi.org/10.1007/978-3-662-49851-4_1.
11. Grus, J. (2019). Data science from scratch- first principles with Python. *O-Reilly*.

12. Shaikh, A., & Ali, R. (2016). Quantum computing in big data analytics: A survey. In *2016 IEEE International Conference on Computer and Information Technology (CIT)*. Nadi, Fiji, pp. 112–115, https://doi.org/10.1109/CIT.2016.79.
13. Wang, Y. (2022). When quantum computation meets data science: Making data science quantum. *Harvard Data Science Review*, *4*(1), https://doi.org/10.1162/99608f92.ef5d8928.
14. Rebentrost, P., Mohseni, M., & Lloyd, S. (2014). Quantum support vector machine for big data classification. *Physical Review Letters*, *113*(3), 130503, https://doi.org/10.1103/PhysRevLett.113.130503
15. Rana, A., Vaidya, P., & Gupta, G. (2022). A comparative study of quantum support vector machine algorithm for handwritten recognition with support vector machine algorithm. *Science Direct, Materials Proceedings*, *56*(Part 4), 2025–2030.
16. Jia, Z.-A., Yi, B., Zhai, R., Wu, Y.-C, Guo, G.-C., & Guo, G.-P. (2019). Advance quantum technologies. *Wiley*, *2*(7–8), 1800077, https://doi.org/10.1002/qute.201800077.
17. Zhou, L., Wang, S.-T., Choi, S., Pichler, H., & Lukin, M. D. (2020). Quantum approximate optimization algorithm: Performance, mechanism, and implementation on near-term devices. *Physical Review X*, *10*(2), 021067.
18. Choi, J., & Kim, J. A tutorial on quantum approximate optimization algorithm (QAOA): Fundamentals and applications. In *2019 International Conference on Information and Communication Technology Convergence (ICTC), IEEE Xplore*, p. 19259347, https://doi.org/10.1109/ICTC46691.2019.8939749.
19. Rabah, K. (2018). Convergence of AI, IoT, big data and blockchain: A review. *The Lake Institute Journal*, *1*(1), 1–18.
20. Viggiano, G., & Brin, D. (2022). *Convergence: Artificial Intelligence and Quantum Computing Social, Economic, and Policy Impacts*. Wiley, p. 320. ISBN 9781394174119.
21. Shamshad, S., Riaz, F., Riaz, R., Rizvi, S. S., & Abdulla, S. (2021). A hybrid architecture for resolving Cryptographic issues in Internet of Things (IoT), Employing Quantum computing supremacy. In *International Conference on Information and Communication Technology Convergence (ICTC),* Republic of Korea, IEEE, pp. 271–276, https://doi.org/10.1109/ICTC52510.2021.9621208.
22. Kan, K., & Une, M. (2021). Recent trends on research and development of quantum computers and standardization of post-quantum cryptography. *Monetary and Economic Studies*, *39*, 77–107.

CHAPTER 4

Reliability and Correctness of Quantum Key Exchange with Secure Encoding

PARTHA SARATHI GOSWAMI[1*] and TAMAL CHAKRABORTY[2]

[1]*Department of Cyber Forensics and Information Security, Behala Government Polytechnic, Kolkata, West Bengal, India*

[2]*Department of Computer Science, Mrinalini Datta Mahavidyapith, Kolkata, West Bengal, India*

*Corresponding author

ABSTRACT

This chapter focuses on the security and reliability of quantum key exchange algorithms with secure encoding. Various DNA encoding schemes have been discussed in combination with Super-increasing Knapsack codes and Fermat codes. Amalgamating more than one coding techniques increases the diffusion and confusion of the underlying communication channel, thereby adding to the overall system robustness. The impact of possible well-known attacks on the system has been critically analyzed. The results show that the proposed methodology works well with respect to the vulnerabilities under observation.

4.1 INTRODUCTION

A numerical one-way trapdoor function, f, is a mapping that is "easy" to compute in a single direction. However, it is "hard" to find $f - 1$ sans a priori knowledge. It is not adequate for a function to be termed one-way just because it is one-to-one. Mathematically, a one-way function can be denoted as

Applications of Quantum Computing in a Variety of Domains. Gunjan Mukherjee, Biswadip Basu Mallik, Rahul Kar Özen ÖZER, Digvijay Pandey, and Binay Kumar Pandey (Eds.)

DOI: 10.1201/9781998511051-4

$\Lambda_i : \beta_i \rightarrow \lambda_i$ where $i \in \text{Im}$ and $\{\text{Im}, \beta, \lambda\} \subseteq \{0,1\}^*, \{0,1\}^*$ being set of all binary strings with finite length.

This function is usually used in asymmetric cryptoanalysis. The key property of these mapping is that, using it a proficiently solvable problem is offered to the participants, while any opponent will face an insurmountable challenge. The barrier of difficulty between authentic and fake players is the foremost notion behind contemporary public-key cryptosystems.

An input message in binary form can be transformed to its corresponding nucleotide base by using a DNA code set. Also, in any quantum transmission medium, security is guaranteed by quantum superposition. A fascinating problem in a quantum cryptosystem is the exchange of the encoded key among the participants in the quantum channel. Combining the encoding schemes such as Fermat Numbers and DNA sequences along with Quantum postulates provides an extra layer of protection. The notion of Watson–Crick's complement of DNA sequences and randomness of the Fermat Numbers can be applied for securing the communication media by virtue of dual encryption.

4.2 RELATED WORKS

Zhang et al. [1] proposed a DNA-based cryptographic methodology combining hamming code with a block cryptogram that offered security for the key that is to be used to enhance a DNA-based method. Here, for securing the data against various attacks, the maximum length matching procedure is used.

Zhang et al. [2] suggested a stenographic technique using DNA cryptosystem and Feistel network. First, to generate the hash digest, the Secure Hash Algorithm (SHA-3) procedure was used and then to generate the "Hill cipher" matrix the chaos-generated sequence was used. Finally, the DNA sequence was used in the Feistel network.

Goswami et al. [3] gave an encryption technique that used DNA encoding scheme in single qubit rotations.

Patnala and Kumar [4] proposed a DNA-based cryptographic protocol that uses DNA codons. An arbitrary DNA lookup table containing the DNA codons was used to replace their corresponding alphabet.

Basu et al. [5] proposed a schema applying the central dogma of molecular biology where they simulated the Genetic Code and additional operations of a DNA sequence. The input text is grouped into 16-bit blocks. To generate the encoded text, the blocks are combined in the arrangement of protein bases.

Davide et al. [6] suggested a scheme that engaged a restricted number of states which is spread over an uncomplicated strategy, which offers a detailed analysis in divergence to comprehensible challenges.

Vagniluca et al. [7] demonstrated an easy low-cost quantum key distribution (QKD) arrangement. The three-step "BB84" procedure was proved using a time-bin encrypting scheme.

Huawang et al. [8] projected a confidential QKD technique. Each photon is produced by the transmitter, while the receptor applies "Fourier transformation" to encipher its key.

Goswami and Chakraborty [9] designed a scheme of a unidirectional trapdoor, which is built using principles of the quantum cryptosystem. During encryption of the secret message, a quantum public key is used while at the time decryption, a private key is used. The one-way trapdoor function is obtained by mapping the bits used in the classical system with their respective quantum states.

Price et al. [10] demonstrated how by decreasing the security of the BB84 protocol, denial of service can be easily detected. They schemed a QKD procedure for detecting unauthenticated users who are trying to intervene in the medium by controlling the nodes and rejecting service irrespective of the number of qubits replaced beyond the finite key limit. By lessening the security of the BB84 protocol, they generated a secured key from a two photon polarization state.

Partha et al. [11] overviewed a secured QKD algorithm on the basis of the properties of monotonically ascending knapsack strings, which were related to the states of the qubit by rotating a three qubits tuple.

Goswami et al. [12] stated a secured QKD algorithm that is combined with an encrypting mechanism which is created on the basis of Fermat Numbers and DNA sequences. The notion of Watson–Crick's complement of DNA sequences and randomness of the Fermat Numbers is applied for securing the communication media by virtue of dual encryption. The key generation process is done by a quantum bit rotation method.

Goswami et al. [13] showed how the concept of quantum computing can be used with a DNA code set to achieve a secured QKD, so that well-known security risks in the communication network can be prevented.

Goswami and Chakraborty [14] gave a glimpse about the concept of using quantum computing and DNA codon encoded with Gödel code to perform the QKD scheme.

4.3 ADSORBATE THE KEY DISTRIBUTION MECHANISM (KDM)

Let $\mathcal{M}$ and K_A denote the Sender's message and key, respectively. Let the receiver's key be denoted by K_B. Let the XOR operation be denoted by the symbol $\oplus$.

The sender conveys a message $\mathcal{M}$ after encoding it via his key K_A. The receiver obtains the encoded text as $\mathcal{M} \oplus K_A$ and in order to validate it, the encoded text is sent back to the sender for authentication. Before sending for authentication to the sender over the transmission channel, the receiver encrypts the encoded text by his key K_B. The sender on receiving the encrypted message $\mathcal{M} \oplus K_A \oplus K_B$ validates it and directs it back to the receiver by encrypting it again with his key K_A. The receiver will accept $\mathcal{M} \oplus K_A \mathcal{M} \oplus K_B \mathcal{M} \oplus K_A = \mathcal{M} \oplus K_B$ and decodes the encrypted message as received using his key K_B as $\mathcal{M} \oplus K_B \oplus K_B = \mathcal{M}$. Thus, the receiver will get the original message $\mathcal{M}$.

The procedure enables both the participants to securely communicate among themselves without the need for sharing the secret keys.

4.4 ALGORITHM FOR KEY GENERATION

A couple of keys, namely, a *Private Key* (K_{py}) and a *Public Key* (K_{pb}) will be generated by each user in the cryptosystem. The algorithm for the key generation process is as under:

Key_Gen:

1. Let m be any arbitrary positive integer such that $m \gg 1$.
2. Let $\beta \in \mathbb{Z}_2^{\mathrm{m}}$ be an arbitrary integer strings set of length $= L$ such that $\beta = \{\beta_1, \beta_2, \beta_3, \ldots, \beta_L\}$ and β_j is selected exclusively from $\mathbb{Z}_2^{\mathrm{m}}$ Suppose S is an arbitrary binary set of strings where $S = \{S_1, S_2, S_3, \ldots, S_L\}$ and $S_{i\in} \{0, 1\}$.
3. Find L qubits from the bases $|\, 0_z\rangle = 0 \otimes^{L}$ by employing the L parallel "Hadamard" operator.
4. Now $\forall\, \beta_{j\in}\, \beta$, rotate $\hat{R}_j \beta_j (a_m))$ by $a_m = \frac{\pi}{2^{m-1}}$ iff $S_j = 1$ so that the jth qubit state
   $|\, \Upsilon \beta_j (a_m)\rangle_j = \hat{R}_j (\beta_j (a_m)) \,|\, 0_z\rangle$ is transformed to
   $|\, \Upsilon\, \beta\, (a_m)\rangle \equiv \hat{R}\, (\beta\, (a_m))\ |0_z\rangle = \cos\frac{\beta(\alpha_m\,)}{2}|\,0_z\rangle + \sin\,(\frac{\beta(\alpha_m)}{2})\,|\,1_z\rangle$
   where $0 \leq \alpha < 2\pi$.
5. Private Key: $K_{py} = \{m, \beta\}$

Public Key:

$K_{pb} = \{L, |\Upsilon_{(pk)\,(am)}\rangle\}$, where L qubit states as $|\Upsilon_{(pk)\,(am)}\rangle \equiv 0 \oplus^{Lj} |\Upsilon\beta_{j\,(am)}\rangle_j$

4.5 KEY DISTRIBUTION MECHANISM

The algorithm below is adopted for KDM.

4.5.1 DNA ENCODING AND DECODING

The rest of the subsection describes the encoding and decoding process.

4.5.1.1 ENCODING OF THE PLAIN TEXT TO DNA ENCODED TEXT

1. Perform Binary conversion of $\mathcal{M}$. (Let the message $\mathcal{M}$ be converted as: $\mathcal{M}$ = 0110 1100).
2. Convert this $\mathcal{M}$ to its DNA equivalent form using Table 4.1.

$$\therefore \mathcal{M} = 0110\ 1100 = \text{CGTA}$$

TABLE 4.1 DNA Code to Binary Translation

DNA Code	Binary Form
A	00
C	01
G	10
T	11

3. Transform $\mathcal{M}$ using the rule: A ⇔ T and C⇔ G.

$$\therefore \mathcal{M} = 0110\ 1100 = \text{CGTA} = \text{GCAT}.$$

4. Translate the above into binary.

$$\therefore \mathcal{M} = 0110\ 1100 = \text{CGTA} = \text{GCAT} = 1001\ 0011$$

Now, substitute the first bit of the four-group code set so obtained by 0 if it is 1 and 1 if it is 0. So, that $\mathcal{M}$ = 0001 1011

The receiver decodes $\mathcal{M}$ using the steps below.

4.5.1.2 DECODING OF THE DNA ENCODED TEXT TO ORIGINAL TEXT

1. Replace the first bit of the four-group code set of the encoded message $\mathcal{M}'$ that is received after DNA encryption and applying the quantum protocol by 0 if it is 1 and 1 if it is 0.

$$\therefore \mathcal{M}' = 0001\ 1011 = 1001\ 0011.$$

2. Convert $\mathcal{M}'$ into the corresponding DNA codons. $\mathcal{M}' = 1001\ 0011$ = GCAT
3. Applying the A⇔ T and C⇔ G [71, 72]. $\mathcal{M}' = 1001\ 0011$ = GCAT = CGTA
4. Convert $\mathcal{M}'$ to binary.

$$\therefore \mathcal{M}' = \text{CGTA} = 0110\ 1100$$

Finally, convert the binary message to its equivalent plain text which is the original message the sender intended to send to the receiver.

4.5.1.3 ENCRYPT AND DECRYPT TECHNIQUES

Let us consider the following states:

$$|00\rangle = |\Psi_A\rangle = \begin{pmatrix} 1 & 1 \\ 0 & 0 \end{pmatrix} \quad 10\rangle = |\Psi_G\rangle = \begin{pmatrix} 0 & 1 \\ 1 & 0 \end{pmatrix}$$

$$|01\rangle = |\Psi_c\rangle = \begin{pmatrix} 1 & 0 \\ 0 & 1 \end{pmatrix} \quad |11\rangle = |\Psi_T\rangle = \begin{pmatrix} 0 & 0 \\ 1 & 1 \end{pmatrix}$$

Now, if the sender's message $\mathcal{M}$ has "n" classical bits, then the encrypted qubit states is defined as follows:

$\mathcal{M} = |i_1\rangle \otimes |i_2\rangle \otimes |i_3\rangle \otimes \ldots \otimes |i_j\rangle$, where $\{i_j \mid i_j = \{00, 01, 10, \text{or } 11\}, j = 1, 2, 3, \ldots, n\}$, $\otimes$ = tensor product.

Since "$2n$" qubits are encrypted using an "*n-bit*" string, the "*jth*" qubit state is given a rotation of $\phi_j = \frac{\pi}{2^{(j-1)}}$ for any constant $n \in \mathbb{N}$, which is selected randomly for any specific qubit. So, the rotation operation $\hat{\rho}(\phi_j)$ is given by

$$\hat{\rho}(\phi_j) = \begin{pmatrix} \cos\frac{\phi_j}{2} & -\sin\frac{\phi_j}{2} \\ \sin\frac{\phi_j}{2} & \cos\frac{\phi_j}{2} \end{pmatrix} \tag{4.1}$$

The angle $(\frac{\phi_j}{2})$ in Equation 4.1 is the encryption key.

Similarly, a rotation by an angle $(-\frac{\phi_j}{2})$ is performed for decoding.

Let λ_S and λ_R represent the respective secret keys of the sender and the receiver. Then, for each session, we have

$$\lambda = \left\{ \frac{\phi_j}{2} \mid 0 \leq \frac{\phi_j}{2} < \pi, j = 1,2,3,\ldots,n \right\}$$

For each instance, the session key is utilized twice—once during the encryption and a second time for the decryption. With the expiry of each individual session, the previous session key is substituted by a fresh key to evade intrusion.

4.6 ENCODING DECODING USING SUPERINCREASING KNAPSACK SEQUENCE

Key Generation:

To generate the key, the encoding–decoding process by means of superincreasing knapsack arrangement is given below

1. Suppose S = $\{S_1, S_2, S_3, \ldots, S_n\}$ be a collection of monotonically ascending terms.
2. Let $P > S_1 +, S_2 +, S_3 + \ldots + S_i$, [$P$ is prime].
3. Let $1 < Q < P$, [Q is prime].
4. Then, Public Key: $R_i = S_i \times Q \bmod p$ and Private Key: $\{S, Q, P\}$.

Encoding

To encode the message, the below-mentioned steps are followed.

1. $\mathcal{M}$ is separated into smaller parts where each part equals the cardinality of the knapsack.
2. Take 1 if the item exists, else take 0.
3. Weigh each of the smaller blocks.
4. The encoded message is the weights that are to be transferred through the communication medium.

Decoding

To decode the message the below-mentioned steps are followed.

1. Compute Q^{-1} so that $Q\,(Q^{-1}) \equiv 1 (\mathrm{mod}\ P)$.
2. Multiply every smaller block by Q^{-1} mod P.
3. In order to obtain $\mathcal{M}$, divide the output of above with S.

4.6.1 THE ENCRYPTION–DECRYPTION PROTOCOL FOR KDM

The protocol for KDM is as follows:

1. Translate $\mathcal{M}$ into binary as per Table 4.2.

TABLE 4.2 Conversion Table for Alphabet to Binary and Character to Binary

Alphabet	Binary	Alphabet	Binary	Character	Binary	Character	Binary
A	01000001	a	01100001	Space	00100000	]	01011101
B	01000010	b	01100010	!	00100001	^	01011110
C	01000011	c	01100011	'	00100010	_	01011111
D	01000100	d	01100100	#	00100011	`	01100000
E	01000101	e	01100101	$	00100100	{	01111011
F	01000110	f	01100110	%	00100101	|	01111100
G	01000111	g	01100111	&	00100110	}	01111101
H	01001000	h	01101000	'	00100111	~	01111110
I	01001001	i	01101001	(	00101000		
J	01001010	j	01101010	)	00101001		
K	01001011	k	01101011	*	00101010		
L	01001100	l	01101100	+	00101011		
M	01001101	m	01101101	,	00101100		
N	01001110	n	01101110	–	00101101		
O	01001111	o	01101111	.	00101110		
P	01010000	p	01110000	/	00101111		
Q	01010001	q	01110001	:	00111010		
R	01010010	r	01110010	;	00111011		
S	01010011	s	01110011	<	00111100		
T	01010100	t	01110100	=	00111101		
U	01010101	u	01110101	>	00111110		
V	01010110	v	01110110	?	00111111		
W	01010111	w	01110111	@	01000000		
X	01011000	x	01111000	[	01011011		
Y	01011001	y	01111001	\	01011100		

2. Encrypt the binary equivalent message $\mathcal{M}$ by converting it to its corresponding decimal form. Perform binary conversion once again. Let this be denoted by T.

3. As the sender's encoded message T comprises n classical bits, the encrypted qubit states can be defined as follows:

$T == |i_1\rangle \otimes |i_2\rangle \otimes |i_3\rangle \otimes , ... , \otimes |i_j\rangle$, where $\{i_j | i_j = \{000, 001, 010, 011, 100, 101, 110 \text{ or } 111\}, j = 1, 2, 3, \ldots, n\}$, $n \in \mathbb{N}$, and $\otimes$= tensor product.

4. For ease of calculation the three-qubit states can be represented as follows:

$$|000\rangle = \begin{pmatrix} 1 & 1 & 1 \\ 0 & 0 & 0 \end{pmatrix} \quad |100\rangle = \begin{pmatrix} 0 & 1 & 1 \\ 1 & 0 & 0 \end{pmatrix}$$

$$|001\rangle = \begin{pmatrix} 1 & 1 & 0 \\ 0 & 0 & 1 \end{pmatrix} \quad |101\rangle = \begin{pmatrix} 0 & 1 & 0 \\ 1 & 0 & 1 \end{pmatrix}$$

$$|010\rangle = \begin{pmatrix} 1 & 0 & 1 \\ 0 & 1 & 0 \end{pmatrix} \quad |110\rangle = \begin{pmatrix} 0 & 0 & 1 \\ 1 & 1 & 0 \end{pmatrix}$$

$$|011\rangle = \begin{pmatrix} 1 & 0 & 0 \\ 0 & 1 & 1 \end{pmatrix} \quad |111\rangle = \begin{pmatrix} 0 & 0 & 0 \\ 1 & 1 & 1 \end{pmatrix}$$

5. For any random constant $n \in \mathbb{N}$, the jth quantum bit state is given a rotation with an angle of φ_j such that $\phi_j = \frac{\pi}{2^{(j-1)}}$. This is possible as the $2n$ qubits are encrypted by a n bit message. Let $R(\varphi_j)$ denote the rotation operation then

$$R(\varphi_j) \begin{pmatrix} \text{con}\varphi_j & \text{con}\varphi_j \\ -\sin\varphi_j & \sin\varphi_j \end{pmatrix}$$

The angle φ_j represents the encryption key. Rotate by angle $(-\varphi_j)$.

Contrary to the "one-time pad" mechanism [15, 16], in KDM, the key is never disclosed.

6. Let us suppose the sender's and receiver's keys be K_s, K_R respectively.

Then, for each individual session, we have

$$\lambda = \{\varphi_j | 0 \leq \varphi_j < \pi, j = 1,2,3,\ldots,n\}.$$

Under any conditions, the session keys are exposed to anyone in the communication network. Each session key is utilized only twice in a session: (1) through encryption and (2) through decryption. With the expiry of an individual session, the earlier key is substituted by generating a fresh key, thereby eliminating the chances of misapplication of any information.

7. At this point, the decoded message is converted to decimal.
8. Decrypt $\mathcal{M}$ using the algorithm for decoding using monotonically ascending knapsack string, as discussed above. Lastly, convert the binary text to plain text using Table 4.2.

4.7 METHODOLOGY

The methodology of KDM is discussed here.

4.7.1 MESSAGE STRING TO DNA ENCODED STRING

To define the algorithm. the steps followed are the following:

1. Perform DNA conversion of $\mathcal{M}$ using Figure 4.1.
2. Translate A ⇔ T and C⇔ G. on the obtained sequence.
3. Convert the result of the previous step using Figure 4.1.

The inverse of the above method is applied during the decoding process.

Letter	Code	Letter	Code	Letter	Code
0	ATA	A	ACT	O	TGT
1	TCT	B	CAT	P	GAG
2	GCG	C	TCA	Q	TAT
3	GTG	D	TAC	R	CAC
4	AGA	E	CTA	S	TGA
5	CGC	F	GCT	T	TAG
6	ATT	G	GTC	U	GAT
7	ACC	H	CGT	V	GTA
8	AGG	I	CTG	W	ATG
9	CAA	J	TGC	X	AGT
start	TTG	K	TCG	Y	GAC
stop	TAA	L	ATC	Z	GCA
	AGC	M	ACA		
.	ACG	N	CTC		

FIGURE 4.1 The DNA conversion set.

4.7.2 *APPLICATION OF FERMAT ENCODING*

1. Let p,q be the cardinality of the DNA string and a randomly selected key.
2. The key is appended to the reversed key.
3. Subdivide S into S_1 and S_2 say. S_1 where S_1 contains the first symbol and the following alternate symbols and S_2 contains the leftover symbols.
4. Applying Fermat encoding F_p with the same cardinality as key K_q , so that

$$|C_s|=(p+q) \bmod 26.$$

5. Combine all the substring to generate the output string.

   The inverse of the above method is applied during the decoding process.

4.7.3 *QUANTUM-ENABLED KDM*

Assuming

$$|00\rangle = \begin{pmatrix} 1 & 1 \\ 0 & 0 \end{pmatrix} = |A\rangle \quad |01\rangle = \begin{pmatrix} 1 & 0 \\ 0 & 1 \end{pmatrix} = |C\rangle$$

$$|00\rangle = \begin{pmatrix} 1 & 1 \\ 0 & 0 \end{pmatrix} = |A\rangle \quad |01\rangle = \begin{pmatrix} 1 & 0 \\ 0 & 1 \end{pmatrix} = |C\rangle$$

Now, if C_s has a cardinality of "n" then its quantum encoding is

$$C_s = |i_1\rangle \otimes |i_2\rangle \otimes |i_3\rangle \otimes' \ldots ' \otimes |i_j\rangle$$

Here, $\{i_j \,|\, i_j = |0^{\otimes 2}, \forall j \in 1,2,\ldots,n\}$

Rotating by an angle $\Upsilon(\varphi_j)$, where $\phi_j = \frac{\pi}{2^{(j-1)}}$., for a random invariant "j" yields the cipher key.

The rotation procedure is defined as

$$R(\Upsilon(\varphi_j)) = \begin{pmatrix} \mathrm{con}\Upsilon(\varphi_j) & \mathrm{con}\Upsilon(\varphi_j) \\ -\sin\Upsilon(\varphi_j) & \sin\Upsilon(\varphi_j) \end{pmatrix}$$

An inverse spin of $(-\Upsilon(\varphi_j))$ depicts the decipher.
Taking"ς_s" and "ς_r" as the key pair, produced per session gives

$$\varsigma = \{\Upsilon(\varphi_j) | 0 \leq \Upsilon(\varphi_j) < \pi, \forall j \in 1,2,\ldots,n\}.$$

4.8 SECURITY ANALYSIS

The following section discusses the reliability and correctness of the preceding algorithms.

4.8.1 *TROJAN HORSE ATTACK*

Trojan horse attack is a kind of malicious code that looks authentic but has the ability to control the communication system [17]. It is intended for damaging, disrupting, or stealing the information in a network media.

When a system is affected by a Trojan horse attack, the attacker engages a portion of the quantum channel to detect the sender's signals [18]. The attacker intrudes into the KDM system by inserting false pulses from random sources and analyzing the backscattered signal with a detector. The detection system of the attacker rests on the specificities of the random source, that is, on its phase. An attacker may have to sometimes eliminate part of the genuine signal to compensate for the inserted loss by an enhanced quantum channel. Figure 4.2 shows how a Trojan horse attack works.

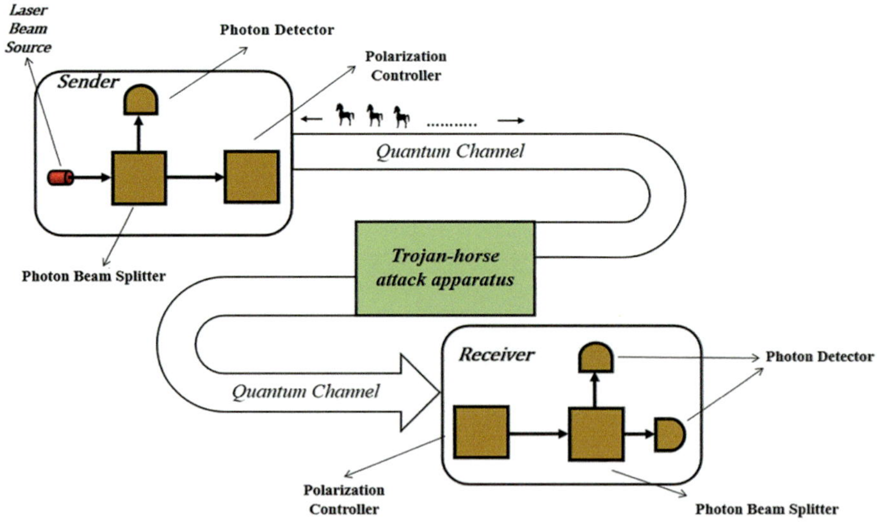

FIGURE 4.2 Trojan horse attack.

The suggested protocol is vulnerable to Trojan horse assaults, also known as invisible photon attacks because it is a two-way communication protocol that allows for the multiple transmission of the same photon. The transmitter and receiver implement extra security measures such as wavelength quantum filters and photon number splitters (PNS) to detect the existence of any attackers in order to protect the protocols from such attacks. The invisible photons transmitted by the attacker are discarded by the wavelength quantum filter, which is set up to only permit the wavelengths associated with the operating wavelength [19]. By splitting each sample photon and detecting the appearance of an abnormally high rate of multiple photons (if any) in the quantum signal, the PNS facilitates the finding of delayed photons.

In the algorithm KDM using Fermat numbers and DNA encoding, as the sender uses a set of two fast-steering mirrors to direct the photon beams, it becomes quite challenging for the attacker to avoid this countermeasure. Moreover, by using *Schmidt–Cassegrain Telescope* where from wave pulse is directed to a prefixed point at the other end after the fast-steering mirrors, it becomes more tough for the attacker. To ascertain uninterrupted message transmission of the KDM system, a few nanometer filtering widths are sufficient as all the sidebands of the pulse and intensity of the modulation are in the range of the filter. This filter is also advantageous for the security of the receiver.

The attackers cannot enter the encryption system because of the nonorthogonality of quantum cipher-strings with computational basis. Hence, the risk of Trojan horse is mitigated.

4.8.2 INDIVIDUAL PARTICLE ATTACK

Individual particle attack is a method of decoding an encrypted message by the attacker by means of entanglement [20] with his own quantum bits.

In the algorithms discussed in the chapters previously, the attackers can only view the qubits randomly as

$$\{|0\rangle \text{ or } |1\rangle\}, \{|00\rangle, |01\rangle, |10\rangle \text{ or } |11\rangle\} \text{ or } \{|000\rangle, |001\rangle, |010\rangle, |011\rangle, |100\rangle, |101\rangle, 110\rangle \text{ or } |111\rangle\}$$

depending on the use of a one-qubit, two-qubit, or three-qubit system.

Thus, it is infeasible for the hacker to break the encoded message as the rotation angle applied by the participants in each session is not known to the attacker. So, all the algorithms are secure from individual particle attack.

4.8.3 MAN-IN-THE-MIDDLE ATTACK

A man-in-the-middle attack [21] is a spying attack where intruders interrupt a prevailing message communication. In a three-pass protocol [22], the intruder introduces himself in the "middle" of the communication by pretending to be both the legitimate participants in any KDM system. As a result, the attackers are now qualified to peep into the sender's state, send a similar fake state to the receiver, and keep doing so until the KDM method is deactivated and an excessively high rate of multiple photons (if any) appear in the quantum signal.

In a man-in-the-middle attack, the attacker manipulates the information unknown to the sender and the receiver, acting to fetch confidential messages and if not cause damage. Figure 4.3 shows the working of a man-in-the-middle attack.

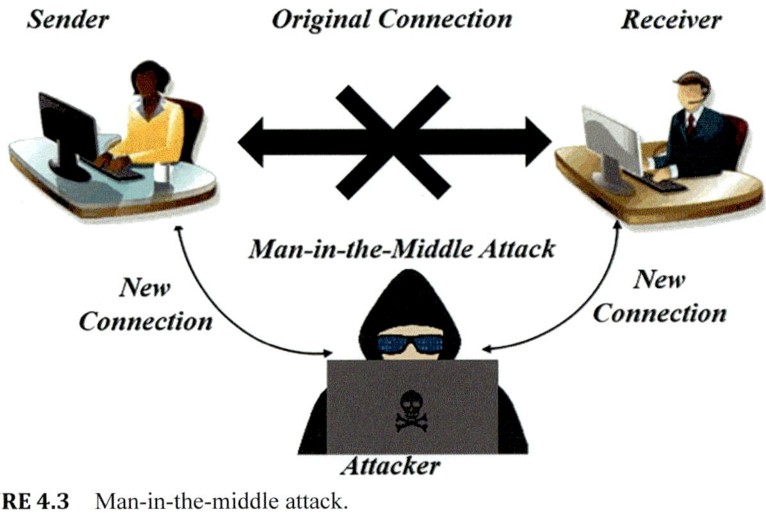

FIGURE 4.3 Man-in-the-middle attack.

It has been observed that a suitable encoding scheme (e.g., Gödel Code) [14] is effective in handling the man-in-the-middle attack. This is done by integrating a three-layered protocol:

1. First, by encrypting the input message string using DNA codons.
2. Second, by generating a cipher-string through an appropriate encoding scheme and then again converting the enciphered code to its binary equivalent code.

3. Third, by giving a trapdoor enabled quantum bit rotation on the qubit tuple state.

Therefore, it becomes problematic for the attacker to decipher the enciphered message, as he is unaware of the encoding mechanism that has been done on the sender's side as well as the decoding mechanism on the receiver's side.

4.8.4 INTERCEPT-RESEND ATTACK

An intercept-resend attack also known as a faked-state attack is an attack that is applied to the QKD protocol with four-state systems [23]. The security of a KDM system is specified by the effectiveness of the process of detection of these possible attacks. Figure 4.4 shows an intercept-resend attack [24].

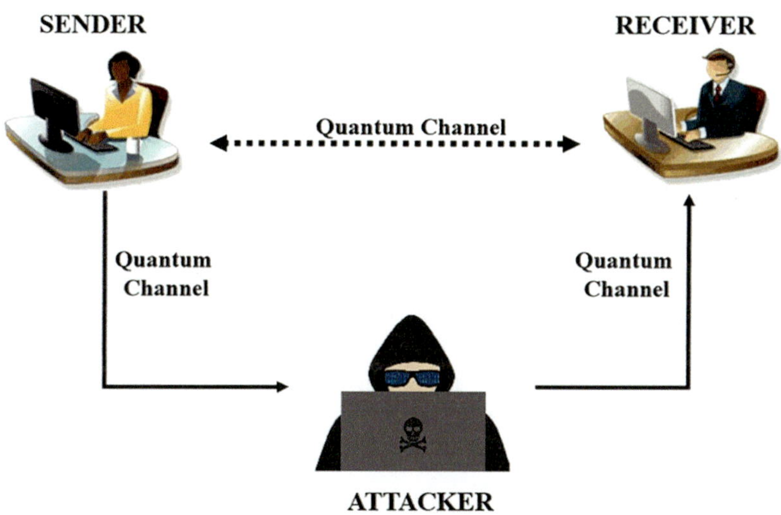

FIGURE 4.4 Intercept-resend attack.

To limit the hackers from duplicating the encrypted text, quantum superposition is used as the basis of conversation in the algorithms discussed previously; therefore, replication of any quantum bit state is not feasible in my quantum protocols.

The quantum states in my protocol for the single qubit state is

$a_0|0\rangle + a_1|1\rangle$ where $a_0$and random variables and $| a_0 + a_1|^2=1$

for the two-qubit state is

$$a_{00}|00\rangle + a_{01}|01\rangle + a_{10|}10\rangle + a_{11}|11\rangle,$$

$$\text{where } a_{ij} \text{ are random variables and } \sum_{i,j} |a_{ij}|^2 = 1$$

and for the three-qubit states is

$a_{000}|000\rangle + a_{001}|001\rangle + a_{010|}010\rangle + a_{011}|011\rangle + a_{100}|\rangle\ 100\rangle + a_{101|}\ 101_{\rangle} + a_{110|}110\rangle + a_{111|}\ 111\rangle$, where a_{ijk} are random variables and

$$\sum_{i,j,k} |a_{ijk}|^2 = 1$$

Thus, it is difficult for the eavesdroppers to duplicate the enciphered message accurately that is being transmitted in a superposition state. Therefore, the algorithms take care of these types of attacks.

4.8.5 PNS ATTACK

Generally, photon rays which remain transmitted in a KDM system have 0, 1, or greater than one photons, which are distributed according to *Poisson's distribution*. If #Photons(Sender) > 1, the hacker splits the ray into two parts using a beam splitter. The attacker keeps the extra photon to perform a quantum nondemolition detection using his quantum detector and transmits the other to the recipient over a lossless network. In cases when the intruder receives an empty pulse, the quantum channel is blocked by him using an optical switch. A diagrammatic representation of the PNS [25] attack is shown in Figure 4.5.

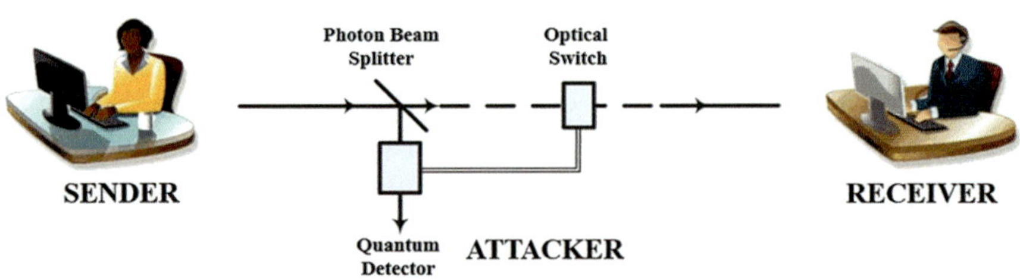

FIGURE 4.5 Photon number splitters.

Here, the eavesdropper seizes the photon(s) until the recipient obtains it and the sender discloses the encoded basis. The intruder can then correctly decode the accumulated photons in the transmitter's base to regain the errorless secret key.

To get rid of this PNS attack there are two likely methods:

1. by using only one photon beam source [26] or
2. by using decoy states as given in [27] and [28].

To check a PNS attack in KDM, the sender uses a set of two fast-steering mirrors.

4.8.6 BEAM SPLITTING ATTACK (BSA)

In the case of BSA [29], the eavesdropper attempts to incorporate a splitter in the quantum network in order to fragment the laser ray and guide a fraction of it, toward recipient over the network. The intruder executes a deferred measurement of the fragmented ray to obtain the secret key. The mechanism is shown in Figure 4.6.

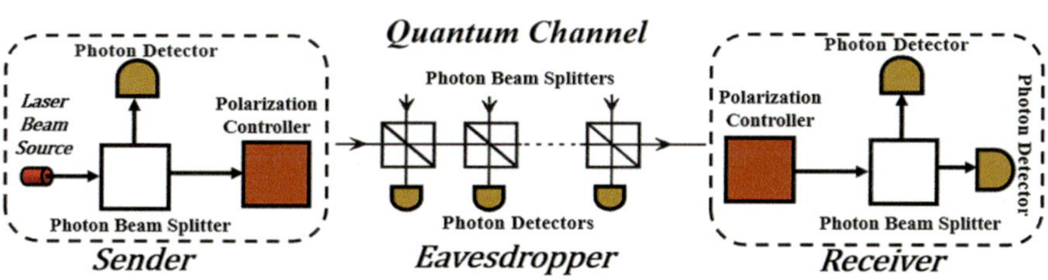

FIGURE 4.6 Beam splitting attack.

However, the BSA turns out to be unsuccessful for a network with greater transmission distance. Hence, this type of attack can be taken care by making the KDM scalable for bigger mediums as in Knapsack Enciphering.

The BSA is checked by inserting a *Schmidt–Cassegrain Telescop*e at the sender's side, which is elaborated in the algorithm.

4.9 CONCLUSION

Distributing the public and private keys between two communicating parties is a tedious cryptographic mission. The entire security apparatus may collapse if a forger/eavesdropper/malicious attacker becomes aware of the key. Hence, secure exchange of keys is of paramount importance. In KDM, laws of quantum physics are exploited to obtain a provably secure method for exchanging encryption keys only known between shared parties. However, KDM faces various critical challenges and threats, namely, Trojan horse, individual particle attack, man-in-the-middle, intercept-resend attack, PNS attack, beam-splitting attack. This chapter provides a detailed discussion of the different aspects of the security threats that can be confronted in a KDM system using secure encoding.

KEYWORDS

- **DNA encoding**
- **information security**
- **quantum cryptography**
- **session key exchange threat analysis**

REFERENCES

1. Zhang, Y., Liu, X., Ma, Y., & Cheng, L.-C. (2017). *An Optimized DNA Based Encryption Scheme with Enforced Secure Key Distribution*. Springer Science and Business Media, LLC.
2. Zhang, X., Zhou, Z., & Niu, Y. (2018). An image encryption method based on the feistel network and dynamic DNA encoding. *IEEE Photonics Journal*, *10*(4), 1–14.
3. Goswami, P. S., Chakraborty, T., & Chatterjee, H. (2018). A novel encryption technique using DNA encoding and single qubit rotations. *International Journal of Computer Sciences and Engineering*, *6*(3), 364–369.
4. Patnala, B. D., & Kumar, R. K. (2019). A novel level-based DNA security algorithm using DNA codons. In *Computational Intelligence and Big Data Analytics*. Springer, pp. 1–13.
5. Basu, S., Karuppiah, M., Nasipuri, M., Halder, A. K., & Radhakrishnan, N. (2019). Bio-inspired cryptosystem with DNA cryptography and neural networks. *Journal of System & Architecture*, *94*, 24–31.
6. Rusca, D., Boaron, A., Curty, M., Martin, A., & Zbinden, H. (2018). Security proof for a simplified Bennett-Brassard 1984 quantum-key-distribution protocol, *Physical Review A*, *98*, 052336.

7. Bacco, D., Vagniluca, I., Da Lio, B., Biagi, N., Frera, A. D., Calonico, D., Toninelli, C., Cataliotti, F. S., Bellini, M., Oxenløwe, L. K., & Zavatta, A. (2019). Field trial of a three-state quantum key distribution scheme in the Florence metropolitan area. *EPJ Quantum Technology*, *6*, 5.
8. Huawang. Q., Tso. R., & Dai. Y. (2019). Quantum secret sharing by using fourier transform on orbital angular momentum. *IET Information Security*, *13*(2), 104–108.
9. Goswami, P. S., & Chakraborty, T. (2020). Design of a quantum one-way trapdoor function. In Mandal, J., & Bhattacharya, D. (Eds.), *Emerging Technology in Modelling and Graphics. Advances in Intelligent Systems and Computing*, Vol. 937. Springer, Singapore. https://doi.org/10.1007/978-981-13-7403-6_48
10. Price, A. B., Rarity, J. G., & Erven, C. (2020). A quantum key distribution protocol for rapid denial of service detection. *EPJ Quantum Technology*, *7*, 8. https://doi.org/10.1140/epjqt/s40507-020-00084-6
11. Goswami, P. S., Chakraborty, T., & Chattopadhyay, A. (2020). Knapsack encoding for secured quantum key distribution protocol. *Modern Physics Letters A*, *35*(36), 2050295.
12. Goswami, P. S., Chakraborty, T., & Chattopadhyay, A. (2021). A secured quantum key exchange algorithm using Fermat numbers and DNA encoding. In *2021 Fourth International Conference on Electrical, Computer and Communication Technologies (ICECCT)*, Erode, India. pp. 1–8, https://doi.org/10.1109/ICECCT52121.2021.9616749.
13. Goswami, P. S., Chakraborty, T., & Chattopadhyay, A. (2022). A nature-inspired DNA encoding technique for quantum session key exchange protocol. In Shandilya, S. K., Wagner, N., Gupta, V., & Nagar, A. K. (Eds.), *Advances in Nature-Inspired Cyber Security and Resilience. EAI/Springer Innovations in Communication and Computing*, Springer, Cham. https://doi.org/10.1007/978-3-030-90708-2_7
14. Goswami, P. S., & Chakraborty, T. (2023). Godel code enciphering for QKD protocol using DNA mapping. *Mathematics and Computer Science*, *1*, 371–394.
15. Watson, J. D., & Crick, F. H. C. (1953). Molecular structure of nucleic acids: A structure for deoxyribose nucleic acid. *Nature*, *171*, 737–738.
16. Crick, F. H. C. (1966). The genetic code–yesterday, today, and tomorrow. *Cold Spring Harb. Quantum Biology*, *31*, 1–9.
17. Deng, F. G., Li, X. H., & Zhou, H. Y. (2005). Improving the security of multi-party quantum secret sharing against trojan horse attack. *Physical Review A*, *72*(4), 044302.
18. Gisin, N., Fasel, S., Kraus, B., Zbinden, H., & Ribordy, G. (2006). Trojan-horse attacks on quantum-key-distribution systems. *Physical Review A*, *73*(2006), 22320.
19. Cai, Q. Y. (2006). Eavesdropping on the two-way quantum communication protocols with invisible photons. *Physics Letter A*, *351*(1–2), 23C25.
20. Kanamori. Y, Yoo. S. M., & Al-Shurman, M. (2005). A quantum no-key protocol for secure communication. In *ACM Southeast Conference (ACMSE-05)*, pp. 92–93.
21. Svozil, K. (2005). Feasibility of the interlock protocol against man-in-the-middle attacks on quantum cryptography. *International Journal of Quantum Information*, *3*(4) 649—654.
22. Yang, L., Wu, L.-A., & Liu, S. (2002). Quantum three-pass cryptography protocol. *Photonics Asia*, 106–111.

23. Erven, C. (2007). On free space quantum key distribution and its implementation with a polarization-entangled parametric down conversion source, UWSpace. http://hdl.handle.net/10012/3021
24. Azuma, H., & Ban, M. (2021). The intercept/resend and translucent attacks on the quantum key distribution protocol based on the pre- and post-selection effect. *International Journal of Quantum Information*, *19*(1), 2150010.
25. Gaidash, A. A., Egorov, V. I., & Gleim, A. V. (2016). Revealing of photon-number splitting attack on quantum key distribution system by photon number resolving devices. *Journal of Physics: Conference Series*, *735*, 012072. https://doi.org/10.1088/1742-6596/735/1/012072
26. Intallura, P. M., Ward, M. B., Karimov, O. Z., Yuan, Z. L. et al. (2007). Quantum key distribution using a triggered quantum dot source emitting near 1.3 μm. *Applied Physics Letters*, *91*(16), 161103.
27. Ma, X., Qi, B., Zhao, Y., & Lo, H.-K. (2005). Practical decoy state for quantum key distribution. *Physical Review A*, *72*(1), 012326.
28. Lo, H.-K., Ma, X., & Chen, K. (2005). Decoy state quantum key distribution. *Physical Review Letters*, *94*, 230504.
29. Dušek, M., Haderka, O., & Hendrych, M. (1999). Generalized beam-splitting attack in quantum cryptography with dim coherent states. *Optics Communications*, *169*(1–6), 103–108.

CHAPTER 5

Deep Dive on Advances in Intelligent Quantum Computing

HEMALATHA P.[1*], MANIKANDAN J.[2], K. JAYASHREE[3], K. DHANALAKSHMI[4], and YONGQING CHANG[5]

[1]*Vel Tech Rangarajan Dr.Sagunthala R&D Institute of Science and Technology, Chennai, Tamil Nadu, India*

[2]*Department of Information Technology, St. Joseph's College of Engineering, OMR, Chennai, Tamil Nadu, India*

[3]*Department of Artificial Intelligence and Data Science, Panimalar Engineering College, Chennai, Tamil Nadu, India*

[4]*Department of Computer Science and Engineering, PSNA College of Engineering and Technology, Dindigul, Tamil Nadu, India*

[5]*College of Marxism, Xingtai Polytechnic College, Xingtai, Hebei, China*

*Corresponding author

ABSTRACT

This chapter deals with the transforming advances in intelligent quantum computing, considering the major emphasis on the synergistic relationship between the classical and quantum computational paradigms. It first considers the basics of quantum principles such as superposition, entanglement, and quantum gates that form the cornerstone for quantum computing. Further, the chapter portrays the development of quantum architectures such as variational quantum eigensolvers and the framework of distributed quantum computing to effectively handle the challenge of large-scale computation. The main issues that have been discussed

Applications of Quantum Computing in a Variety of Domains. Gunjan Mukherjee, Biswadip Basu Mallik, Rahul Kar Özen ÖZER, Digvijay Pandey, and Binay Kumar Pandey (Eds.)

DOI: 10.1201/9781998511051-5

pertain to quantum error correction techniques developed and put into place, which are designed to sustain system fidelity. Advanced quantum algorithms were presented, including QAOA, whose solutions for optimization problems exist. Machine learning integrated with quantum systems is discussed as well, showing the potential of hybrid approaches to solve challenges in data-intensive environments. It gives an overview of the insights from experimental investigations into quantum gates, scalable quantum systems, and quantum memory. These studies emphasize the optimization of performance, minimizing computational overheads, and overcoming current technological limitations. Applications of quantum computing in real life are discussed, underlining the transformative potential of quantum computing in cryptography, chemical modeling, and artificial intelligence. The chapter concludes with a look to the future in the field, presenting trends and challenges such as scalable implementation and quantum-classical integration. This chapter thus lays a critical foundation for both researchers and practitioners in making sense of not only the present status but also the future possibilities in intelligent quantum computing, thereby encouraging further innovation and exploration in this fast-advancing domain.

5.1 INTRODUCTION

In contrast to conventional calculations, quantum computing technique provides essentially distinct answers to computation issues and allows for more effective issue resolution. Quantum data processors may be accessible economically in a short time-frame, based on encouraging experimental findings [1–10]. Shor's prime factor finding [11] is one among the best well-known examples of the capabilities of quantum computers. Classical computing's superiority over quantum computing may be shown in the RSA algorithm's record-breaking performance [12]. In this computation world, computation tasks' solution finding would take millenniums. On the other hand, quantum computing devices might resolve it in a quick turnaround time [11, 13]. When this technique was first developed in 1994, it sparked the "big bang" of quantum calculations, which led to quantum computing techniques and the ability to evaluate quantum computers. There are many distinct pieces that make up a quantum computer—the operational ones are identical to those in regular computers, although in the device layer, they are radically distinct. Quantum manipulations are carried out by the utilization of quantum registers in a computer environment that uses quantum physics. For the quantum register, quantum states are intertwined, but for the network, they create quantified superpositions. There is a substantially distinct structure attribute than what is found in a standard computer as a result of these events. Since the quantum derivative will not be applied for umpteen number of gates, the no-cloning theory and other quantum hardware constraints need new circuit design approaches as well [5, 10]. The quantum gates of a quantum computer are reversible and execute a single function on the quantum systems. There are now just a few of quantum computers operating in a laboratory context [1, 3–8]. While this progress has been steady, there are numerous advanced technologies that might give it a major bump up. Lesser quantum computers connect with each other through the quantum bus to create large-scale quantum computers that are dispersed. A novel generation of technologies will allow quantum computers to be downsized during the upcoming few years. In terms of both design and speed, this is extremely reminiscent of the many stages in the history of traditional computers.

5.2 QUANTUM-BASED COMPUTATION

The core idea behind quantum computers is founded on the idea of quanta in information. Computers of this kind are able to execute computations because information is stored in a manner that may be represented with "quantum states," which can be used for quantum phenomena [14–18]. Multiple ways quantum systems can appear in the physical world (atom energy levels, spin, polarization). It is feasible to depict every potential classical value concurrently in a collection of n quantum states in superposition because the system is d-dimension where the d is always set to be as 2, which is the case for qubit systems. Quantum states in quantum circuit computations can often be described as entangled systems, signifying each quantum system depends on and influences each other's state. This reversible computation principle is at the heart of quantum calculations. Theoretically, the intial state can be obtained from the output states generated from the revesible calculations [19]. Classical systems allow for the design of reversible circuits, which require a specific number of inputs and outputs per reversible gate. Furthermore, these systems feature one-to-one mappings between inputs and outputs: each input corresponds to its respective output. Quantum computing systems likewise abide by these principles, enabling transformations of input quantum states through one-step operations on the quantum circuit and providing reversibility through a series of quantum gates. Use of a second NOT-gate to retrieve original input. Ancilla states are ignored when determining output. Subsequently, classical numerical values derived from the quantum register are used for final computations. Quantum algorithms, which utilize quantum computation principles, are designed to maximize speedups (exponential, polynomial, or super polynomial) over traditional algorithms, as evidenced by existing research. The prime factorization issue, for example, shows that quantum algorithms may be used to tackle a number of issues that are now unsolvable using classical techniques. It is important for quantum computers to meet certain physical requirements. The DiVincenzo criteria [21] are the main rules for this. If the quantum registers can be expanded, they must be set to a known state at the outset.

They also need to have a universal gate set that can run any kind of quantum algorithm, and they must be capable of keeping their consistency and accuracy for long processes. When it comes to quantum computing, they are the foundational principles. Figure 5.1 shows a conceptual representation of quantum computing progress. The functional layer encompasses classical and quantum technologies with similar objectives, while their physical layers differ greatly. Quantum computation follows specific rules set forth by DiVincenzo criteria which require physical properties of quantum registers, gates, circuits, and memory used within quantum computers following specific physical layer characteristics required to implement successful quantum computers. The issue of quantum computing difficulty has been examined from a variety of angles. Classical computers cannot successfully replicate quantum computers, according to a study published in [22] on the computational complexity of linear optics. Additionally, the scientists proposed a computational framework that uses a linear-optical networking to create identical photons that are passed across the network, and then counted in each phase. They further looked at the possibility of implementing the concept utilizing existing photonics and optics technologies. The researchers came to the conclusion that the suggested approach can handle sampling issues and seek difficulties that are traditionally unsolvable [23].

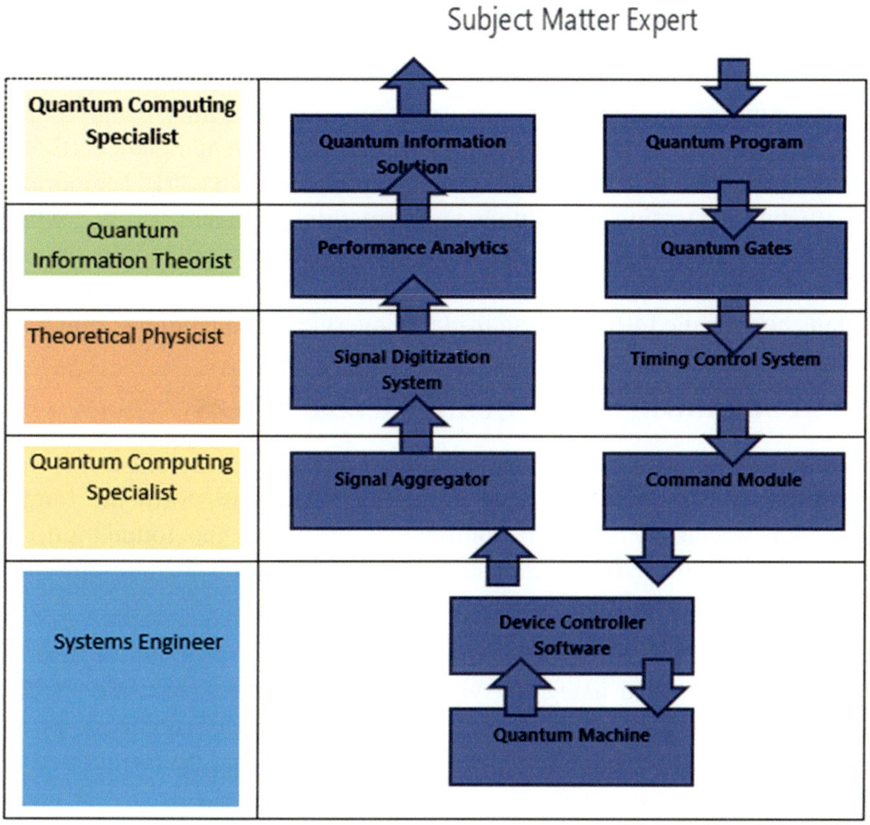

FIGURE 5.1 Schematic representation of quantum computer integrated with cloud computing.

5.3 RELATED REVIEW

This literature review presents several key works in quantum computation and information. Deutsch's groundbreaking work [24] centers around quantum mechanics and universal quantum computers. Feynman's study [25] explores simulating quantum computation using conventional computers, emphasizing Feynman's no-cloning theorem [26]. Feynman highlights Unruh's work from 1995 as providing insight into how quantum computers maintain consistency. Vittorio et al. [31] offer an in-depth exploration of the advantages and disadvantages of quantum computing, with DiVincenzo's groundbreaking 2000 study on quantum calculations available here; for prime factorization using quantum computers [11]. Quantum algorithms are extensively discussed in Ref. [32], with [33] providing more details on algebraic issues. [34] provides an overview of current developments in quantum algorithms while [35] explores entanglement's role in speeding up quantum computing. Quantum spin systems have long been studied concerning matrix product states, projected sets of entangled particles, and variational renormalization group approaches [36, 37]. Temporally unstructured quantum computing is thoroughly discussed in [37], while [38] presents universal blind quantum computing as a potential solution. To deal with multiparty delegated quantum computation challenges [39] details how, while [40] offers an in-depth overview of quantum simulation.

5.4 BUILDING BLOCK OF QUANTUM COMPUTERS

Quantum logic gates, quantum storage devices, processors, control and measurement devices, and error mitigation techniques form the fundamental elements of quantum computers—providing the foundation for exploring recent advancements in this domain. Figure 5.2 presents this block diagram containing these essential components:

- **Input Data:** This component represents the problem or task to be addressed using the variational quantum eigensolver (VQE) algorithm, whether that means computational chemistry problems, optimization issues, or anything that can be formulated as an eigenvalue problem.
- **Quantum Circuit Block:** In VQE, the quantum circuit represents the gates and operations applied to an initial quantum state. Usually, this consists of an ansatz with predefined sets of gates applied sequentially over time to achieve optimality in operation.
- **Variational Parameters:** Variational parameters form part of an ansatz and should be modified iteratively during optimization to find their optimum values that minimize an objective function.
- **Objective Function:** An objective function measures the difference between quantum states obtained from an electronic circuit and their target states, typically related to solving an eigenvalue problem. Optimizing this objective function aims at minimization.
- **Classical Optimizer:** The classical optimizer block uses classical optimization algorithms, such as gradient-based or evolutionary

ones, to adjust the variational parameters of quantum circuits based on feedback from its objective function, updating parameters accordingly.

- **Convergence Criteria:** This component tests whether the optimization process has reached convergence. By evaluating objective functions and their respective minimum values, as well as other conditions related to termination conditions and optimality thresholds, convergence criteria verify if optimization processes have successfully reached equilibrium.
- **Output Results of VQE Algorithm:** The output from the VQE Algorithm is an optimized set of parameters that minimize the objective function. These represent solutions to the problem being tackled.

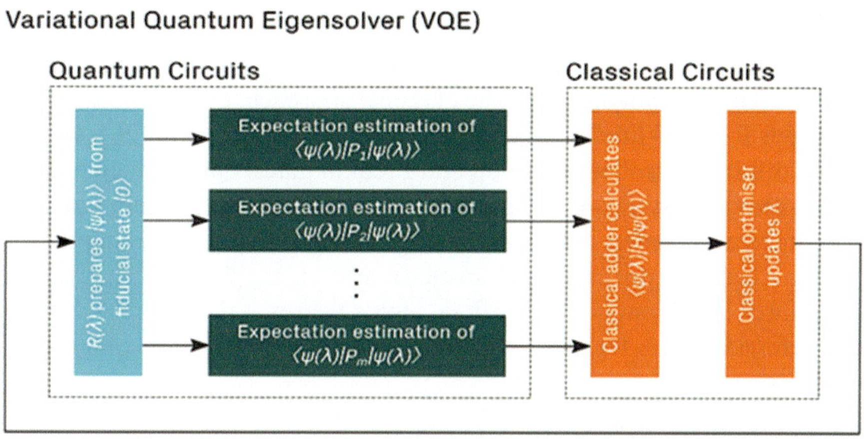

FIGURE 5.2 Block diagram of quantum computing using variational quantum eigensolver.
Source: riverlane. https://www.riverlane.com/blog/the-full-quantum-computing-stack

5.4.1 QUANTUM-BASED GATES

Quantum computing utilizes quantum gates as computational elements to perform operations on quantum states by drawing upon principles of quantum mechanics. A quantum circuit can be broken down into Toffoli or Fredkin gates [14–15, 17–19] that act like NOT or CNOT gates to simulate 3-bit gates; any such combination can achieve universal quantum computation [18, 19]. Quantum gates' reversibility eliminates unnecessary states and retains only useful outputs. Quantum gates may be implemented using various physical layers, from ion traps and superconductor quantum dots to donor-based computation systems and topological quantum computing components, as discussed in Section 5.3. However, practical implementations remain challenging in dealing with quantum gate defects, thus necessitating effective quantum error-correction algorithms [8, 10]. Researchers investigated the quantum benefits offered by shallow networks, showing that constant-depth quantum circuits outshone their classical counterparts. Researchers discovered that conventional probabilistic circuits require logarithmic depth when handling this issue, while constant-depth quantum circuits can offer a deterministic solution. Operating locally on a two-dimensional array and employing only 1- and 2-qubit gates has proven sufficient [25]. Instantaneous quantum polynomial-time (IQP) circuits performed admirably under physically motivated constraints, underscoring their difficulty in simulating using conventional approaches. Researchers discovered IQP circuits that can be constructed on a square lattice of *n* qubits and demonstrated how sampling from their noise distribution can be mimicked using a polynomial-time classical approach. Furthermore, design strategies for high-fidelity 3-qubit gates were investigated in [26], specifically Toffoli, Controlled-Not-Not, and Fredkin gates. Quantum computing relies heavily on quantum gates for mitigating errors and handling experimental quantum data, and the approach put forth here to implement machine learning principles achieved an astounding 99.9% accuracy rate using three superconducting artificial atoms nearby—providing an invaluable reference point for increasing fault-tolerance in quantum computing.

5.4.2 MEMORY-BASED QUANTUM

There are *n* stationary quantum states in quantum circuit computing, and this is how quantum memories are formed. It is possible to interpret data in a quantum register stored in quantum memory. Quantum memories may be produced using a variety of diverse ideas. Topological quantum memory [27] is an intriguing technique that uses an array or torus of quantum states to accomplish its goals [28]. To create a sustainable logical quantum system, such quantum systems are entangled in a certain way. Recent advancements in this field include the demonstration of a room-temperature quantum bit memory with a memory retention time of 1 sec [29] and a proposed design for a large-scale quantum computer that incorporates both atomic memory and photonic interconnects [30]. Furthermore, the authors introduced a framework utilizing n qubits to manage superpositions of N memory cells; their quantum random access memory (QRAM) design significantly reduces retrieval overhead as designed. A better resilient QRAM technique may be built using these findings, which simultaneously reduces the amount of power required for addressing by an exponential amount. A quantum photonic implementation was the final step in the project. Quantum annealing recall is used to examine associative memory' exponential capability [32]. A conceptual approach of associative memory, which can retain a sublinear number of memories, has been shown to have exponential storage capacity by applying quantum annealing in this study. Their method was also used for the Dwave processor, which included an on-board quantum annealing mechanism. In Ref. [28], recurrent neural networks are used to study the maximization of dynamical decoupling for quantum memory. When the authors worked on this project, they used conventional machine learning methodologies that use recurrent neural networks to make dynamic decoupling sequences better. They say that this is a simple strategy for cutting down on quantum memory errors. People who looked at the models said that, with certain knowledge and a certain way to do iterations, they could help rectify errors in quantum memory. Here, quantum memristors are explained in [33]. They are resistors with memory that change their resistance based on how many times they have been crossed by electricity. An ongoing measurement response system is used to regulate the decoherence methodology in the suggested framework. The writers also proved how memory effects are still present in the quantum realm, and also that superconducting circuits are the most suitable devices for implementing them in practice. According to the authors' conclusion, the newly proposed concept of quantum memristor may be employed as a core component for neuromorphic quantum computing and quantum simulations of non-Markovian systems. They are resistive quantum components that can store data about their previous dynamics. In Ref. [34], the researchers assessed the implementations of quantum memristors that made use of superconducting circuits. If supercurrents are negated, the scientists devised a quantum gadget whose permissive activity results from quasiparticle-induced tunneling. Quantification of quantum memory retention has been provided by the authors, and they found that hysteretic activity may be achieved using already implemented measurement methodologies in superconducting quantum circuits. Qubit-based memcapacitors and meminductors have been suggested in [35] for further study. The capacitive and inductive devices, according to the researchers, have extraordinary capabilities for quantum computing (superconducting charge and phase qubits are quantum versions of memory capacitive and inductive systems). According to the current study, certain qubit-based devices display strange hysteresis patterns under certain input conditions. The major finding of this study is that using qubit-based quantum devices, memcapacitive and meminductive systems can be broadened.

5.4.3 CPU-BASED QUANTUM

Quantum CPUs utilize a quantum bus to communicate among the parts of a quantum computer that work together. Quantum CPUs can be looked at from a computing point of view by looking at the parts that make them up: quantum adders. These reversible quantum adders can be used in a wide range of architectures, such as those that use quantum Fourier transform-based adders or linear-time adders. They can also be used to make different kinds of calculations, like quantum carry-save adders, carry-lookahead adders, conditional sum, and carry-select adders [19]. If you want to do quantum computing, you can furthermore make the classical adders into quantum adders with changeable structures and multiple implementation methods. Even though all of the quantum adders employ ancilla quantum states and are reversible, the varying operating methods, circuit depths, latencies, and efficiency of each one raise a number of outstanding issues when attempting to realize their cooperative operations [36, 37].

Meter III [19] used Shor's prime factorization method to examine five distinct qubit connectivity topologies. Figure 5.2 depicts the fundamental gate construction of this algorithm. Its main aim is to increase the probability of finding desired outcomes (represented by red dots in Quantum Register A). Among all variables considered, its optimal efficiency has been shown across many parameters.

The study concluded that linear interconnection provides adequate efficiency for modest nodes (up to five logical qubits). When the number of bits factorized reaches several hundred, more complex networks become unnecessary. Notably, quantum adders demonstrated outstanding effectiveness: They enabled factorization of 6000-bit numbers at one million times faster speeds than binary-carry digit processing (BCDP) modular exponentiation technique used by BCDP modular exponentiation method. Furthermore, this study also explored the characteristics of quantum adders, with a special focus on secure state transfer using an approximate quantum adder [38]. Researchers employed a decoherence-protected mechanism in depolarizing quantum networks to facilitate photonic quantum state transmission via approximate quantum adders employing spontaneous parametric down converters to implement examined protocols; researchers noted a higher success rate with this approach than traditional quantum teleportation methods for distances below certain thresholds.

With the use of evolutionary methodologies, the authors examined estimated quantum adders in [39]. A genetic algorithm-based optimization technique for estimated quantum adders was provided by the writers, as well as the theoretical features of these devices. The findings, according to the writers, allow for greater effectiveness and accuracy than was previously conceivable with some earlier regimens. IBM's Quantum Experience was used to build an approximate quantum adder. Quantum information handling can be improved by using approximation quantum adders, according to the study's writers.

Vermersch et al. [40] investigate a mechanism for transferring quantum states across noisy photonic and phononic waveguides. The scientists devised a technique for reliably transferring a photon's quantum state from one cavity to another over an unlimited single-dimensional waveguide. According to the findings of the authors, this data may be conveyed while being impervious to arbitrary noise put into the waveguide (e.g., thermal noise). The authors examined a cavity QED configuration in which atoms or single atoms were used as quantum memories. A variety of phononic quantum data handling domains might benefit from the methods and outcomes presented, according to the authors.

In Ref. [41], the writers investigated the use of quantum adders and evolutionary approaches to realize quantum autoencoders. There is a relevant link between estimated quantum adders and quantum autoencoders, as the authors have noted. In this study, the scientists discovered that evolutionary techniques may be used to create efficient approximation quantum adders. The findings also have practical implications, as quantum autoencoders may be created for a wide range of beginning states, and programmable quantum platforms can be used to build them.

For a reversible floating-point adder in quantum processing, the challenge of space-efficient structure was examined by the writers in [42]. Research on experimental low-power computing and quantum computation has underscored the need for reversible logic, as the authors noted.

The writers developed a quantum computer reversible floating-point adder that is both space-efficient and time-efficient. Using the suggested approach, binary quantum computation and costly unit architecture may be improved. The writers recommended cost-cutting and fault-tolerant circuit designs as part of their work. Quantum computation implementations and experimentation are examined as two conflicting and cooperating technology directions [43]. Considering this conclusion, classical computers will somehow serve a significant role in the future, although they are constrained by thermodynamics and quantum phenomena.

5.4.4 QUANTUM-BASED ERROR CORRECTION

Greater fidelity and acceptable coherence times can be achieved with the advancement of error-correction algorithms for quantum computing. An inaccuracy in a classical computer system is very different from one in a quantum computation system [44]. Quantum error rectification remains an outstanding issue despite a variety of physical methods being developed for the numerous quantum hardware implementations to provide safe, fault-tolerant quantum computing. Input data quantum states and syndrome quantum states, which are utilized to recognize incorrect information, are commonly employed in quantum error-correction systems. Physically encoded quantum states are unique from their logical counterparts in experimental quantum computing because they are encoded in multiple physical states that reflect one logical quantum state. It is possible to alter the existing quantum error-correction codes (like models of topological error correction, etc.) to meet the needs of diverse physical implementations of the program.

A faulty lattice was investigated by the authors of [45] in order to investigate the issue of surface code error rectification. According to the authors, the impetus for developing such inaccuracy rectification systems stems from the fact that quantum computer implementations would be prone to loss in the type of physically flawed quantum states. Because of this, adaptive error correction algorithms will be critical in the implementation of quantum computations in practice as well as the development of quantum computing systems in theory. In this study, the writers replicated single-fault lattices and lattices that were statically arranged on a grid. There is a less detrimental impact on the lattice from a static loss near the perimeter than a static loss in the center, according to the writers. Researchers also examined several metrics for forecasting quantum chip functionality and found that the depth of a lattice's deepest stabilizer circuit had the highest link with postcorrection inaccuracy levels. As a consequence, experiments using quantum computing will consider the findings extremely useful. Using a deformation-based surface algorithm, the writers in [46] investigated the issues of state injection, lattice surgery, and dense packing. Short error chains linking the super stabilizers were detected by utilizing a deformation-based surface code developed by the authors of the study. Quantum computers can use near proximity of logical qubits, according to the findings. Deformation-based surface code was also explored by the authors, as was the conversion procedure from defect-based surfaces. The findings are especially useful for large-scale experimental quantum computing. Quantum sample difficulty of learning with mistakes was examined in [44]. A quantum learning method with a polynomial sample and time complication was discovered by the authors to be effective for a learning issue. There are some ramifications for cryptography in the findings, as the writers have determined.

Using silicon-based surface code quantum computers, Albrecht et al. [47] investigated the operational issues. Surface code quantum computing with solid state spins was shown to be feasible by demonstrating the contradiction between qubit–qubit interaction separation and qubit–qubit interaction separation at a nanometer resolution. For mechanical separation, the suggested approach makes use of probe spins and comprises a process for correcting errors caused by incorrect spin placement. They confirm that this design addresses a large number of challenges in solid-state quantum computation and gives qubit densities multiple orders of magnitude more than existing systems. Condensed matter systems have quasiparticle excitations known as "Majorana zero modes," which were investigated in [48]. Such Majorana zero modes are of critical importance because they can be utilized to develop failure-tolerant quantum computers. Their concept incorporates an experimental technique known as the "Coulomb-Blockage Spectroscopy" in order to produce superconducting Coulomb Islands (also known as "Majorana islands") in nanowire segments. The framework presented by the writers helps to elucidate the trivial-to-topological changeover in limited systems and to examine the advanced aspects of topological protection findings. Error correction in superconducting circuits can lengthen the lifespan of a quantum bit, according to the researchers. For the implementation of the qubits, Schrödinger cat states are superimposed over each other to encode them.

Using a feedback control mechanism, a quantum error-correcting process is put into practice in this way: Corrected qubit lifetimes of 320 μs were achieved in the suggested system. Such findings demonstrate the advantages of hardware-efficient qubit encoding instead of typical quantum fault rectification approaches, according to the authors.

Boixo et al. [49] investigate the issue of quantum supremacy, which is described as the ability of quantum devices without fault rectification to accomplish a well-defined computing job that is above the capability of presently existing conventional computers. The challenge of sampling from the outcome distributions of (pseudo-) random quantum networks was investigated in this study by the authors. In accordance with the authors' findings, sampling the distribution needs a high-cost numerical simulation of the circuit to be performed. It is worth noting that this cost grows exponentially in proportion to the count of qubits in the system. The authors conducted an analysis of quantum circuits with up to 42 qubits. Near-term quantum devices with 50 superconducting qubits can attain quantum supremacy, according to the authors. Researchers in the study [50] used machine learning to characterize decohering quantum systems. They studied the decoherence consequences of adaptive characterization techniques, in which measurement parameters are modified based on information feedback. Measuring with a larger sample size reduces estimation inaccuracy by an order of magnitude, as the authors have shown. A paradigm for dealing with substantial initial parameter ambiguity and flaws in the readout of decohering quantum systems was also created by the researchers. Using quantum autoencoders, Farhi et al. [51] were able to compress quantum data more efficiently than ever before. Autoencoders are designed to map input data into a lower-dimensional point so that the original data may be retrieved with reasonable probability from the mapped point. To conduct these actions on quantum data, the researchers developed an approach of a quantum autoencoder. Utilizing conventional optimization procedures, the authors discovered that they could train the parameters of the quantum autoencoder. As an added feature, the authors proved their findings in the context of quantum systems compression.

5.5 LARGE-SCALE-BASED QUANTUM COMPUTING

Complex quantum computations require a large-scale quantum computer, prompting ongoing efforts to develop such a system. The spatial arrangement of quantum states necessitates larger physical spacing and more extensive building blocks in the physical layer compared to traditional transistor technology. Consequently, instead of a single monolithic quantum computer (macro-architecture), a distributed approach is adopted, wherein multiple smaller quantum computers (micro-architecture) are interconnected in a specific network topology to facilitate distributed computations. Various models for large-scale quantum architectures are possible, as the chosen model for implementing quantum fault tolerance in the physical layer influences the available theoretical structures.

5.5.1 GATE MODEL QUANTUM COMPUTERS

There are numerous levels of quantum gates in gate-type quantum computers that execute quantum calculations. The input quantum systems are subjected to a single unitary function at every quantum gate. Due to hardware limits like the no-cloning principle, which prevents a particular quantum system from participating in multiple quantum gates at the same time [5], the gates are applied in rounds. The achievable circuit depth of current gate-based quantum computers (e.g., Google, MIT) relies on the reliability of the quantum gates and the specific qubit-to-qubit coupling scheme employed in the qubit systems. Figure 5.3 illustrates the architectural configuration of gate model quantum computers.

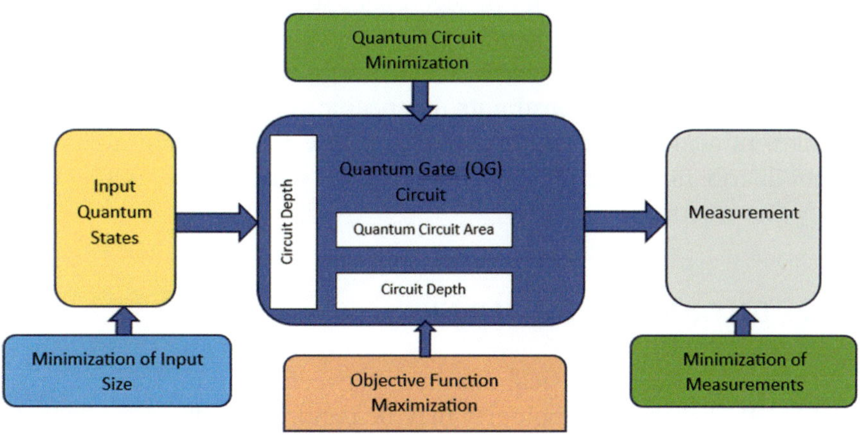

FIGURE 5.3 Gate model quantum computers.

Source: Adapted from Ref. [14]

According to [52], a quantum method for efficiently solving multimodal optimization issues is specified as the so-called Quantum Approximate Optimization Method. According to the authors, the quantum algorithm provides approximated answers, and the operation principle of the method relies on a positive integer to function. Such a positive integer enhances the accuracy of the quantum method, according to the authors' statement. Unitary gates whose locality is no more than the objective function's locality are included in the quantum circuit, as described by the researchers (the objective is to obtain the best of the objective purpose). It has been shown that within their structure, the quantum circuit's length develops linearly. The writers evaluated the quantum algorithm's functionality on normal graphs, and determined that it had significant advantages beyond conventional methods. Quantum approximate optimization algorithm (QAOA) was implemented to a well-defined multimodal issue by the researchers in [53]. A series of linear equations are used as the input system in the examined concept, each of which has precisely 3 Boolean variables, and each of them produces the result which is either 0 or 1 depending on whether the total of the variables mod 2 is equal to zero or one. To authors, traditional methods fail to solve the input problem as fast and professionally as the authors' quantum technique does. The QAOA was used in [54] by the writers to investigate the importance of quantum supremacy. A gate-model quantum computer can perform this method, as described in the study. A combinatorial optimization issue is fed into the algorithm, and it returns a string as the result. In accordance with the authors' claims, this output string meets a significant portion of the total quantity of possible clauses. The writers demonstrated that the suggested quantum method has well-defined efficiency constraints for specific situations. Because of this, no conventional device can accurately imitate the quantum algorithm's output distribution. The Quantum Adiabatic Algorithm was used to better verify this assertion.

5.5.3 DISTRIBUTED TOPOLOGIES

Given the significant physical distances between quantum states in space [9, 10, 19], distributed topologies may be required for extensive calculations. Distributed architecture disperses quantum algorithms and fault rectification procedures among smaller interconnected quantum computers linked by a quantum bus (such as optical fibers or wireless quantum channels). Effective distributed quantum computing frameworks, applications, fault rectification techniques, and measurement mechanisms are vital for successful quantum control and measurement mechanisms. Quantum computers are connected via system area networks, using relevant protocols to manage and govern them within this paradigm (classical protocols are also supported). To cover larger distances, quantum-wide area networks or metropolitan area networks may also be formed to connect more distant quantum computers.

Much research has been undertaken on quantum computing designs and methodologies [10]. This study thoroughly evaluates different building approaches and experimental concepts of quantum error correction to create scalable quantum computation. Hypothetically, a million-qubit quantum computer was proposed [55]. Unfortunately, research shows that such computers require striking an equilibrium between large-scale integration of elements and hardware stability to function successfully. By employing the appropriate modeling techniques, this equilibrium can be evaluated. Researchers created a performance simulation based on quantum logic operations executed on real-world quantum hardware with limited computing resources. This study demonstrated how Shor's algorithm could be applied to factorize a 1024-bit integer with a basic budget of 1.5 million qubits, as well as show how a trapped-ion quantum computer could factorize 2048-bit integers within 5 months [55].

Additionally, the authors developed a paradigm for distributed secure quantum machine learning [56]. This paradigm allows conventional users to directly assign distant quantum machine learning tasks to quantum servers. The authors presented a protocol utilizing a remote photon quantum computing processor to ensure no eavesdroppers gain access to sensitive data using quantum mechanics' principles as protection. Researchers also explored how feedforward neural networks could be generalized to quantum states [57]. Reversibility, an essential property of conventional neurons, was extended into the quantum domain. The research revealed autoencoder and teleportation algorithms using quantum networks, enabling the compression of quantum states into minimal qubits. Furthermore, light can be used as an implementation medium to implement quantum neuron modules with real-world applications being explored by researchers.

Researchers investigating quantum dots as potential candidates for building quantum neural networks based on dipole-dipole connections [58] tested whether their use could be viable and flexible; their implementation involved GaAs-based quantum dot qubits with phonon reservoirs to ensure consistency of over 100 ps in liquid nitrogen temperatures of 77 K, even while being kept consistently consistent at very cold temperatures when kept for testing at very cold temperatures; researchers concluded this implementation was three times more powerful than current millikelvin temperatures implementations [61, 64, 70, 72]. Researchers in [58] investigated whether quantum dots can be used successfully in creating quantum neural networks using dipole-dipole connections, with GaAs-based quantum dot qubits using GaAs-based quantum dot qubits connected by dipole–dipole connections utilizing dipole–dipole connections; the implementation was found both viable and flexible while keeping core neural network consistency for 100 ps or below liquid nitrogen temperature conditions (77 K). They concluded their implementation was three times more powerful than current implementations operating at millikelvin temperatures (7 K). More significantly, quantum computing has been applied in machine learning applications. The Pharmacogenomic Database was utilized in the work to design and develop a predictive machine for thyroid cancer among South Asian populations using deep convolution neural networking [59]. In large-scale nano-scale technologies, quantum dot cellular automata (QCA) subdue the shortcomings of integrated circuits by adopting alternative technologies like Hack AL U [60]. Also in nanoelectronics, QCA provides a path for designing electronic devices concerning quantum-mechanical aspects [61] In recent days, quantum annealing has depicted the efficacy of solving modern-day computations [62].

5.6 RESULTS AND DISCUSSION

Calculations were carried out using density functional theory and wave function theory calculations on intermediates and transition states involved in catalysis to provide us with all the information necessary for analysis and interpretation in this section. Next, we explored quantum phase estimation's computational costs when making accurate chemical predictions across small active spaces of 52–65 orbitals and larger active spaces. Furthermore, we addressed runtime requirements and qubit resources associated with critical intermediates/transition states in catalysis processes.

$$x_{(i,\sigma)}G = \Sigma ij,_{\sigma}\ gijx_{(i,\sigma)}x_{(j,\sigma)} + \frac{1}{2}\Sigma ijkl, \sigma\rho gijkl_{(i,\sigma)}x_{(k,p)}x_{(l,p)}x_{(j,\sigma)} \quad (5.1)$$

Equation 5.1 indicates that molecular orbitals within an orbital subspace known as the active space are described by 1- and 2-electron integrals calculated over this space. To accurately identify which orbitals form part of this active space, strongly correlated orbitals must first be identified; automated measurements of orbital entanglement are often employed as an effective means for this task, although exact values for alternative orbital spaces are not crucial.

Measures of orbital entanglement, pair-orbital mutual information, and occupancy numbers demonstrate that the ground states of catalyst architectures investigated in this study are not predominantly governed by static correlation. Thus classical quantum chemistry tools like coupled cluster methods provide rapid and precise calculations within their chosen basis set limits, creating a formidable challenge for quantum approaches to overcome. We aim to develop a universal quantum computing strategy that effectively handles static correlation and potential future correlated problems economically.

Whether the chosen dimensions for our dynamic orbital space do not follow conventional electron correlation trends, their nonadherence did not significantly hinder resource evaluation. Our ability to select an active space of strongly correlated orbitals ranging from 5–16 remained undamaged. The main goal of this research was to gain a deeper insight into how quantum algorithms perform on real-world chemical problems of various sizes and complexities; Table 5.1 presents experimental results highlighting energy estimation and error rate relationships. The expanding expanse of the orbital space wherein the precise wave function is produced is represented by the variable size. It follows that in order to establish an appropriate testing environment we must pick active space widths that are arbitrary in terms of the appropriate balancing between static and dynamic correlation. It was necessary to include weakly correlated orbitals in order to expand active space sizes above the conventional limitation. Also, the comparison over cost of Toffoli and truncation threshold for estimation of phase is given in Figure 5.4. Figure 5.5 provides minimized Toffoli cost of each configuration of the catalytic cycle with respect to active space size.

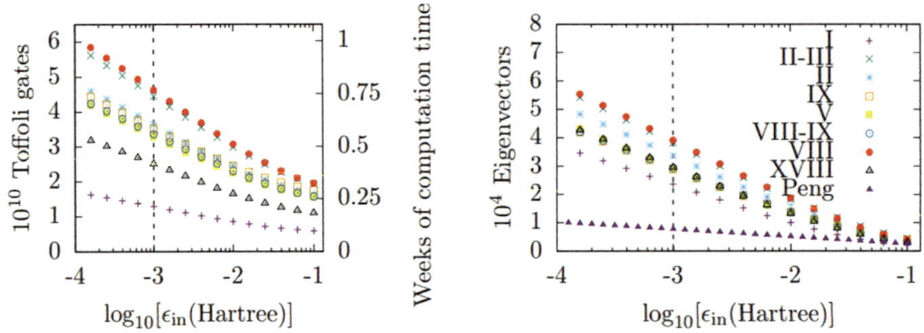

FIGURE 5.4 Cost of Toffoli vs truncation threshold for estimation of phase.

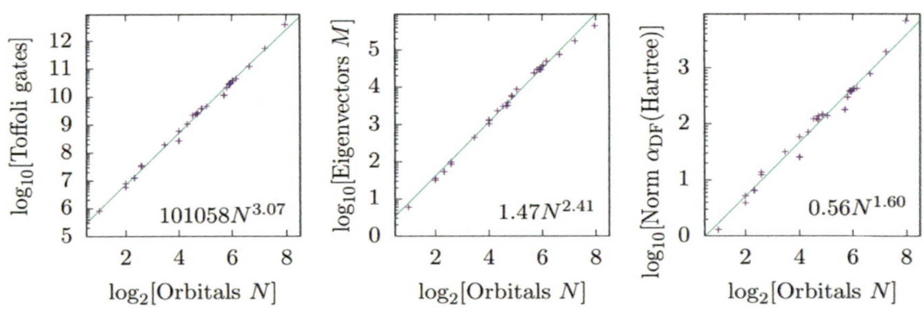

FIGURE 5.5 Evaluating Toffoli cost scaling models to identify which configurations have minimal Toffoli cost scaling.

TABLE 5.1 Entire Toffoli Gates for Energy Estimation Level with Respect to Error Occurred

Structures	Orbitals	Electrons	Toffoli	Negative Rate	∝(Per Hartree)	Using Very Less Qubits	Qubits Toffolis/10^{10}
I	53	47	614	24.343	188.3	3300	1.3
II–III	63	72	735	34.543	378.4	4300	5.4
IV	65	73	785	39.454	432.1	4400	4.3
V	66	65	645	29.343	372.3	3400	4.5
VI–VIII	59	73	797	39.545	384.4	4500	4.4
VIII–IX	65	45	656	28.442	394.5	4600	5.2
IX–X	64	64	659	28.454	345.2	4700	5.2
XI	630	64	806	29.343	275.6	4900	5.5

5.7 CONCLUSION

In conclusion, this chapter has provided a thorough insight into significant developments within intelligent quantum computing, exploring various contributions made over time, including fundamental principles related to quantum computation and information, characteristics of quantum communication systems as well as new advancements made within quantum algorithms. Researchers such as Deutsch, Feynman, DiVincenzo, and Shor have been recognized for their groundbreaking achievements and profound insights within quantum computing. Entanglement's importance, temporally unstructured quantum computing's difficulties, and multiparty delegated quantum computation's potential have all been thoroughly covered in recent discussions. Also included herein is an in-depth examination of both the advantages and drawbacks of quantum computing, an update on ongoing advancements in quantum algorithms and simulation, and exciting advances in this exciting domain of simulation. All these developments illustrate that intelligent quantum computing holds great promise to revolutionize various fields and pioneer new frontiers of scientific and technological exploration.

KEYWORDS

- **machine learning**
- **deep learning**
- **noisy intermediate-scale quantum**
- **quantum approximate optimization algorithm**

REFERENCES

1. Barends, R., Kelly, J., Megrant, A., Veitia, A., Sank, D., Jeffrey, E., White, T. C., et al. (2014). Logic gates at the surface code threshold: Superconducting qubits poised for fault-tolerant quantum computing. arXiv preprint *arXiv:http://arxiv.org/abs/1402.4848.*
2. Biamonte, J., Wittek, P., Pancotti, N., Rebentrost, P., Wiebe, N., & Lloyd, S. (2017). Quantum machine learning. *Nature*, *549*(7671), 195–202.
3. Debnath, S., Linke, N. M., Figgatt, C., Landsman, K. A., Wright, K., & Monroe, C. (2016). Demonstration of a small programmable quantum computer with atomic qubits. *Nature*, *536*(7614), 63–66. https://doi.org/10.1038/nature18648.
4. DiCarlo, L., Chow, J. M., Gambetta, J. M., Bishop, L. S., Johnson, B. R., Schuster, D. I., Majer, J. et al. (2009). Demonstration of two-qubit algorithms with a superconducting quantum processor. *Nature*, *460*(7252), 240–44. https://doi.org/10.1038/nature08121.
5. Farhi, E., Goldstone, J., Gutmann, S., & Neven, H. (2017). Quantum algorithms for fixed qubit architectures. arXiv preprint *arXiv:1703.06199.*

6. Higgins, B. L., Berry, D. W., Bartlett, S. D., Wiseman, H. M., & Pryde, G. J. (2007). Entanglement-free Heisenberg-limited phase estimation. *Nature*, *450*(7168), 393–396.
7. Monz, T., Nigg, D., Martinez, E. A., Brandl, M. F., Schindler, P., Rines, R., Wang, S. X., Chuang, I. L., & Blatt, R. (2016). Realization of a scalable Shor algorithm. *Science*, *351*(6277), 1068–1070.
8. Ofek, N., Petrenko, A., Heeres, R., Reinhold, P., Leghtas, Z., Vlastakis, B., Liu, Y. et al. (2016). Extending the lifetime of a quantum bit with error correction in superconducting circuits. *Nature*, *536*(7617), 441–445.
9. Devitt, S. J., Greentree, A. D., Stephens, A. M., & Meter, R. V. (2016). High-speed quantum networking by ship. *Scientific Reports*, *6*(1), 36163.
10. Van Meter, R., & Devitt, S. J. (2016). Local and distributed quantum computation. arXiv preprint *arXiv:1605.06951*.
11. Shor, P. W. (1999). Polynomial-time algorithms for prime factorization and discrete logarithms on a quantum computer. *SIAM Review*, *41*(2), 303–332.
12. Rivest, R. L., Shamir, A., & Adleman, L. (1978). A method for obtaining digital signatures and public-key cryptosystems. *Communications of the ACM*, *21*(2), 120–126.
13. Proos, J., & Zalka, C. (2003). Shor's discrete logarithm quantum algorithm for elliptic curves. arXiv preprint. *arXiv: quant-ph/0301141*.
14. Imre, S., & Gyongyosi, L. (2012). *Advanced Quantum Communications: An Engineering Approach*. John Wiley & Sons.
15. Imre, S., & Balazs, F. (2005). *Quantum Computing and Communications: An Engineering Approach*. John Wiley & Sons.
16. Imre, S. (2013). Quantum communications: Explained for communication engineers. *IEEE Communications Magazine*, *51*(8), 28–35.
17. Nielsen, M. A., & Chuang, I. L. (2010). *Quantum Computation and Quantum Information*. Cambridge University Press.
18. Nielsen, M. (2000). *Quantum Computation and Quantum Information*. Cambridge University Press.
19. Meter III, R. D. V. (2006). Architecture of a quantum multicomputer optimized for shor's factoring algorithm. arXiv preprint *arXiv: quant-ph/0607065*.
20. DiVincenzo, D. P. (2000). The physical implementation of quantum computation. *Fortschritte der Physik: Progress of Physics*, *48*(9–11), 771–783.
21. Aaronson, S., & Arkhipov, A. (2011). The computational complexity of linear optics. In *Proceedings of the Forty-third Annual ACM Symposium on Theory of Computing*, pp. 333–342.
22. Levin, L. A. (2003). One-way functions. *Problemy Peredachi Informatsii*, *39*(1), 103–117.
23. Bravyi, S., Gosset, D., & König, R. (2018). Quantum advantage with shallow circuits. *Science*, *362*(6412), 308–311.
24. Bremner, M. J., Montanaro, A., & Shepherd, D. J. (2017). Achieving quantum supremacy with sparse and noisy commuting quantum computations. *Quantum*, *1*, 8.
25. Zahedinejad, E., Ghosh, J., & Sanders, B. C. (2016). Designing high-fidelity single-shot three-qubit gates: A machine-learning approach. *Physical Review Applied*, *6*(5), 054005.
26. Dennis, E., Kitaev, A., Landahl, A., & Preskill, J. (2002). Topological quantum memory. *Journal of Mathematical Physics*, *43*(9), 4452–4505.

27. August, M., & Ni, X. (2017). Using recurrent neural networks to optimize dynamical decoupling for quantum memory. *Physical Review A*, *95*(1), 012335.
28. Maurer, P. C., Kucsko, G., Latta, C., Jiang, L., Yao, N. Y., Bennett, S. D., Pastawski, F. et al. (2012). Room-temperature quantum bit memory exceeding one second. *Science*, *336*(6086), 1283–1286.
29. Monroe, C., Raussendorf, R., Ruthven, A., Brown, K. R., Maunz, P., Duan, L - M., & Kim, J. (2014). Large-scale modular quantum-computer architecture with atomic memory and photonic interconnects. *Physical Review A*, *89*(2), 022317.
30. Giovannetti, V., Lloyd, S., & Maccone, L. (2008). Quantum random access memory. *Physical Review Letters*, *100*(16), 160501.
31. Santra, S., Shehab, O., & Balu, R. (2016). Exponential capacity of associative memories under quantum annealing recall. arXiv preprint *arXiv*:1602.08149.
32. Pfeiffer, P., Egusquiza, I. L., Di Ventra, M., Sanz, M., & Solano, E. (2016). Quantum memristors. *Scientific Reports*, *6*(1), 29507.
33. Salmilehto, J., Deppe, F., Di Ventra, M., Sanz, M., & Solano, E. (2017). Quantum memristors with superconducting circuits. *Scientific Reports*, *7*(1), 42044.
34. Shevchenko, S. N., Pershin, Y. V., & Nori, F. (2016). Qubit-based memcapacitors and meminductors. *Physical Review Applied*, *6*(1), 014006.
35. Büch, H., Mahapatra, S., Rahman, R., Morello, A., & Simmons, M. Y. (2013). Spin readout and addressability of phosphorus-donor clusters in silicon. *Nature Communications*, *4*(1), 2017.
36. Veldhorst, M., Hwang, J. C. C., Yang, C. H., Leenstra, A. W., de Ronde, B., Dehollain, J. P., Muhonen, J. T., et al. (2014). An addressable quantum dot qubit with fault-tolerant control-fidelity. *Nature Nanotechnology*, *9*(12), 981–985.
37. Gatti, G., Barberena, D., Sanz, M., & Solano, E. (2017). Protected state transfer via an approximate quantum adder. *Scientific Reports*, *7*(1), 6964.
38. Li, R., Alvarez-Rodriguez, U., Lamata, L., & Solano, E. (2017). Approximate quantum adders with genetic algorithms: An IBM quantum experience. *Quantum Measurements and Quantum Metrology*, *4*(1), 1–7.
39. Vermersch, B., Guimond, P.-O., Pichler, H., & Zoller, P. (2017). Quantum state transfer via noisy photonic and phononic waveguides. *Physical Review Letters*, *118*(13), 133601.
40. Lamata, L., Alvarez-Rodriguez, U., David Martín-Guerrero, J., Sanz, M., & Solano, E. (2018). Quantum autoencoders via quantum adders with genetic algorithms. *Quantum Science and Technology*, *4*(1), 014007.
41. Nguyen, T. D., & Meter, R. V. (2014). A resource-efficient design for a reversible floating point adder in quantum computing. *ACM Journal on Emerging Technologies in Computing Systems (JETC)*, *11*(2), 1–18.
42. Van Meter, R. (2014). Quantum computing's classical problem, classical computing's quantum problem. *Foundations of Physics*, *44*(8), 819–828.
43. Lidar, D. A., & Brun, T. A. eds. (2013). *Quantum Error Correction*. Cambridge University Press.
44. Nagayama, S., Fowler, A. G., Horsman, D., Devitt, S. J., & Meter, R. V. (2017). Surface code error correction on a defective lattice. *New Journal of Physics*, *19*(2), 023050.
45. Nagayama, S., Satoh, T., & Van Meter, R. (2017). State injection, lattice surgery, and dense packing of the deformation-based surface code. *Physical Review A*, *95*(1), 012321.

46. O'Gorman, J., Nickerson, N. H., Ross, P., Morton, J. J. L., & Benjamin, S. C. (2016). A silicon-based surface code quantum computer. *npj Quantum Information*, *2*(1), 1–14.
47. Albrecht, S. M., Higginbotham, A. P., Madsen, M., Kuemmeth, F., Jespersen, T. S., Nygård, J., Krogstrup, P., & Marcus, C. M. (2016). Exponential protection of zero modes in Majorana islands. *Nature*, *531*(7593), 206–209.
48. Boixo, S., Isakov, S. V., Smelyanskiy, V. N., Babbush, R., Ding, N., Jiang, Z., Bremner, M. J., Martinis, J. M., & Neven, H. (2018). Characterizing quantum supremacy in near-term devices. *Nature Physics*, *14*(6), 595–600.
49. Stenberg, M. P. V., Köhn, O., & Wilhelm, F. K. (2016). Characterization of decohering quantum systems: Machine learning approach. *Physical Review A*, *93*(1), 012122.
50. Romero, J., Olson, J. P., & Aspuru-Guzik, A. (2017). Quantum autoencoders for efficient compression of quantum data. *Quantum Science and Technology*, *2*(4), 045001.
51. Farhi, E., Goldstone, J., & Gutmann, S. (2014). A quantum approximate optimization algorithm. arXiv preprint *arXiv:1411.4028*.
52. Farhi, E., & Harrow, A. W. (2016). Quantum supremacy through the quantum approximate optimization algorithm. arXiv preprint *arXiv:1602.07674*.
53. Ahsan, M., Van Meter, R., & Kim, J. (2015). Designing a million-qubit quantum computer using a resource performance simulator. *ACM Journal on Emerging Technologies in Computing Systems (JETC)*, *12*(4), 1–25.
54. Sheng, Y.-B., & Zhou, L. (2017). Distributed secure quantum machine learning. *Science Bulletin*, *62*(14), 1025–1029.
55. Wan, K. H., Dahlsten, O., Kristjánsson, H., Gardner, R., & Kim, M. S. (2017). Quantum generalisation of feedforward neural networks. *npj Quantum information*, *3*(1), 36.
56. Altaisky, M. V., Zolnikova, N. N., Kaputkina, N. E., Krylov, V. A., Lozovik, Y. E., & Dattani, N. S. (2016). Towards a feasible implementation of quantum neural networks using quantum dots. *Applied Physics Letters*, *108*(10), 103108.
57. Sajeev, V., Hima Vyshnavi, A. M., & Krishnan Namboori, P. K. (2020). Thyroid cancer prediction using gene expression profile, pharmacogenomic variants and quantum image processing in deep learning platform-a theranostic approach. In *2020 International Conference for Emerging Technology (INCET)*, Belgaum, India, pp. 1–5, https://doi.org/10.1109/INCET49848.2020.9154041.
58. Aadhithya, A. A, Akshaya, J., Ghaayathri Devi, K., Nithesh, B., Jyothish Lal, G., & Soman, K. P. (2021). Implementation of Hack ALU using quantum dot cellular automata. In *2021 Fourth International Conference on Microelectronics, Signals & Systems (ICMSS)*. IEEE, pp. 1–7.
59. Prasanna S. A, Madhava Reddy, B., & Ramesh, S., R. (2021). Design of combinational arithmetic circuits using quantum dot cellular automata. In *2021 5th International Conference on Trends in Electronics and Informatics (ICOEI)*. Tirunelveli, India, pp. 117–122, https://doi.org/10.1109/ICOEI51242.2021.9453069.
60. Venugopalan, A. K., Karishmah, R. K., Pillai, R. S., Sreedev, D., Balachandran, V., & Bhattacharjee, P. (2021). Study of quantum annealing and the type of related applications. In *2021 IEEE Pune Section International Conference (PuneCon)*. IEEE, pp. 1–6.

CHAPTER 6

Applications of Quantum Computing in the Field of Data Science

ELAKKIYA ELANGO[1*], GNANASANKARAN NATARAJAN[2*], SUNDARAVADIVAZHAGAN BALASUBRAMANIAN[3*], MOHAMED IMRAN KAREEM BASHA[4*], and BALASUBRAMANIAN SHANMUGANATHAN[5*]

[1]*Department of Computer Science, Government Arts College for Women, Sivaganga, Tamil Nadu, India*

[2]*Department of Computer Science, Thiagarajar College, Madurai, Tamil Nadu, India*

[3]*Department of Information Technology, University of Technology and Applied Sciences, Al Mussanah, Oman*

[4]*Department of Computer Application, Merit Haji Ismail Sahib, Arts and Science College, Pernambut, Vellore, Tamil Nadu, India*

[5]*Department of Distance Education, Alagappa University, Karaikudi, Tamil Nadu, India*

*Corresponding author

ABSTRACT

To fulfill the demands of their companies, professionals must keep up with the most recent tools, technologies, and trends in their industry. The world of technology is continuously changing. Quantum computing is a specific invention which is attracting a lot of interest due to its potential to influence how data will be handled and processed in the future. The whole data science pipeline depends on computing, from data collection and

Applications of Quantum Computing in a Variety of Domains. Gunjan Mukherjee, Biswadip Basu Mallik, Rahul Kar Özen ÖZER, Digvijay Pandey, and Binay Kumar Pandey (Eds.)

DOI: 10.1201/9781998511051-6

maintenance through processing and analysis to final communication or response predicted on the collected insights. Moreover, computing difficulties are frequently linked to statistical analysis. Comparing quantum algorithms to conventional ones, the former gain more computational effectiveness (with quicker speed) at the price of statistical effectiveness (with greater variation). Data science methodologies can aid in understanding and optimizing this trade-off as well as identifying generic tools for accelerating quantum algorithms' computing speed. These resources, which might take the form of tangible objects, digital data, or mathematical components, are used to examine how effective they are at accelerating computing.

6.1 INTRODUCTION

Quantum computing has emerged as a game-changing technology in the always-changing field of data science due to the pursuit of more potent computing paradigms. Once thought to be beyond the capabilities of classical computers, quantum computing uses the ideas of quantum physics to accomplish computations. The subject of data science is one of the most promising areas where this paradigm shift may be applied to solve complicated challenges, as it presents previously unheard-of potential across multiple domains. While classical computing techniques are powerful at managing large datasets and running complex algorithms, they have inherent drawbacks when faced with specific kinds of issues. Computational approaches that can quickly process, evaluate, and extract insights from data are desperately needed as the volume and complexity of data continue to rise.

With its special capacity to take advantage of quantum superposition and entanglement, quantum computing has the potential to completely transform how we tackle problems involving large amounts of data. This investigation into the use of quantum computing in data science is a practical answer to the increasing needs of our data-driven society rather than just a theoretical endeavor. This is where data science and quantum computing converge, offering a potentially transformative synergy that can change the analytics, machine learning, and artificial intelligence landscape. This exploration of the quantum domain of computing holds the potential to improve data processing speed and efficiency while also opening up previously unthinkable avenues for problem-solving.

This chapter explores the complexities of using quantum computing in data science. It does so by examining the underlying ideas of quantum algorithms, their possible effects on pattern recognition and data analysis, and the usefulness of the technology for sectors looking for novel approaches to their most difficult data-centric issues. Come along on this thrilling journey as we explore the unexplored aspirations of applying quantum computing to data science, bringing in an entirely novel phase of computational discoveries and opportunities.

6.1.1 LITERATURE SURVEY

Understanding quantum computing's applications in data science requires familiarity with the core literature on the technology. Understanding the special ideas of quantum mechanics that underpin quantum computing is made possible by the works of pioneers like Richard Feynman and David Deutsch [5, 12]. The field's foundational works, Shor's and Grover's algorithms, are thoroughly examined, emphasizing their potential utility in resolving challenging computing issues, such as those arising in data science. A substantial amount of research examines the relationship between machine learning and quantum computing. Prominent contributions are made to the field of quantum algorithms specifically for machine learning problems by scholars such as Wittek and Lloyd [3].

Regarding data categorization, clustering, and regression, quantum machine learning holds the potential to significantly accelerate specific algorithms through exponential growth. Examining these studies offers insights into how quantum-enhanced machine learning approaches are developing. New paradigm-challenging data structures and algorithms are introduced by quantum computing. Quantum databases, quantum search algorithms, and quantum parallelism are examined in the literature by Lov Grover and others, providing insight into their possible uses in data storage, retrieval, and manipulation. Gaining knowledge of these quantum data structures is essential for knowing how data science procedures might be revolutionized by quantum computing. Data science is full of optimization problems, and quantum computing is quite good at solving them.

The research on quantum optimization algorithms offers perspectives on the way to use quantum computers to find effective solutions for data-centric problems like choosing features, hyperparameter tuning, and combinatorial optimization issues. This includes the Quantum Approximate Optimization Algorithm (QAOA). A fundamental quantum phenomenon that has significant effects on data security is quantum entanglement. The literature on quantum key distribution and quantum cryptography describes how data storage and transmission security can be improved by quantum computing. To fully comprehend the possible influence of quantum computing on maintaining data integrity and confidentiality in the quantum era, one must have an in-depth knowledge of these quantum cryptography techniques. Analyzing the literature on real-world applications of quantum algorithms for data science jobs sheds light on recent successes and difficulties.

In the framework of data science applications, researchers like Alán Aspuru-Guzik and Hartmut Neven have investigated the practical issues and constraints of current quantum hardware through their exploration of quantum computing applications on platforms like IBM Q and Google's Sycamore [19]. Examining case studies and quantum computing applications across a range of industries, such as finance, healthcare, and logistics, provides a useful viewpoint on how quantum computing might be applied to solve practical data science problems. The body of research on applications unique to particular industries offers insight into the revolutionary potential of quantum computing for data-driven decision-making. The potential future of quantum-enhanced data science is based on the combination of fundamental quantum principles, algorithmic advances, and practical considerations. The reviewed literature paves the way for more investigation and growth in this dynamic and quickly developing multidisciplinary topic.

6.2 SCOPE AND SIGNIFICANCE

6.2.1 SCOPE

- **Algorithmic Advancements:** This research explores the possible uses and effectiveness of state-of-the-art quantum algorithms, such as Grover's Algorithm, Shor's Algorithm, and QAOA, in resolving data science problems.
- **Machine Learning Paradigms:** This area of study looks at how quantum computing and machine learning interact, exploring

quantum-enhanced methods for regression, classification, clustering, and neural networks as well as their potential to advance data science approaches.

- **Data Structure and Manipulation:** The potential of quantum data structures and algorithms for data storage, retrieval, and manipulation is investigated. This study looks at how traditional data management techniques can be revolutionized by quantum computing.
- **Data Security and Cryptography:** The study delves deeply into the function of quantum entanglement in quantum cryptography, highlighting its importance in bolstering data security and confidentiality and clearing the path for secure interaction in the modern age of quantum computing.
- **Optimization in Data Science:** The scope includes optimization issues that are specific to data science, like feature selection and hyperparameter tuning, with an emphasis on assessing how well quantum algorithms perform when optimizing solutions to data-centric problems.
- **Platforms and Real-World Implementations:** The chapter assesses the current state of the art concerning real-world implementations on quantum computing platforms, like IBM Q and Google Sycamore, and provides information about the advantages, disadvantages, and considerations that should be made when integrating quantum solutions into real-world data science tasks.
- **Challenges and Future Directions:** A key component of the scope is identifying and tackling the problems associated with quantum computing for data science, with a focus on fault tolerance, scalability, and ethical issues. Future directions for developing quantum-enhanced data science approaches are examined in this chapter.
- **Industry Applications:** The study explores particular uses of quantum computing in a range of industries, including case studies that show how quantum technologies are applied to data science problems unique to a certain business.

6.2.2 SIGNIFICANCE

- **Transformative Potential:** Because of its potentially revolutionary nature, it is crucial to comprehend how quantum computing is applied in data science. The ability of quantum algorithms to solve problems at previously unheard-of speeds will revolutionize processes including data processing, pattern recognition, and decision-making.
- **Enhanced Computational Efficiency:** The research is noteworthy for demonstrating how quantum computing can resolve the drawbacks of traditional computing paradigms and pave the way for new approaches to managing massive and complicated datasets. This can lead to an exponential increase in computational efficiency in data science jobs.
- **Developments in Machine Learning:** The investigation of quantum machine learning methods is extremely important since it opens the door to new machine learning paradigms. Quantum-enhanced algorithms may perform better than their conventional equivalents, providing new methods for solving data-driven problems.
- **Secure Data Communication:** To comprehend how quantum computing may provide secure data communication, it is essential to look at the function of quantum entanglement in data security. For businesses and organizations that handle sensitive data, this has important ramifications.
- **Optimization in Data-driven Decision Making:** The study's emphasis on data science optimization problems is noteworthy for sectors looking for effective solutions for feature selection, hyperparameter tuning, and other optimization problems. This will ultimately lead to more informed and data-driven decision-making processes.
- **Real-world Implementations:** Evaluating real-world platforms and implementations offers insights into the difficulties and viability of incorporating quantum computing into data science workflows. This knowledge is crucial for directing businesses thinking about implementing quantum technology.
- **Overcoming Obstacles and Creating the Future:** Determining hurdles and suggesting alternatives is crucial in helping

practitioners, researchers, and industry stakeholders create the future of quantum-enhanced data science. This feature adds to the current discussion on the viability and endurance of quantum solutions.

6.3 FOUNDATIONS OF QUANTUM COMPUTING

- **Overcoming Challenges and Defining the Future:** Practitioners, researchers, and industry stakeholders must work together to identify impediments and provide solutions in order to shape the direction of quantum-enhanced data science in the future [18]. This feature contributes to the ongoing debate on the durability and practicality of quantum solutions.
- **Principles of Quantum Mechanics:** Discovered in the early 1900s, quantum mechanics presents a probabilistic understanding of the physical world. Wavefunctions are intricate mathematical constructs that represent the likelihood of discovering particles in various states and are used to characterize quantum states. In the quantum domain, measurement creates an inherent uncertainty because particles do not have fixed attributes until they are measured. This is a fundamental break from classical determinism.
- **Quantum Bits (Qubits) and Quantum Gates:** Qubits are the quantum equivalent of the traditional bits of computing, which stand for 0s and 1s. Qubits, in contrast to classical bits, are capable of being in a superposition of states, simultaneously representing 0 and 1. The computing potential of quantum systems is greatly increased by this special characteristic. Building blocks of quantum circuits, quantum gates use operations that take advantage of quantum physics to modify qubits.
- **Quantum Entanglement and Superposition:** Quantum superposition enables qubits to exist in several states at once. This property allows the simultaneous investigation of several options in quantum calculations. Another quantum phenomenon called entanglement connects qubits so that, regardless of their distance from one another, the state of one instantaneously affects the state of the other. The foundation for producing highly linked quantum states is this interdependence.

- **Quantum Parallelism:** The capacity of qubits to exist in superpositions gives rise to quantum parallelism. Quantum computers are able to investigate several solutions at once, in contrast to classical computers that assess options one after the other. The possibility of quantum speedup—a phenomenon in which quantum algorithms perform better than their classical counterparts for specific computational tasks—is supported by this parallelism.
- **Quantum Algorithms and Circuits:** Similar to classical logic gates, quantum gates control qubits to carry out particular tasks. Combining these gates can create quantum circuits, which are collections of operations that carry out quantum algorithms. Well-known quantum algorithms that use quantum parallelism to solve problems tenfold quicker than classical algorithms include the Simon's algorithm and the Deutsch-Jozsa algorithm. These algorithms demonstrate the potential of quantum computing.

Comprehending these fundamental concepts is important for maneuvering across the complex terrain of quantum computing. These ideas will be the basis for understanding the quantum algorithms and approaches that have the potential to completely change the way we handle and analyze large datasets as we continue to explore the use of quantum computing in data science.

6.3.1 QUANTUM BITS (QUBITS) AND QUANTUM GATES

Quantum bits, or qubits, are the fundamental building blocks of quantum computing, and quantum gates allow for the manipulation of these bits [16]. Gaining an understanding of these components is essential to appreciating the special computational powers that quantum systems provide.

- **Classical Bits Versus Quantum Bits:**
  - **Classical Bits:** Bits are used in classical computers to process information. Bits can be in one of two states: 0 or 1. Classical logic gates are used to alter information, and computations are carried out in a sequential fashion.
  - **Quantum Bits (Qubits):** The quantum equivalents of classical bits, or qubits, have an amazing characteristic known

as superposition. Qubits, in contrast to classical bits, are multistate entities that can concurrently represent 0 and 1. Quantum systems have exponentially greater processing capacity because of their intrinsic duality.

- **Qubit Quantum Superposition:**
  - **Superposition:** A superposition of states is possible for qubits to exist in. This implies that a qubit may indicate a combination of 0 and 1 until it is measured. One important aspect that sets qubits apart from classical bits is their capacity to investigate numerous options simultaneously.
- **Quantum Entanglement:** Apart from superposition, qubits can also be entangled, which is a phenomenon in which the states of two qubits are intimately coupled, irrespective of their physical distance from each other. Formation of strongly coupled quantum states is made possible via entanglement.
- **Quantum Circuits and Quantum Gates:**
  - **Atomic Gates:** The basic components of quantum circuits are known as quantum gates. These gates apply quantum mechanical operations to qubits, changing their states in the process. The Hadamard gate, the phase gate, and the Controlled NOT (CNOT) gate are examples of notable quantum gates.
  - **Quantum circuits:** To carry out particular calculations, quantum gates are placed in a series known as a quantum circuit. These circuits utilize entanglement and superposition to carry out quantum algorithms. The quantum computation's output is determined by the layout and interaction of the gates.

To fully utilize quantum computing, one must comprehend the dynamics of qubits and the functions of quantum gates. Quantum systems have the capacity to continuously explore large solution spaces due to their superposition and entanglement properties, which may lead to a computational speedup not possible with conventional computers. Effective use of qubits and quantum gates is the foundation of quantum algorithms, which have the potential to be used in data science and other fields to solve challenging problems.

6.3.2 QUANTUM SUPERPOSITION AND ENTANGLEMENT

Entanglement and quantum superposition are two noteworthy characteristics that set quantum systems apart from classical ones [13]. The extraordinary computing capacity of quantum computers is based on these ideas, which are fundamental to the behavior of quantum particles.

- **Quantum Superposition:**
  - **Definition:** A quantum system is capable of being in more than one state at once, a phenomenon known as quantum superposition. In contrast, a particle in a conventional system is in a fixed state.
  - **Qubits and Superposition:** Qubits can exist in a superposition of 0 or 1 in quantum computing. This makes it possible for quantum computers to handle data in parallel and investigate several options at once.
  - **Mathematical Representation:** A typical mathematical expression for a qubit's state in superposition is a linear combination of its base states. A qubit in superposition, for instance, could be written as $|\psi\rangle=\alpha|0\rangle+\beta|1\rangle$, where the numbers α and β are complex.
  - **Quantum Entanglement:** Despite their physical separation, two or more qubits can have a distinct correlation in which the state of one is directly related to the value of the other. This phenomenon is known as quantum entanglement.
  - **Entangled Qubits:** Regardless of their distance from one another, entangled qubits possess a common state in which the measurement of one right away determines the state of the other.
  - **EPR Paradox:** The Einstein–Podolsky–Rosen (EPR) conundrum is a well-known example of entanglement in action, illustrating the nonlocal and correlated properties of entangled particles.
  - **Bell's Inequality:** Bell's inequality shows that entanglement defies a number of traditional presumptions regarding coupled systems. The existence of entanglement has been verified by tests using Bell's inequality.

- **Quantum Computing Applications:**
  - **Quantum Parallelism:** For some applications, quantum computers may process information more quickly than classical computers because to the concepts of superposition and entanglement.
  - **Quantum Algorithms:** Using superposition and entanglement, quantum algorithms, including Grover's and Shor's algorithms, can solve problems tenfold quicker than their classical equivalents.
- **Difficulties and Prospects:**
  - **Quantum Decoherence:** Entanglement and superposition are sensitive to the fact that are capable of being broken by outside forces, resulting in a phenomenon called quantum decoherence. Managing and reducing decoherence is a major obstacle to the development of useful quantum computers.
  - **Quantum Communication:** The security of cryptographic keys is ensured by entangled states, which has consequences for secure communication via quantum key distribution.

They serve as the foundation for quantum computing and are the key to unlocking its ability to solve intricate issues at rates that traditional computers are unable to match. In the quest for useful quantum technology, researchers are still tackling the difficulties of controlling and maintaining these fragile quantum states.

6.3.3 QUANTUM CIRCUITS AND QUANTUM ALGORITHMS

The structural frameworks that coordinate the manipulation of quantum bits, or qubits, via quantum gates are known as quantum circuits [2]. These circuits serve as the building blocks for quantum algorithms, which use the laws of quantum mechanics to accelerate calculations exponentially when compared to their classical counterparts.

- **Quantum Gates:**
  - **Basic Operations:** Fundamental Functions. The fundamental components of quantum circuits are quantum gates, which carry out particular actions on qubits. The purpose of these

procedures is to take advantage of quantum concepts such as entanglement and superposition.

  - **Hadamard Gate:** It is a basic gate that converts a qubit from its classical states of $|0\rangle$ and $|1\rangle$ to a superposition state, thus enabling superposition.
  - **Controlled NOT (CNOT) Gate:** It is a type of two-qubit gate in which the state of one qubit is dependent upon the state of the other. This gate is essential for creating entangled states.

- **Quantum Circuits:**
  - **Gate Configuration:** A series of quantum gates applied to qubits make up a quantum circuit. The circuit's computation is determined by the placement and sequence of these gates.
  - **Quantum Parallelism:** Quantum circuits use the entanglement and superposition concepts to carry out calculations concurrently across several states. This enables the simultaneous exploration of a large solution space by quantum algorithms.
  - **Representation:** Visual illustration of quantum circuits is common; boxes stand in for quantum gates and horizontal lines for qubits. The qubits' states are affected by each gate in the computation, which proceeds from left to right.

- **Quantum Algorithms:**
  - **Shor's Algorithm:** The Algorithm of Shor is a novel quantum algorithm that challenges conventional computers by factoring big numbers effectively. Shor's algorithm illustrates the possible quantum advantage by having consequences for cracking specific encryption techniques.
  - **Grover's Algorithm:** A quadratic speedup over classical methods is provided by this quantum search algorithm. It is frequently used to search databases that are not sorted, providing notable improvements in computing performance for some workloads.

- **Quantum Computational Complexity:**
  - **Exponential Speedup:** Compared to their most well-known classical equivalents, quantum algorithms frequently show

exponential speedup. This is explained by quantum systems' capacity to process data concurrently across several states.

- **Complexity Classes:** Bounded-error quantum polynomial time or BQP is one of the complexity classes introduced by quantum computing that effectively classifies tasks that a quantum computer can solve.

- **Quantum Error Correction:**
  - **Challenges of Quantum Decoherence:** Difficulties Errors brought on by external circumstances can cause quantum states to lose their coherence. Maintaining the integrity of quantum calculations requires the use of quantum error correcting techniques.
  - **Fault-Tolerant Quantum Circuits:** One important field of research to guarantee the dependability of quantum algorithms in the presence of mistakes is the development of fault-tolerant quantum circuits.

They use the fundamentals of quantum mechanics to carry out calculations that are intrinsically difficult for classical computers. At the forefront of the search for useful and scalable quantum computing technology is the investigation and optimization of quantum circuits and algorithms.

6.4 QUANTUM ALGORITHMS IN DATA SCIENCE

By utilizing the ideas of quantum physics to carry out computations that would prove impractical for conventional computers, quantum algorithms have a chance to completely transform some areas of data science. Qubits, the building blocks of quantum computing, are capable of existing in several states at once because of the superposition phenomenon [10]. This enables quantum algorithms to investigate several options concurrently, possibly leading to exponential acceleration for specific kinds of computations. The following are a few data science applications and quantum algorithms:

- **Grover's Algorithm:**
  - **Goal:** Compared to the finest classical algorithms, Grover's algorithm is meant for searching an unsorted database quadratically faster.

- **Application in Data Science:** Grover's approach can be used to expedite unsorted database searches, which can be performed four times faster than using traditional algorithms.

- **Quantum Machine Learning (QML):**
  - **Objective:** QML is to improve conventional machine learning algorithms by utilizing the concepts of quantum computing.
  - **Application in Data Science:** Linear algebra problems, considered essential to machine learning, are among the tasks that quantum algorithms can be used for. Algorithms for quantum machine learning have the potential to accelerate some tasks, such as handling linear equation systems and inverse matrix.

- **Quantum Support Vector Machines (QSVM):**
  - **Objective:** It aims to handle specific kinds of machine learning classification problems more quickly than traditional techniques.
  - **Application in Data Science:** For binary classification tasks, QSVM can be applied, and in certain instances, it is anticipated to offer a quadratic speedup over standard support vector machine algorithms.

- **Quantum Principal Component Analysis (QPCA):**
  - **Objective:** It is to minimize the dimensionality of data by the use of a quantum algorithm for principal component analysis, a method that is widely applied in classical data analysis.
  - **Application in Data Science:** Large-scale dimensionality reduction projects involving data might gain advantage from a speed boost provided by quantum principal component analysis.

- **Algorithms for Quantum Clustering:**
  - **Goal:** Algorithms for quantum clustering seek to cluster together similar data points.
  - **Application in Data Science:** Tasks like pattern identification and consumer segmentation may benefit from the use of quantum clustering algorithms.

It is noteworthy that we continue to be in the early phases of developing viable quantum computers with an adequate amount of stable qubits. Furthermore, not every data science projects will benefit from using quantum algorithms, and researchers are now investigating the drawbacks and possible uses of quantum computing. Researchers and data scientists will probably look at new approaches to using quantum algorithms to solve difficult issues as quantum technology continues to progress.

6.5 QUANTUM MACHINE LEARNING

The multidisciplinary area of QML aims to improve upon classical machine learning algorithms in specific applications by fusing quantum computing with machine learning approaches [1]. Combining quantum computing and machine learning tries to accomplish tasks that would prove impossible for classical computers by utilizing the special qualities of quantum systems, such as superposition and entanglement.

The following are some important ideas and methods in the field of quantum machine learning:

- **Quantum Representation of Data:** Qubits, the building blocks of quantum computers, are multistate particles that exhibit superposition. In contrast with classical bits, this feature can be used to store and analyze data in an entirely novel manner. Methods for encoding data quantum attempt to take advantage of this benefit for particular kinds of calculations.
- **Machine Learning with Quantum Algorithms:** Quantum algorithms, such as Grover's algorithm, QSVM, and QPCA, are intended to execute machine learning tasks at a possible speed advantage over classical algorithms. Solving linear algebraic problems, especially frequently arising machine learning computations, is the primary emphasis of these methods.
- **Quantum Neural Networks:** The quantum equivalents of conventional neural networks are known as quantum neural networks (QNNs). To represent and process information, they make use of quantum states and gates. QNNs may effectively represent intricate relationships in data and could be beneficial in some situations.

- **Quantum Feature Maps:** Quantum kernel techniques for machine learning employ quantum feature maps. By converting classical data into a quantum state, they make it possible for quantum algorithms to process the data and maybe find nonlinear patterns more quickly than they could with classical techniques.
- **Quantum Variational Algorithms:** Optimization issues, especially encountered in machine learning frequently, are solved using variational algorithms, which include the Quantum Variational Eigensolver. Quantum circuits and quantum states can be optimized for particular machine learning applications using these approaches.
- **Quantum Generative Models:** The goal of quantum generative models is to create fresh data samples that bear similarities to a given dataset. In order to generate sample from probability distributions, quantum computers might be advantageous. This could result in generative models that are more effective.

It is vital to remember that real-world quantum computers having sufficient amounts of stable qubits are still in the initial stages of research as of the information we have cutoff in January 2022. Development on quantum machine learning is ongoing, and scientists are trying to figure out what quantum computers can and cannot do to improve machine learning tasks. Researchers are attempting to create more reliable quantum algorithms and comprehend the particular circumstances in which quantum advantages manifest themselves as quantum technology progresses.

6.5 QUANTUM DATA STRUCTURES AND ALGORITHMS

By utilizing the ideas of quantum mechanics to overcome the constraints of traditional computing, quantum data structures and algorithms provide an innovative method to information processing. The qubit, or quantum bit, is the fundamental component of quantum [15]. Because of this special property, one can design quantum data structures that are essentially different from traditional ones. Information in quantum computing is a complicated superposition of states rather than just a binary string of 0s and 1s. Similar to conventional registers, quantum registers group qubits together to collectively represent quantum states.

This idea is expanded upon by quantum arrays that enable simultaneous manipulation and storing of numerous quantum states. These quantum data structures serve as the foundation for algorithms that take advantage of quantum computing's built-in parallelism. Grover's method is a well-known example of a quantum algorithm that overcomes classical constraints in quest of information. Grover's approach demonstrates the capability of quantum parallelism by searching unsorted databases quadratically quicker than classical algorithms. Furthermore, Shor's algorithm effectively factors enormous numbers, demonstrating the exponential speedup possible with quantum computing and presenting a potential threat to traditional cryptography techniques.

A key component of many quantum calculations, such as Shor's algorithm, is the Quantum Fourier Transform, an efficient quantum method that computes the discrete Fourier transform. Another important approach for estimating the eigenvalues of unitary operators—which are necessary for resolving issues like linear systems of equations—is quantum phase estimation. Inspired by conventional random walks, quantum walks find usage in quantum algorithms related to optimization and search problems. The integration of quantum computing principles with machine learning tasks is explored via quantum machine learning algorithms, like quantum neural networks and support vector machines, which provide the possibility of increased computational efficiency. Variational quantum algorithms, such as the QVE, are becoming more and more popular for optimization applications as quantum computers develop.

A method that utilizes adiabatic quantum processing called quantum annealing can be beneficial in combinatorial optimization problems. Additionally, quantum data structures and algorithms explore new fields such as quantum image processing, which applies a quantum perspective to image-related activities by analyzing and processing quantum images using quantum computing approaches. Although quantum data structures and algorithms are still in their early stages of development, research is being driven by the possibility of exponential speedup for specific challenges. The field of information processing and computational problem solving is set to undergo a radical change as quantum data structures and algorithms become more widely used and feasible. This is especially true when quantum computers with adequate qubits and error correction become available.

6.7 QUANTUM ENTANGLEMENT AND DATA SECURITY

A key event in quantum physics is known as quantum entanglement, which occurs when a number of particles connect to the point where their states are directly related to one another, independent of their distance from one another [4, 11]. This special relationship between entangled particles serves as the foundation for several aspects of quantum encryption and has significant implications for data security. The following are the main ideas behind quantum entanglement and how they relate to data security:

- **Basics of Quantum Entanglement:** Quantum entanglement is a quantum phenomenon in which entangled particles' properties (such as spin, polarization, or other quantum states) start to correlate. Despite the great distances between these particles, the states of the two are instantly influenced by one another.
- **Quantum Superposition:** A quantum superposition of states contains entangled particles. This implies that both entangled particles exist in a combination of all possible states until one of them is measured.
- **Quantum Measurement and Instantaneous Correlation:** Regardless of the physical distance between two entangled particles, the state of one particle can be immediately derived from the state of the other. It appears that this phenomenon overcomes the limitations of traditional information transport.
- **Bell's Theorem:** This theorem defines the bounds on the classical correlations between particles that are entangled. Experimental proof of nonclassical nature of entanglement is given by Bell inequalities violations.
- **Quantum Cryptography:** To guarantee secure communication, quantum cryptography techniques make use of quantum entanglement. Quantum Key Distribution (QKD) is a single such protocol that uses entangled particles to generate a secret key that is shared between two parties. The entangled particles would be disturbed by any attempt to listen in on the conversation, indicating the presence of an intruder.
- **Quantum Key Distribution (QKD):** QKD techniques use quantum entanglement to create a secret key among two parties.

One such protocol is the popular Bennett-Brassard 1992 (BBM92) protocol. The quantum characteristics of entangled particles are necessary for the security of the key distribution, and the principles of quantum mechanics.

- **Applications of Quantum Cryptography:** Quantum entanglement finds application in a number of quantum cryptographic applications, such as quantum coin flipping for equitable and secure decision-making, QKD for secure communication, and quantum secret sharing for sharing confidential information among several parties.
- **Entanglement-Based Quantum Networks:** Scientists are investigating the creation of quantum networks that link quantum computers and provide reliable interaction over larger distances by means of entangled particles.

  Quantum Hacking Detection: Entanglement concepts can be used to identify quantum communication eavesdropping. The correlation would be disrupted by any third party effort to determine the number of entangled particles, warning the communication parties about any security breaches.
- **Future Quantum Technologies:** Entanglement-based systems and protocols are anticipated to be essential for safeguarding data transit and communications in the quantum era as quantum technologies develop.

A novel form of data security is brought about by quantum entanglement, which makes it possible to create secure communication channels and identify possible eavesdroppers. The special properties of entanglement are probably going to be further investigated and used in innovative ways to improve the security of data transfer as quantum technologies advance.

6.8 OPTIMIZATION PROBLEMS IN DATA SCIENCE

Data science's foundational optimization challenges are important in many situations where determining the optimal answer from a range of options is the objective. These issues come up in a variety of disciplines, including statistics, operations research, machine learning, and decision-making [6, 14]. The following are the main ideas behind data science optimization problems:

- **Objective Function:** The quantity that needs to be optimized is specified by the objective function. This could be any indicator in data science that indicates the caliber of a solution, such as the precision of a machine learning model or the effectiveness of a clustering approach.
- **Decision Variables:** The variables or parameters that can be changed in order to maximize the objective function are known as decision variables. These comprise the components of the remedy that are being optimized.
- **Feasible Region:** The collection of all potential decision variable pairings that meet the optimization problem's constraints is known as the feasible region. Not every combination can result in workable or legitimate solutions.
- **Constraints:** The requirements that the solution must meet are known as constraints. These might involve limitations on the decision variables' values that correspond to constraints or requirements found in the actual world.
- **Local and Global Optima:** A solution is considered optimal within a particular section of the viable space if it is a local optimum. The finest option available throughout the whole feasible space is known as a global optimum.
- **Linear Programming:** In a linear programming issue, the constraints and the goal of the functions are both linear. It is extensively employed in fields like operations research.
- **Nonlinear Optimization:** Nonlinear optimization deals with nonlinear constraints or objective functions. This area includes a large number of real-world challenges, particularly in machine learning.
- **Convex Optimization:** Convex objective functions and constraints are the subject of convex optimization. Numerous optimization techniques have been created for convex optimization because convex problems have favorable mathematical characteristics.
- **Integer Programming:** By limiting the values of decision variables to integers, integer programming goes beyond linear programming.

It is frequently applied to issues in discrete optimization and other situations where variables must have whole-number values.

- **Quadratic Programming:** This technique works with linear restrictions and quadratic goal functions. It finds use in a number of industries, including as engineering and banking.
- **Optimization Algorithms:** Algorithms are techniques for determining the best course of action. Some examples of optimization methods used in data science include particle swarm optimization, simulated annealing, gradient descent, and genetic algorithms.
- **Hyperparameter Tuning:** In machine learning, this technique entails fine-tuning a model's hyperparameters to maximize performance. This is frequently handled as an optimization issue.
- **Global Optimization in Machine Learning:** To determine the ideal set of hyperparameters across a broad range of options and guarantee the highest model performance, global optimization techniques are employed in machine learning.
- **Optimization in Deep Learning:** Training deep learning models requires careful consideration of optimization. Neural network weights are frequently optimized using gradient descent variations as Adam, RMSprop, and stochastic gradient descent.
- **Metaheuristic Optimization:** Complex optimization issues that traditional methods can find difficult to solve are solved by metaheuristic optimization algorithms like simulating annealing, swarm intelligence, and genetic algorithms.

Data science optimization challenges are widespread and varied, requiring a combination of domain-specific knowledge, mathematical modeling, and algorithm design to develop efficient and affordable solutions. To gain useful knowledge from data and make wise decisions, it is essential to be able to enhance processes and models.

6.8.1 PRACTICAL IMPLEMENTATIONS AND HARDWARE CONSIDERATIONS

When implementing optimization issues in data science, hardware infrastructure concerns are frequently made when putting the algorithms into practice [8]. The effectiveness and scalability of optimization strategies can be strongly impacted by these factors. Here are important things to think about:

- **Algorithm Selection:** The kind of objective function, the restrictions, and the specifics of the problem—all influence the optimization method selection. Gradient-based techniques like gradient descent might be useful for some issues, but metaheuristic algorithms like genetic algorithms or particle swarm optimization might be needed for others.
- **Hardware Architecture:** An important consideration is the hardware architecture that the optimization techniques will operate on. Different features of specialized hardware, such as field-programmable gate arrays (FPGAs) or quantum computers, as well as conventional CPUs and graphical processing units (GPUs).
- **Parallelization:** To improve computing performance, several optimization algorithms may profit from parallelization. GPUs, for example, may greatly speed up some optimization processes and therefore ideal for parallel processing.
- **Distributed Computing:** Frameworks for distributed computing, like Apache Spark or Dask, are capable of being used for large-scale optimization issues. These frameworks make it possible to run algorithms in parallel on several nodes or computer clusters, which makes managing large datasets easier.
- **Quantum Computing:** This is a young field with the potential to solve some optimization problems tenfold quicker than with traditional computers. For combinatorial optimization challenges, quantum algorithms such as the QAOA are being investigated.
- **Memory Considerations:** The dataset's size and the optimization algorithm's memory needs must match the amount of memory that the system has available. Performance bottlenecks might result from insufficient memory, particularly when working with large-scale datasets.
- **GPU Acceleration:** GPUs are frequently used to speed up optimization operations, especially in machine learning and deep learning applications. They are well-suited for parallel computing.

Parallelizable tasks can be programmed efficiently on GPUs, thanks to libraries like CUDA.

- **Quantum Hardware Restrictions:** Qubit coherence times, gate fidelities, and connectivity restrictions are examples of the unique hardware restrictions that apply to quantum computers. These considerations impact the kinds of optimization issues that are capable of being performed efficiently on existing quantum hardware as well as the selection of quantum algorithms.
- **Energy Efficiency:** Energy efficiency is a crucial factor to take into account because optimization issues can be computationally demanding. Selecting low-power CPUs or specific hardware accelerators can have an effect on the system's overall energy usage.
- **Hybrid Techniques:** Research is being done on hybrid techniques that blend classical and quantum computing. For instance, complicated problems can be solved by combining variational quantum algorithms with conventional optimization algorithms.
- **Real-time Constraints:** Optimization algorithms sometimes have to deliver solutions within very tight time limits, like in control systems or real-time decision-making. In these situations, the processing speed and efficiency of the hardware become crucial.
- **Scalability:** Scalability concerns are about the extent to which an optimization method can manage escalating computing demands or data volumes. For applications where the scale and complexity of problems may change over time, scalability is essential.
- **Robustness and Error Management:** In quantum computing, where qubits are prone to mistakes because of decoherence and other circumstances, robust implementations should take error management techniques into account. Using quantum error-correcting methods is crucial to keeping quantum calculations reliable.
- **Algorithmic Complexity:** The optimization algorithm's complexity should be in line with the hardware resources available, as determined by the algorithm's time and space needs. Selecting the appropriate hardware combinations requires an understanding of the algorithmic complexity.

The optimization of problems necessitates a careful assessment of the essence of the problem, the algorithmic properties, and the hardware capabilities [7]. The field of practical implementations is constantly changing because to advancements in distributed computing frameworks, GPU technology, and quantum computing. These developments present novel opportunities for tackling intricate optimization problems in data science.

6.8.2 CHALLENGES AND FUTURE DIRECTIONS

These are significant obstacles in the ever-changing field of data science optimization problems that scholars and practitioners are working hard to overcome. At the same time, the discipline is positioned for revolutionary expansion, with bright future prospects that could fundamentally alter our approach to tackling complicated problems [17]. It is essential to navigate these obstacles and take advantage of these chances if optimization in data science is to advance.

6.8.2.1 CHALLENGES

- **Computational Complexity:** Handling optimization problems' computational complexity is a recurring difficulty. Finding effective algorithms becomes more difficult as issues get bigger, requiring creative solutions to deal with complex mathematical structures and massive information.
- **High-Dimensional Data:** The optimization landscape is complicated by the persistent problem of high-dimensional data. The curse of dimensionality, which occurs when the search space grows exponentially and makes it more difficult to identify the best solutions, is something algorithms have to deal with.
- **Noisy Data:** Noise is a constant in the world of real-life data. The uncertainties posed by noisy data must be handled by optimization algorithms, which call for the creation of strong methods that can identify trustworthy patterns among the noise.
- **Identification of Global Optima:** One of the primary challenges still is discerning between local and global optima. In order to extract the best possible results from a variety of landscapes, algorithms must traverse complicated solution spaces; hence, ensuring convergence to the global optimum is essential.

- **Interpretability:** As optimization algorithms become more complicated, interpretability becomes a worry. Maintaining actionable insights and fostering confidence in optimization results require finding a balance between complex models and interpretability.
- **Resource Constraints:** It is always difficult to optimize when faced with limitations in time or computational power. For algorithms to be useful in the real world, they must be modified to function well under resource limitations.
- **Dynamic Environments:** Dynamic environments are those in which parameters change over time and are present under numerous real-world circumstances. Developing algorithms capable of dynamically reacting to evolving data is necessary to handle the difficult task of adapting optimization algorithms to changing situations.
- **Integration with Domain Knowledge:** One of the ongoing challenges in optimization algorithms is the successful integration of domain knowledge. Resolving real-world issues with a greater comprehension of the underlying issues requires balancing data-driven techniques with expert knowledge.

6.8.2.2 FUTURE DIRECTIONS

- **Impact of Quantum Computing:** Optimization issues could undergo radical changes as a result of the development of practical quantum computing. Investigating how quantum algorithms, such the QAOA, can achieve exponential speedup for particular jobs is the direction of current research.
- **Hybrid Approaches:** By fusing established optimization techniques with cutting-edge innovations like quantum or neuromorphic computing, it is possible to solve complicated issues in novel ways that take advantage of the advantages of many paradigms.
- **Explainable AI and Optimization:** A potential path that fits with the larger explainable AI trend is to improve the interpretability of optimization models. Building models that offer obvious insights into the decision-making process is crucial to gaining the trust and comprehension of users.

- **Evolutionary Algorithms:** Natural selection served as the inspiration for these algorithms, which are becoming more and more popular for addressing optimization problems. It is anticipated that more studies will examine these algorithms' potential, particularly with regard to managing complicated, large-scale issues with a variety of solution spaces.
- **Metaheuristic Advancements:** It is expected that metaheuristic algorithms, including projected annealing, genetic algorithms, and particle swarm optimization, will keep making progress. These algorithms are essential for solving optimization problems in a variety of fields.
- **Machine Learning Integration:** A rapidly developing field is the integration of machine learning methods, such as deep learning and reinforcement learning, with optimization algorithms. An increased level of adaptability and data-driven optimization solutions could result from such integration.
- **Privacy-Preserving Optimization:** As worries about data privacy rise, it is becoming increasingly important for the area to develop optimization methods that can work with encrypted or privacy-preserving data.
- **Sustainable Optimization:** Reducing environmental impact and optimizing for sustainability are future-focused factors. Creating optimization models for sustainable decision-making that take ecological and resource restrictions into account is probably going to be the main focus of research efforts.
- **Human-in-the-Loop Optimization:** Using interactive and cooperative frameworks to incorporate human expertise into the optimization process is a promising avenue for the future. These methods seek to develop solutions that respect human limitations and preferences.
- **Benchmarking and Standardization:** It is critical to provide standard assessment criteria and benchmark datasets for optimization challenges. Aims made in this field will assist in helping to develop the field going forward by enabling equitable comparisons between various algorithms.

Realizing the entire potential of optimization for tackling intricate, real-world problems will depend on overcoming these obstacles and embracing these future directions as the discipline of optimization in data science continues to develop. Both researchers and practitioners are at the vanguard of a dynamic journey where advancement is primarily driven by innovation and collaboration.

6.9 INDUSTRY APPLICATIONS AND CASE STUDIES

Optimization problems are powerful instruments that drive efficiency, cost-effectiveness, and strategic decision-making in the dynamic business environment [9]. Applications are made in a variety of industries, and each one poses a different set of difficulties that optimization algorithms are precisely able to solve. The subsequent case studies and industry applications highlight the critical role that optimization plays in resolving real-world issues:

- **Transportation and Logistics:** Planning routes is a critical function of optimization algorithms in the field of transportation and logistics. These algorithms are used by UPS, FedEx, and other companies to figure out the best routes for delivery trucks. These businesses increase customer satisfaction and operational efficiency by cutting delivery times and fuel usage.
- **Manufacturing:** Production scheduling is one area where optimization is heavily utilized in manufacturing. For example, automakers use optimization algorithms to plan their production schedules. This guarantees the effective use of resources, reduces downtime, and facilitates the smooth achievement of production goals.
- **Managing Inventory:** It is one area of supply chain management where optimization is frequently used. Based on demand projections, retailers—including market leaders like Amazon—optimize their inventory levels. This reduces holding expenses and guarantees that the products are supplied exactly when needed.
- **Finance:** Modern Portfolio Theory is an example of how optimization is used in the financial sector to design portfolios. These

algorithms are used by investment firms to build portfolios that optimize returns for a specific degree of risk, supporting strategic decision-making in the fast-paced world of finance.

- **Telecommunications:** Network structure and design are handled by telecom corporations through optimization. In telecommunications, the optimization of network topologies improves total data transmission efficiency by maximizing coverage and minimizing interference.
- **Energy:** Power grid optimization is one area in which optimization algorithms are used. These algorithms are used by utilities to distribute power in an efficient manner while minimizing losses, balancing loads, and avoiding overloading transmission lines. Healthcare: Hospital resource allocation is one area of healthcare where optimization is used. In order to provide timely patient treatment while reducing operating expenses, optimization algorithms aid in the effective scheduling of staff, the allocation of operating rooms, and the use of equipment.
- **Agriculture:** Crop planning using precision agriculture uses optimization. Crop planting, irrigation, and resource distribution can all be optimized by farmers to maximize yields, decrease resource use, and protect the environment.
- **Retail:** To optimize shelf space, retailers use optimization algorithms. Retailers carefully assign shelf space based on consumer behavior and sales data, making sure that popular products are prominently displayed to promote sales.
- **E-commerce:** To fulfill orders, e-commerce systems use optimization. Algorithms choose the most economical route from many warehouses to complete client orders, saving money on shipping and expediting delivery.
- **Human Resources:** Workforce scheduling is optimized in human resources. Employers maximize worker schedules by taking into account operational requirements, labor rules, and worker preferences in order to strike a balance between productivity and worker happiness.

- **Urban Planning:** Traffic flow optimization is one area in which cities use optimization in urban planning. Traffic signal timings are created by algorithms to control traffic, enhance flow, shorten travel times, and use less fuel.
- **Environment:** Waste management relies heavily on optimization, particularly when it comes to scheduling waste collection trucks' most effective routes. Optimization enhances operational efficiency and reduces fuel consumption, both of which support sustainable waste management techniques.
- **Education:** Educational establishments use algorithms to optimize class schedules in order to reduce conflicts with scheduling, maximize resource use, and suit student preferences. This guarantees a more efficient learning environment for both teachers and students.

These case studies and industry applications highlight how optimization has a revolutionary effect on a variety of industries. The prospects of optimizing methodologies and advancing technology to tackle intricate problems and stimulate innovation in industry applications are encouraging.

6.10 CONCLUSION

When summed up, data science optimization is a dynamic discipline that spurs efficiency and innovation in a variety of businesses. Optimization algorithms become indispensable tools while navigating the complex terrain of real-world situations. They solve issues with anything from portfolio development in finance to route planning in transportation. Applications for optimization can be found in a wide range of industries, including manufacturing, supply chain management, healthcare, and more. There are still issues to be solved, such as the computing complexity of large-scale issues and the requirement for reliable answers when dealing with noisy data. Ongoing research and innovation, however, ensure that optimization keeps evolving and adapting to the always-changing demands of business.

Future-focused, integrating cutting-edge technology like machine learning and quantum computing has a lot of potential. Quantum algorithms have the potential to yield previously unattainable speeds, and the combination of optimization and machine learning methods improves flexibility and data-driven decision-making. The quest for sustainable optimization and explainable AI highlights the dedication to openness, morality, and long-term environmental effects. The given industry applications and case studies demonstrate the concrete effects of optimization, ranging from optimizing healthcare resource allocation and supply chain efficiency to boosting energy grid efficiency and transforming e-commerce logistics. Optimization is not just a theoretical idea; it is a force that shapes how industries function and make choices.

The future of optimization in data science is characterized by a dedication to tackling complexity, embracing technology breakthroughs, and promoting cross-disciplinary collaboration as we stand at the crossroads of difficulties and possibilities. Researchers, practitioners, and business executives come together on this never-ending path of discovery to open up new vistas and develop ground-breaking solutions that will lead to more intelligent, effective, and sustainable decision-making in the future. Optimization continues to be a pillar in this ever-changing environment, leading us to creative solutions that go beyond the boundaries of what was previously thought to be feasible.

KEYWORDS

- **quantum machine learning**
- **quantum data analysis**
- **quantum data visualization**

REFERENCES

1. Ayoade, O., Rivas, P., & Orduz, J. (2022). Artificial intelligence computing at the quantum level. *Data*, *7*(3), 28. https://doi.org/10.3390/data7030028.
2. Bayerstadler, A., Becquin, G. et al. (2021). Quantum technology and application consortium—QUTAC., Industry quantum computing applications. *EPJ Quantum Technology*, *8*, 25. https://doi.org/10.1140/epjqt/s40507-021-00114-x

3. Biamonte, J., Wittek, P., Pancotti, N., Rebentrost, P., Wiebe, N., & Lloyd, S. (2016). Quantum machine learning. *Nature. 549*, 195–202. https://doi.org/10.1038/nature23474.
4. Davids, J., Lidströmer, N., & Ashrafian, H. (2022). Artificial intelligence in medicine using quantum computing in the future of healthcare. In *Artificial Intelligence in Medicine*. Springer International Publishing, Cham, pp. 423–446.
5. Deutsch, D. (1985). Quantum theory, the Church-Turing principle and the universal quantum computer, proceedings of the royal society of London. *Series A, Mathematical and Physical Sciences, 400*, 97–117.
6. Dodig-Crnkovic, G. (2023). On the foundations of computing. *Computing as the Fourth Great Domain of Science. Global Philosophy, 33*(1), 16.
7. Kahanda, G., Patel, V., Parikh, M., Ippolito, M., Solanki, M., & Ahmed, S. (2023). The future era of quantum computing. In *Cybersecurity in the Age of Smart Societies: Proceedings of the 14th International Conference on Global Security, Safety and Sustainability, London, September 2022*. Springer International Publishing: Cham, pp. 469–484.
8. Kashyap, P. (2023). *Applied Quantum Computers: Learn About the Concept, Architecture, Tools, and Adoption Strategies for Quantum Computing and Artificial Intelligence (English Edition)*. BPB Publications.
9. Kaushik, K., & Kumar, A. (2023). Demystifying quantum blockchain for healthcare. *Security and Privacy, 6*(3), e284.
10. Mallow, G. M., Hornung, A., Barajas, J. N., Rudisill, S. S., An, H. S., & Samartzis, D. (2022). Quantum computing: The future of big data and artificial intelligence in spine. *Spine Surgery and Related Research, 6*(2), 93–98. https://doi.org/10.22603/ssrr.2021-0251.
11. Preskill, J. (2023). Quantum computing 40 years later. In *Feynman Lectures on Computation*. CRC Press, pp. 193–244.
12. Feynman, R. P. (1986). Quantum-mechanical computers. *Foundations of Physics, 16*, 507–531.
13. Sanders, B. (2023). Quantum computing for data science. *Journal of Physics: Conference Series, 2438*, 012007. https://doi.org/10.1088/1742-6596/2438/1/012007.
14. Susindhar, A. V., Soni, G., & Tyagi, A. K. (2023). A review on recent trends in quantum computation technology. *Handbook of Research on Quantum Computing for Smart Environments*, IGI Global Scientific Publishing, pp. 48–64.
15. Winker, T., Groppe, S., Uotila, V., Yan, Z., Lu, J., Franz, M., & Mauerer, W. (2023). Quantum machine learning: Foundation, new techniques, and opportunities for database research. In *Companion of the 2023 International Conference on Management of Data (SIGMOD '23). Association for Computing Machinery,* New York, NY, USA. pp. 45–52. https://doi.org/10.1145/3555041.3589404
16. Tripathy, B. K. & Singh, A. (2023). Role of quantum computing in a data analytics environment. https://doi.org/10.4018/978-1-6684-6821-0.ch014.
17. Ur Rasool, R., Ahmad, H. F., Rafique, W., Qayyum, A., Qadir, J., & Anwar, Z. (2023). Quantum computing for healthcare: A review. *Future Internet, 15*(3), 94.
18. Wang, Y. (2022). When quantum computation meets data science: Making data science quantum. *Harvard Data Science Review, 4*(1). https://doi.org/10.1162/99608f92.ef5d8928

19. Yudong, C., Jhonathan, R., & Alan, A.-G. (2018). Potential of quantum computing for drug discovery. *IBM Journal of Research and Development*, *62*(6), 6–1.

CHAPTER 7

Possibilities Offered by Quantum Computing in the Field of Renewable Energy

SUDIPTA ADHIKARY[1], KAUSHIK CHANDA[2], KAUSHIK BANERJEE[1], and GUNJAN MUKHERJEE[2*]

[1]Department of Law, Brainware University, Kolkata, West Bengal, India

[2]Department of Computational Sciences, Brainware University, Kolkata, West Bengal, India

*Corresponding author

ABSTRACT

Traditional computers, using "classical" computing concept, are unable to execute certain forms of information processing that are possible with quantum computing. Quantum computing is based on the law of quantum physics. As a consequence, quantum computers implement strategies for the resolution of problems, unavailable to traditional computers. Mostly, quantum problems are solvable in physics, and so, the mismatch is found between the traditional research and the practical challenges that need to be solved. Renewable energy is a potential area with ample scope for contribution and exploration for further research. Considering the distributed resources management and that of fluctuation of weather-dependent generation flows, the adoption and scaling up of renewable resources is supposed to be present in an electrical grid with a number of new issues. So, future challenges lie with control management of these resources. The major issues are therefore some difficulties associated with renewable sources of energy, simulation, scheduling, dispatch, and reliability

Applications of Quantum Computing in a Variety of Domains. Gunjan Mukherjee, Biswadip Basu Mallik, Rahul Kar Özen ÖZER, Digvijay Pandey, and Binay Kumar Pandey (Eds.)

DOI: 10.1201/9781998511051-7

evaluations. The crucial challenge is concerned with potential future problems with the scalable technologies to overcome using quantum computing. This chapter will provide an overview of the potential research areas focusing on connection between the quantum computing and renewable energies highlighting the future applications of dual fields.

7.1 INTRODUCTION

Interest in quantum computing has increased in both academia and industry in recent years. The emerging discipline of quantum computing in computer science uses quantum mechanical concepts to carry out calculations that classical computers just cannot handle. New hardware like superconducting devices, trapped ions, and photonics are essential to the functioning of these computers. Therefore, quantum computers can implement strategies for addressing problems that conventional computers cannot. Quantum methods that can address more complex issues without significantly increasing computing time are the most intriguing. This may be utilized to solve issues more quickly while spending the same amount of time overall [1].

Significant progress has been made by leading companies such as Rigetti and D-Wave in the development of quantum hardware manufacturing. While scientists and engineers are intrigued by the potential of quantum computing, completely error-corrected quantum computers that mimic the behavior of these theoretical constructions are likely still years away. In addition, the quantum computer bypasses any improvement of the speed involved in traditional classical computing instances like addition of two integers or any other generic mathematical computation. For these reasons, it is crucial to look for problems with important answers that are also challenging to solve using conventional classical technology and exhibit the kind of structure that indicates the effectiveness of the quantum approach. Within the next decade, it is anticipated that NISQ devices will become accessible [2], and might solve myriad of such relevant issues. For the sake of demonstrating the problem-solving capability of quantum computing, it is important to pick excellent near-term challenges that are still tiny and require special formulation. Figure 7.1 depicts the broad strokes of a renewable energy environment, including potential quantum computing applications in certain industries. Twenty states and Districts of Columbia (D.C.) had "renewable portfolio standards" in place by the end of 2018 that required a particular amount of power from renewable sources. In the upcoming decades, Districts of

Columbia have set ambitious goals to transition their energy systems entirely to renewable sources. The shift from centralized, large-scale thermal power generation to decentralized, fluctuating renewable sources such as wind and solar necessitates a substantial revamp of the technological framework that underpins our current power system. For such a massive undertaking to be completed quickly, efficiently, and ethically, it requires the undivided focus of scientists, engineers, and others.

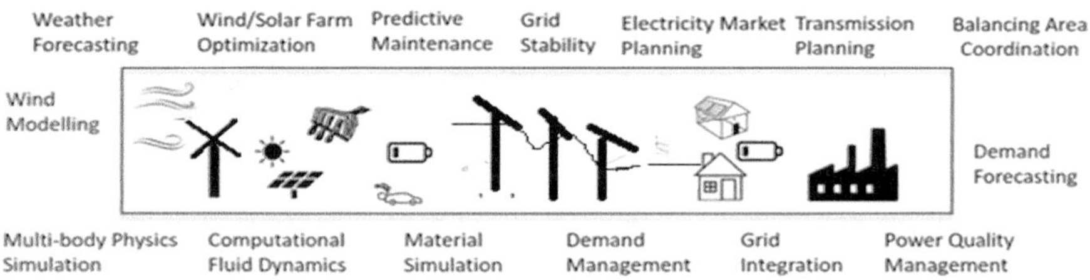

FIGURE 7.1 Natural resources such as the sun and the wind are examples of renewable energy. Materials called photovoltaics can convert solar energy into usable power. When solar power is not accessible, having a place to save energy for later use is essential

Source: Adapted from Ref. [39].

In this study, an attempt has been made to merge these two frontiers of innovation in technology. We highlight many ways in which the growing discipline of quantum computing might aid in the shift to renewable energy. To begin, quantum computer's ability to run simulation algorithms bears the potential to revolutionize computational chemistry, which might have significant implications for fields like energy storage and photovoltaic material development. Furthermore, as power grids become increasingly intricate, we consider the stability and dependability of the electricity network. In this regard, quantum search and linear systems analysis offer potential solutions with promising prospects. In terms of regulations, the FERC has compiled a selection of articles that shed light on the current conventional methodologies and difficulties within these domains. Common to the challenges we uncover is concern over the scalability of existing computing methods in the face of growing demands on the power supply. We seek to solve several energy system issues using quantum computing, which can provide superior-scaling algorithms in these fields. Table 7.1 provides a brief overview of these topics before going further.

The most relevant and significant aspects to be addressed in such discussion fields are integrating the most promising quantum mechanics

TABLE 7.1 Summarized Some of the Most Pressing Issues in the Field of Renewable Energy

	Problem	Influence or Consequences Related to Energy	Existing Obstacles or Difficulties Presently Faced	Methodology Based on Principles of Quantum Mechanics
Quantum Chemistry [33, 35, 36]	Calculate the energy levels of molecules	Emerging battery chemistries and innovative solar cell technologies	Calculating the characteristics of materials with strong correlations poses significant challenges	Quantum variational eigensolvers
Forecasting (NCAR, 2021), [49]	Predict forthcoming conditions by analyzing previous and present circumstances	Enhanced strategies for managing fluctuations in solar or wind power	The unpredictable nature of meteorological challenges constrains the forecast accuracy and timeframes for renewable energy generation	Quantum variational eigensolvers
Planning and Dispatch (Federal Energy Regulatory Commission, 2021)	Discover economically efficient methods to align electricity supply and demand while minimizing losses	Achieving lower electricity costs, seamless integration of intermittent renewable sources, and reduced reliance on reserve capacities	The increasing presence of distributed energy resources adds complexity to power system modeling	Quantum annealers utilizing variational techniques
Stability and Reliability (NERC, 2021)	Assess the resilience of the system against failures, where the system's state is determined by its accuracy	Reduced frequency of power outages, implementation of cost-effective reliability measures, and enhanced system resilience	The rapid deployment of inverter-based resources can result in instabilities occurring over shorter time periods	Grover's search algorithm is suitable for medium-term searches, while the HHL algorithm is designed for solving linear systems over longer timeframes

concepts with practical challenges via the interdisciplinary study of quantum computing and operations research. Analysis of algorithms to determine what kind of feasible and attainable gains in computational performance may be expected from using quantum computers.

While precise theoretical knowledge of quantum performance is yet unavailable, potential techniques can be identified through the experimental realization of fundamental implementations of quantum computing for challenges related to renewable energy where the aspect of quantum application has triggered a big leap compared to the contribution of the traditional computing paradigm.

7.2 BACKGROUND OF THE STUDY

The subsequent sections provide a brief summary of the present state and challenges confronted by the renewable energy and quantum computing sectors. To make this work as accessible as possible to specialists in both fields, we include background information that seasoned practitioners are already aware of. We will discuss some of the optimization issues in the remainder of this study. Due to its reliance on heuristics, the classical technique is difficult to compare since it may perform well in certain circumstances but poorly in others. Figure 7.2 attempts to map the landscape of computing issues by highlighting presence and absence of hard problems that quantum computers may solve.

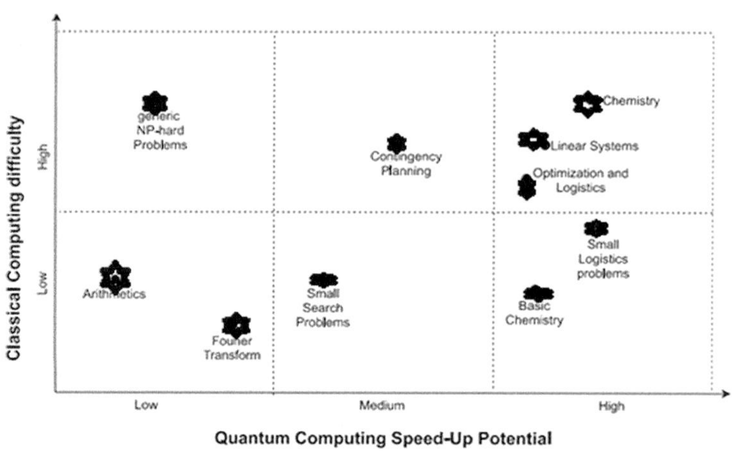

FIGURE 7.2 Comparison of classical difficulty with hypothetical quantum speedups for three levels of difficulty.

Source: Adapted from Ref. [39].

7.3 VARIABLE RENEWABLE ENERGY

Fossil fuels were produced millions of years ago via chemical processes that cannot renew on human timeframes and continue to provide most of the world's energy today. On the other hand, renewable energy comes from naturally occurring energy flows that may be harnessed without diminishing a finite supply. This chapter uses the term "renewable energy" to describe sources like wind, water, and sun.

Bioenergy, despite being a renewable resource and historically serving as the main energy source before fossil fuels, exhibits characteristics more akin to conventional fuels in the contexts we are examining. Mitigating the catastrophic consequences of climate change by lowering carbon dioxide and methane emissions is a pressing imperative within the realm of renewable energy. In the middle of all the talked about global warming, renewable energy sources' prices have dropped dramatically over the past decade. The average cost of solar photovoltaic energy worldwide, considering various factors, such as installation, operation, and maintenance costs fell from $0.085/kWh in 2010 to $0.55/kWh in 2018 (International Renewable Energy Agency, 2021), as reported by IRENA. An instance chart showing cost decreases is presented in Figure 7.3; in 2017, the US Department of Energy successfully achieved its SunShot cost targets for utility-scale solar power generation three years ahead of the scheduled 2020 deadline (NREL, 2016) (DOE SETO, 2021).

The unpredictable and challenging-to-predict nature of the natural energy flows gives rise to various issues for the power grid (NREL, 2016). Solar power generation, for instance, is weather-dependent. Moreover, the transition from a small number of large-scale, centralized power producers to numerous small-scale, decentralized generators, such as rooftop solar, presents significant challenges for grid systems to manage (NREL, 2016). Compared to a system with fewer, bigger power plants, the control difficulties posed by a system with many smaller resources are more complex and difficult to address. Another difficulty arises from eliminating traditional power's reliance on the mechanical inertia that huge, rotating turbines produce. Therefore, anticipating, controlling, and stabilizing the grid provide unique challenges due to renewable energy. To effectively address this issue, energy storage and other technologies would greatly benefit from robust computational resources that can analyze and implement optimal strategies, leveraging accurate forecasts of utility load

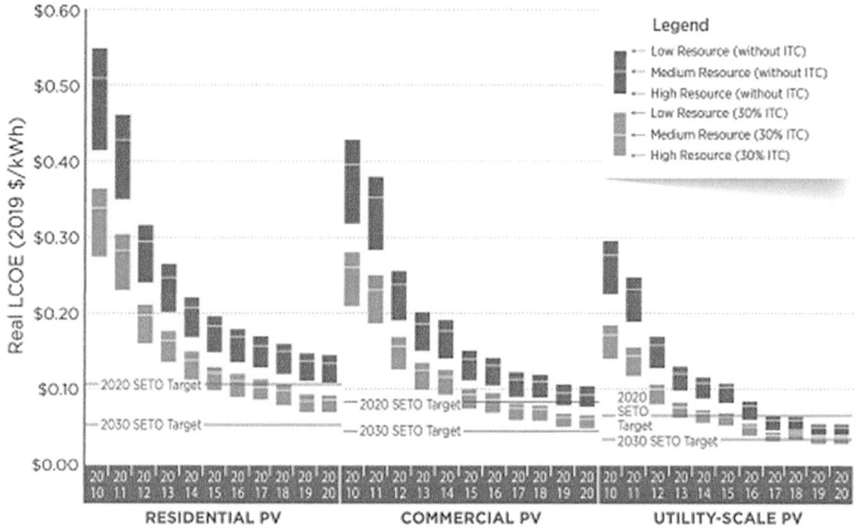

FIGURE 7.3 Cost reductions in photovoltaics over the past decade are graphically depicted across three deployment sizes and with varying degrees of solar resource availability. Reference [9] chart used for illustration.

Source: Adapted from Ref. [39].

and renewable energy output. Such resources would maximize efficiency and cost-effectiveness.

7.4 QUANTUM COMPUTING: OVERVIEW

While a simplistic explanation would define quantum computers as machines utilizing the unique principles of quantum physics to perform computations, this oversimplifies the intricacies of the subject. In fact, traditional computers, including the one that has been used to compose this study, also depend on fundamental principles of quantum mechanics, as the behavior of semiconductors seems to be crucial to their functioning and can only be comprehended through quantum principles. In contrast, quantum computing relies on a fundamentally quantum type of information storage, the quantum bit (or qubit). Superposition, interference, and entanglement are three quantum phenomena that may be exploited with the help of qubits. Figure 7.4 depicts these characteristics.

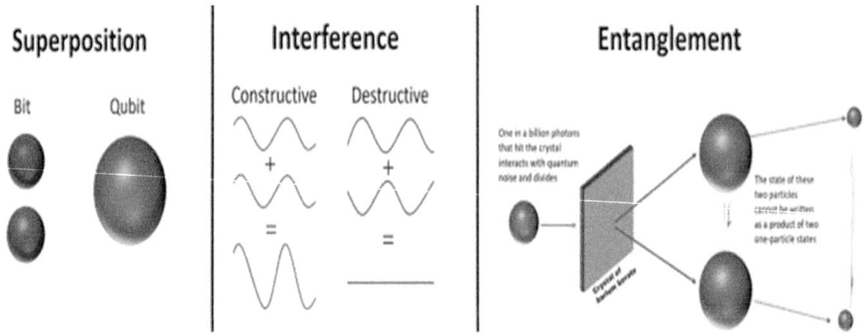

FIGURE 7.4 A basic diagrammatic description of key quantum characteristics that pave the way for quantum computing. The ability to coexist in two distinct states is known as superposition. Waves have additive and subtractive qualities, known as interference, that allow for state control.

Source: Adapted from Ref. [39].

Superposition is a concept from quantum physics that describes the simultaneous existence of two seemingly incompatible states in which quantum objects might exist. In contrast to a conventional coin, whose outcomes are "heads" or "tails," a quantum coin can have both possible outcomes simultaneously. Thus, a quantum computer's quantum bits (qubits) are not constrained to the 0/1 binary of classical bits but may take on an infinite number of exotic and potentially useful superposition configurations. Interference enters the picture after superposition has been created. The outcome of measuring a qubit must be either zero or one. The likelihood of an event is calculated by adding up all the "could have occurred" scenarios, which are shown as superposition states. Positive and negative contributions to a result from different superposition states are possible because the states can constructively and destructively interact to boost and dampen respective consequences, respectively. Therefore, the signatures of several different superposed states can be included in a single result from a cleaver measurement.

Lastly, entanglement stands out as one of the captivating aspects of quantum physics. Einstein famously referred to it as a "spooky interaction at a distance" due to its ability to link two quantum systems in a way that their quantum states act as a unified entity rather than separate occurrences. Consequently, employing reductionist methods to break down quantum systems into manageable components poses a significant challenge. Only *N* bits of information are needed to indicate the classical state of *N* bits;

this is simply the 0/1 value of each bit. Many of the recently popularized quantum technologies are outside the scope of this article. There are theoretical reasons within the quantum computing field that it would be possible to execute quantum computing with less energy consumption than classical computing. However, it is still unclear whether these energy reductions can be effectively implemented in practical systems, as they necessitate significant additional resources for cooling and control equipment (IEEE Spectrum, 2015). Furthermore, there are proposals for a "quantum heat engine" that could store and manipulate energy in ways beyond the capabilities of classical engines, potentially achieving higher levels of efficiency. Nevertheless, research in this field is still in its nascent stages [12]. Our emphasis lies on quantum computing, specifically information-processing techniques, rather than quantum sensing or communication.

7.5 HARDWARE FOR QUANTUM COMPUTING

Similar to how "0" and "1" symbolize binary in traditional computing, a qubit is an abstract mathematical notion that can assume diverse manifestations within different quantum systems. There must be a dominant, industry-wide, standardized qubit platform since no large-scale, general-purpose quantum computer exists. Here, we look at the various quantum computing hardware options available today. For those who wish to learn more, an instructional paper is available in Ref. [13]. Superconducting materials, often aluminum, are used to construct a common type of qubit. Transmons, mons, and fluxonium qubits are all examples of technology that fall under this category [14]. The D-Wave System, the foundation of Google and IBM's hardware development, and superconducting qubits are already in use.

By virtue of their zero electrical resistance, qubits derived from superconducting materials possess the distinctive capability to store quantum information through the arrangement of electromagnetic fields. Using microwave pulses at gigahertz frequencies, the qubit states may be controlled. However, keeping the qubits a few degrees above absolute zero necessitates huge cooling and vacuum systems to preserve the superconductivity. The speed with which superconducting qubits may be controlled is a major benefit. Due to the fabrication process, however, challenges arise with producing consistent and uniform devices to be replicated. Constant recalibration of devices is required, and the data stability lives of superconducting qubits are short. The quantum information contained in a superconducting qubit becomes largely ineffective within a few milliseconds [15]. Decoherence describes this situation. The field of trapped-ion quantum computing evolved from the study of atomic physics and clocks, which won the Nobel Prize in Physics in 1989 (The Nobel Prize in Physics, 1989). There has been economic interest in trapped-ion quantum computing from companies like lonQ.

Laser pulses may change an atom's electron state and store quantum information in this state. The benefit of using trapped ions is that all the atoms of the same isotope and charge given by Nature are similar, making the characteristics of each qubit the same. Furthermore, trapped-ion quantum computers may have easier connection to a fiberoptic network since they link to optical laser pulses. While trapped-ion qubits can last for seconds, far longer than their superconducting counterparts, their manipulation takes significantly longer [17]. Numerous additional qubit technologies are out there, but they are receiving less commercial attention now. Companies like Postquantum and Xanadu are now exploring the economic viability of photonic qubits, which use very stable photons to store quantum information. However, generating the necessary interactions between these qubits for computational purposes makes it exceptionally challenging. There is a positive outlook regarding the potential rapid scalability of semiconductor spin qubits due to their reliance on the same semiconductor physics that forms the foundation of current computer chips. However, the control and computation technologies for these systems are at a different stage of development compared to superconductors and trapped ions. Finally, scientists have been working on topological quantum computing for a while. Quantum information stored in a topological quantum computer would be ordered stably across large distances and does not require error correction. However, researchers still need to build topological qubits and use them to execute computations.

7.6 QUANTUM COMPUTING ALGORITHMS

A quantum computer is not magically superior to a conventional computer in any general-purpose task. Adding two integers on a quantum computer is expected to be slower than on a conventional computer, and it is also unlikely that quantum computing would provide any benefits for human applications. To perform computations beyond the capabilities of classical machines, quantum computers exploit the peculiarities of quantum physics, including superposition, interference, and entanglement. When the quantum machine's inherent physics provides algorithmic benefits over established classical alternatives, we speak about a quantum speedup. You can utilize a quantum computer to solve a larger issue, conduct more calculations in the same amount of time, or take your time looking for the best possible answer rather than relying on a quicker quantum device. Arithmetic quantum circuits (for addition, multiplication, and division) are required for a hardware implementation of quantum algorithms. Thapliyal et al. are working on the development of quantum arithmetic circuits that are optimized for T-count, T-depth, and qubit cost [19, 20]. These quantum arithmetic circuits may be utilized to create computational tools for green energy that leverage quantum computing. The speed of quantum acceleration can vary depending on the task at hand. Let us say a regular computer takes a specific amount of time to complete a task of size N. In comparison, a quantum computer designed for the same task would be faster by a factor that is determined by a polynomial function of N (Check out Grover's algorithm below.)

Experiencing an exponential increase in speed with N, a quantum speedup signifies a substantial improvement in efficiency. However, due to the ongoing development of quantum complexity theory, it remains uncertain whether exponential quantum speedups are achievable. Furthermore, it is worth noting that advancements in conventional software can help minimize the potential impact of such quantum speedups. Quantifying the speedup requires a comparison to the most effective classical method currently available. For example, consider the recommendation algorithm, sometimes called the "Netflix problem." It was formerly thought that the quantum best algorithm for this issue would be significantly faster than the conventional best method, given its economic significance to e-commerce and entertainment corporations. A UT-Austin undergraduate named Ewin Tang found a new classical method in 2018 ("Major Quantum Computing Advance Made Obsolete by Teenager," 2019) [21] that completely negated the quantum speedup. The creation of a quantum-capable database and "quantum random access memory" (qRAM) poses substantial challenges to achieving efficient quantum computation [22].

This holds particularly true for algorithms that are specifically designed for machine learning or database search tasks. In such cases, the effectiveness of input/output architectures becomes crucial as they enable seamless communication between quantum and classical devices [23].

In addition, a noteworthy obstacle in attaining resilient and expandable quantum systems lies in the advancement of coherent networking protocols to ensure dependable transfer of quantum information between devices. Experimental implementations of networking protocols have involved the transmission of photons through optical fibers [24, 25]. While quantum communication methods like the key distribution example given earlier share similarities with quantum networking, quantum networking designed to allow many computers to communicate quantum data have more stringent technological requirements. This work provides a high-level overview of how quantum computers may be used in the renewable energy sector. Many algorithms and algorithm families will be discussed or used in this work. Annealing refers to a class of algorithms that employ quantum processes to locate low-energy optimization solutions. Quadratic unconstrained binary optimization codes can solve these issues. Quantum adiabatic optimization algorithms (QAOAs) are one example of a hybrid quantum-classical technique used in these algorithms. It needs to be determined how much of a quantum speedup can be achieved using these techniques.

Quantum annealing relies on a system starting in a well-defined, easily-replicated state. The optimization issue is encoded in the quantum computer's energy landscape, with severe consequences for breaking limits. According to the adiabatic theorem of quantum mechanics, when a quantum computer is operated at a slow enough pace, it will ultimately reach the state with the lowest energy. Remarkably, this lowest energy state also corresponds to the optimal solution for the problem at hand [26]. Specialized quantum computers like the D-Wave machines or general-purpose quantum computers equipped with digital quantum simulation techniques can be effectively utilized to investigate annealing approaches. These advanced computing systems enable the exploration and experimentation with various annealing techniques and algorithms. Minima and near-minima can be found in a vast but finite problem space using annealing-based quantum computers. Quantum annealing alone cannot solve complex problems, but when combined with other approximate mathematical programming paradigms, we can get close to the optimal solution.

D-Wave's capabilities have been demonstrated to surpass traditional solutions, such as simulated annealing, for two NP-hard graph problems that can be effectively solved using the architecture of a quantum computer. These achievements showcase the superior performance of D-Wave in tackling complex computational challenges that fall under the NP-hard category [27, 28]. In addition to the existing technologies, nonlinear optical resonators have been leveraged to develop "analog" quantum computers aimed at solving optimization problems. These alternative technologies provide an avenue for constructing quantum computing systems that operate in an analog manner, offering potential solutions to optimization challenges [29], besides D-Wave's superconducting-based technology.

Grover's algorithm, a technique for database search, offers a quantum speedup that scales proportionally to the square root of the database's size. The methodology developed by Grover falls under the category of amplitude amplification or amplitude estimation techniques. This approach belongs to a broader class of procedures aimed at enhancing and estimating the amplitudes involved in quantum computations.

Harrow–Hassidim–Lloyd (HHL) is a method described extracting information from linear system solutions, leading to a substantial reduction in the time needed to solve a system of N equations from scaling linearly with N to scaling logarithmically with N. This approach is part of a set of algorithms designed specifically to tackle linear system problems using quantum computers. Many of these approaches have undergone extensive examination in the realm of machine learning, where optimization and other fundamental operations are frequently employed. However, it is crucial to emphasize that there is currently a lack of definitive outcomes available for quantum machine learning applications.

Shor's algorithm is an efficient method of factoring big numbers, which might be used to crack RSA and other public-key cryptosystems. Although our work does not involve the use of Shor's algorithm, it is noteworthy due to its profound impact on the field of quantum computing. The discovery of Shor's algorithm in the early 1990s significantly accelerated research in this area. Shor's algorithm belongs to a group of algorithms that effectively address problems related to "hidden subgroups." These methods constitute quantum algorithms but are likely to represent just a small part of a larger quantum computing infrastructure. Calibration and control are two traditional problems that must be resolved before quantum computers can be built and operated. In several proposed approaches, there is a utilization of "hybrid" quantum-classical algorithms. These algorithms involve integrating a small-scale quantum algorithm, which may be more feasible in the near term, as a subroutine within a larger conventional algorithm. This combination of quantum and classical components offers a practical and effective approach, particularly in the short term.

This study discusses different "time frames" that may be used to show quantum algorithms. However, we warn that even the near-term possible algorithms and techniques we describe will likely be presented mainly in research contexts to validate quantum computing hardware and software approaches. Quantum computing is unlikely to see widespread commercial implementation soon, at least not to solve practical issues. Annealing and other near-term quantum computing methods are closer to the demonstration phase than their longer term counterparts, even if full adoption may still need larger, more durable hardware. Technologies that are regarded as potential prospects for the distant future, like the HHL algorithm, would require substantial advancements in quantum technology before they can be effectively showcased. Key milestones, such as the realization of fault-tolerant quantum computers, would serve as crucial prerequisites for these advanced technologies to materialize.

7.7 POSSIBLE APPLICATION AREAS IN ENERGY SYSTEMS

We propose that joint efforts in these areas can drive advancements in quantum computing while also contributing to the advancement of power systems and renewable energy. Acknowledging the widespread skepticism surrounding the practicality of quantum technologies in the near term, we have adopted a more flexible framework. Although some of the suggested research paths may prove unproductive, researchers can only discover the areas where quantum computing can make the most significant contributions by exploring the landscape. We present the discussed issues in Table 7.2 for reference.

7.8 SIMULATION AND FORECASTING

The simulation of intricate molecules and structures poses a significant challenge for classical computers, as highlighted by physicist Richard Feynman in his renowned 1982 speech [30]. Given that nature operates

TABLE 7.2 Quantum Approaches and Algorithms for Problem Solving: A Summary

	Explanation	Potential Grid Challenges
Quantum Annealing (QA)	Leveraging quantum tunneling for optimal solution discovery	Unit commitment maintenance schedule
		Quantum annealing (QA) system to explore the deepest energy states for optimal solution discovery
		Optimization of resource planning, load scheduling, and machine learning in quantum computing
QAOA	Utilizing classical optimization of quantum hamiltonians for annealing-inspired hybrid quantum-classical optimization	Same as QA
Amplitude estimation (Grover's)	Advanced sampling method outperforming classical Monte Carlo: accelerated search algorithms for efficient database solution discovery	Contingency analysis

on quantum variables, researchers in the field of quantum computing are actively exploring techniques for simulating complex systems. In this study, we delve into the potential of quantum computers in domains such as material design and complex forecasting.

7.9 MATERIAL DESIGNS

7.9.1 DESCRIPTION OF PROBLEM

To properly design batteries and materials, knowledge of molecular characteristics is essential. The development of materials and technologies is crucial to energy generation and storage which relies on chemistry. Photovoltaic (PV) material manufacturing and research into alternative battery chemistries are two such examples. Researchers in photovoltaics are constantly exploring the feasibility of developing novel materials like perovskite photovoltaics. However, there remain challenges regarding product dependability and longevity (OOE SETO, 2021), although perovskites are adaptable and have the potential for high-efficiency and low-cost manufacturing. Multijunction cells, hot-carrier solar cells, intermediate-band solar cells, and multiple exciton generation [32] are some application areas involving concerned methods for mitigating these losses. Problems with high performance, longevity, and ecological awareness are not uncommon. Solar energy may be stored as hydrogen by water splitting in electrolysis, for instance, which is a promising emergency technology for solar energy storage. Today's batteries, though, rely heavily on lithium-ion technology. Resources, trash management, and privacy are the only issues concerning these technologies where resource wastage can be minimized, using industrial real estate to address issues with production [32].. Maximum efficiency, durability, and development over the next several years are required. It is not unusual to come across concerns regarding the environmental implications of quantum computing technology. Short-term solutions, like annealing, may be available to address these issues; however, emergency technologies for solar energy are closer to the demonstration phase and may require larger, more robust hardware even if their eventual storage is developed. Meanwhile, modern batteries are mostly based on lithium-term prospects, such as HHL, which will necessitate substantial ion technologies. There are, however, some valid reasons to be wary about using these technological developments in quantum technology just yet.

Instead of anticipating precise timelines for quickly developing technologies, we have placed each innovation on a short-, medium-, and long-term schedule according to the perceived complexity of the hardware required to execute it and the associated cost. High-fidelity molecular modeling is essential for next-generation battery technologies [34]. Limitations of classical computers in accounting for quantum effects in molecular processes leading to the infeasibility of exact computation using the Schrödinger equation for electron interactions in small molecules have been observed [33].

7.9.2 CURRENT HURDLES AND OVERVIEW OF QUANTUM APPROACH

Quantum computing in the field of chemistry is deemed ideally suited for modeling the Schrödinger equation, which controls the dynamics of issues on a chemistry-sized scale. The wave function of a system with two electrons can be approximatively calculated by multiplying the wave function of a single electron by itself. However, with their superposition feature, qubits can model quantum objects like electrons. They can, for instance, carry out intricate simulations of the molecules that make up inorganic systems. Classical computers are constrained to approximate solutions that rely on approximations of electron interactions. In early efforts to capture chemical behavior, variational quantum eigensolvers (VQE) emerged as a hybrid quantum/classical method. VQE represents a significant step in utilizing quantum approaches to address the complexities of chemical systems [36]. The algorithm demonstrated its effectiveness by successfully calculating the electronic states of the water molecule and efficiently solving other test problems. VQE algorithms provide the ground state, including both its energy and the arrangement that produces it. The crystalline structures underlying photovoltaics are only one example of a condensed matter problem that might benefit from this work's extension to bigger molecules and computational exploration. Since these VQE algorithms are NISQ-scale devices, they are vulnerable to attack by quantum devices in the next 1–5 years, even if modest instances are being developed. It is estimated that between 100 and 1000 fully linked qubits with low error rates would be necessary to handle intriguing issues, such as biomolecule simulations [35]. Accelerated VQE (a-VQE) was developed by Wang et al. [37] to bridge the gap between VQE and quantum phase estimation (QPE). The authors demonstrate that relative to the number of samples and overall execution time, a-VQE is superior to VQE [37]. Distributed quantum computers of variable scale using the accelerated variational quantum Eigen-solver method was proposed by DiAdamo et al. [38]. The group hopes to figure out how to link many individual quantum computers to scale up to an enormous amount of processing power. Full digital modeling of the quantum Hamiltonian allows for more accurate and stable computations. These computations excel at dynamic simulations, such as investigating how a chemical reaction occurs. However, error correction is likely a decade away from being included in digital quantum simulators.

7.10 ADVANCED FORECASTING

7.10.1 DESCRIPTION OF PROBLEM

Utilities utilize a variety of forecasts in order to run the electrical grid efficiently. The prediction of power demand (or load) has historically been the most prevalent type of forecast needed. In the past, these models relied on calendar data to conclude seasonal and daily consumption, but today, sophisticated statistical and machine-learning models [40] are used instead. Forecasting the availability of renewable energy sources like wind and solar power introduces a new layer of complexity. Moreover, considering the dynamic nature of the power system, historical data holds limited value in predicting future actions. Numerous factors, including generators, solar and wind power, water generation, and load curtailment, contribute to maintaining system stability. Accurate forecasting plays a vital role in managing the fluctuations of solar and wind resources, enabling more reliable, robust, secure, and cost-effective integration of renewable energy. Wind and solar generation forecasting tools rely on a combination of meteorological observations, numerical weather prediction models, analysis of atmospheric processes, and statistical analysis to provide precise predictions. These measurements serve as inputs for physical models that generate power generation forecasts. However, due to the vast amount of data and accuracy required to simulate the intricate physics involved, achieving a perfect atmosphere simulation is unfeasible. Therefore, approximation models are employed to find acceptable solutions within a reasonable timeframe. Weather stations gather essential information such as pressure, temperature, and wind speed, which are fed into physics models based on fluid dynamics to make predictions. However, it is important to note that as the prediction horizon is extended further into the future, forecasts become progressively less accurate due to the system's chaotic nature and the inherent limitations of initial measurements. Predictions must be made on timescales ranging from hours to minutes to weeks in order to assess grid dependability and determine pricing in day-ahead energy markets. as well as dynamic energy markets. The New England grid operator (ISO-NE) estimates that lowering the inaccuracy of solar forecasts might save tens of millions of dollars [42]. Both public and private sector researchers are actively engaged in investigating the potential of advanced machine learning techniques for solar forecasting. These efforts aim to enhance the accuracy and reliability of solar energy predictions [43, 44]. The Navier-Stokes nonlinear partial differential equations find application in a range of fields such as weather prediction, wind-blade interactions, and hydrodynamics. These equations are employed to model and study the complex dynamics involved in these systems. There have been preliminary experiments employing the gate model [45–47] and annealing [48] in this emerging field of quantum computing.

7.10.2 QUANTUM APPROACH AND CHALLENGES

For quantum techniques to be successful in forecasting, it is crucial to identify crucial nodes where quantum computers can potentially enhance or accelerate the performance of challenging computational tasks. In such cases, utilizing previously developed VQE could be a viable option. Unlike classical computing, which experiences conjectured exponential scaling for highly chaotic problems, quantum approaches offer an alternative paradigm for addressing these computational challenges [49], There is a possibility of extending the use of VQE to address nonlinear problems, enabling the method to scale polynomially with the number of qubits. Short-term weather forecasting heavily relies on accurately representing atmospheric phenomena to estimate solar and wind power generation. Nonlinear partial differential equations and deep neural networks drive atmospheric dynamics. Quantum computing could speed up and improve weather prediction using the weather research and forecasting (WRF) model. Offloading these equations or training these models on quantum technology could do this (NCAR, 2021). Such efforts would include the construction of hybrid quantum-classical computers that make heavy use of current technologies. When processing massive amounts of data, hybrid approaches are viable options. It is possible to solve only the computationally intensive sections of a challenging machine learning algorithm using a quantum computer, while the rest of the algorithm is solved using classical methods [51]. This signifies that advancements in quantum machine learning techniques can greatly contribute to the development of accurate and efficient forecasting methods for integrating renewable energy sources into existing power systems.

7.11 TASK SCHEDULING AND ASSIGNMENT

7.11.1 PROBLEM STATEMENT

Addressing the power demand challenge encompasses various time scales and responsibilities within the nation's electrical grid management. This includes day-to-day operations, day-ahead planning, and long-term capital enhancement strategies. One of the primary optimization challenges is identifying the most cost-effective electricity provider to meet specific demands. However, operators face numerous constraints, such as transmission limits, safety and reliability requirements, and environmental policy mandates like renewable portfolio standards. Minute-by-minute decision-making involves tackling a range of optimal power flow (OPF) problems. One notable example is the alternating current optimal power flow (AC OPF), which optimizes both actual and reactive power while considering transmission losses based on electromagnetic physics in steady-state power flow. The nonlinearity of the power flow equations makes this a challenging problem to solve, but the rewards might be substantial. Even modest improvements in AC OPF systems might save the American electricity grid billions of dollars each year, according to ARPA-E's GRIDDATA initiative (ARPA-E, 2021). Power system modeling and control requirements double with the number of active nodes, making for a challenging optimization issue described in SETO's ENERGISE grant opportunity. Members of the electrical power supply chain (DOE-EERE, 2021). Day-ahead power forecast inaccuracies can contribute to another major issue in the energy system: unit commitment. When committing to a unit, operators must weigh operational, technical, economic, and environmental factors like thermal line restrictions to choose which units will be brought online and readied to begin generating power. Reserve needs, node balancing limitations, and maximum allowable voltages. Therefore, the unit commitment determines the limitations of the real-time AC OPF computation. This issue calls for the resolution of a nonconvex mixed-integer linear programing problem. Integrated resource planning, which deals with longer time horizons, analyzes the suite of upgrades, including transmission building and new generating capacity needed to fulfil all anticipated increased demand. The new grid delivers significant changes to the power business, with the availability of highly scattered resources becoming increasingly unpredictable, necessitating efficient and resilient resource allocation algorithms. In each of these examples, the prevalence of renewable resources presents a challenge for using conventional computing methods. The challenge is made more difficult by the advent of renewable resources, especially dispersed resources like rooftop solar, which must be managed independently. Scheduling and dispatch must consider the stochastic nature of renewable resources due to their inherent fluctuation. Furthermore, the power grid is becoming more intelligent with the widespread deployment of sensors that transmit data to decision-makers, the emergence of energy storage enabling new grid functionalities, the growing demand for electricity from electric vehicles, and the integration of devices capable of adjusting demand in response to utility requirements or costs. Thanks to these novel aspects, there are now more options to consider, making it more difficult to zero in on the best course of action. Compared to steady-state studies, which only consider time-invariant models and fail to capture transitions between states, dynamic analyses add another layer of complexity.

7.11.2 PRESENT CHALLENGES AND OVERVIEW OF QUANTUM COMPUTING

Approach scheduling and dispatching of complex systems are NP-hard issues (ARPA-E, 2021) when considered in their complete complexity. This means that no "efficient" solution exists that can precisely solve the N-buses issue in a polynomial time in N. Approximations, simplifying assumptions, and heuristics are often used to tackle the issues in practice. Some methods assume the impedance qualities of the electrical network to decouple variables that have some physical connection; for instance, "DC OPF" is a linearization of the AC OPF that assumes constant voltages. These heuristics can quickly solve typical problems but can only handle some scenarios. Therefore, operators risk making manual corrections when the system deviates from expected behavior due to the problem's ignored parts. In practice, this raises the possibility of a grid operator making a mistake or, less dramatically, of market inefficiencies. QA and QAOA are two quantum computing methods worth investigating for solving these challenging optimization problems. These algorithms, detailed in the "Algorithms" section, use the innate propensity of a system to choose the state with the lowest energy to find optimum solutions to optimization issues. While QA embeds the problem into the quantum system's energy landscape, QAOA is an approximation approach that uses a conventional optimization loop to determine the best path to the lowest energy states. Quantum annealer optimization techniques are discussed and illustrated in Refs. [27–29]. Annealing and kindred optimization issues have attracted much attention, but their computational potential is hard to assess. Differences in efficiency across quantum annealing algorithms need to be better understood conceptually. Both QAOA and more conventional heuristic methods. There has to be a lot more study done, both theoretically and empirically, to figure out what benefits quantum computers may provide.<

7.12 STABILITY AND RELIABILITY

7.12.1 DESCRIPTION OF PROBLEM

Constraints on dependability and stability in the power system were discussed in the section on scheduling and dispatch. These norms ensure that consumers always have access to clean, dependable power. The North American Electric Reliability Council (NERC) has set a goal of one day of unintentional outage per 10 years (NERC, 2021) to ensure that the electricity grid is reliable enough to keep up with consumer demand. For example, the voltage at the usage locations cannot deviate by more than 5% from the nominal value (120 V in the United States) and must remain within the requirements of the American National Requirements Institute (ANSI). This necessitates not only the presence of spare power capacity if any generation is disconnected but also the rapid availability of that excess power capacity to prevent a collapse of the system owing to a mismatch between supply and demand. When a producing or transmission asset fails, the grid must withstand a transient disruption and establish a new steady-state solution. This may be represented in terms of the electrical system's normal modes, and it should be shown that any excitations away from the equilibrium state would naturally damp out over time scales of milliseconds to minutes. Persistent or amplified excitations may be harmful to machinery.

7.13 CURRENT CHALLENGES AND DESCRIPTION OF QUANTUM

7.13.1 APPROACH

Several algorithms discovered by quantum computer scientists may be of value to the electrical power engineer concerned with system stability and dependability. Grover's approach, one of the most well-known quantum algorithms, allows for a V.N. speedup while searching a database of N entries. While Grover's approach was originally developed to improve the power grid's reliability, it may be easily adapted to solve other sorts of search issues as well. Such algorithms allow for fast searching and evaluating of multiple configurations or objects against a specified function. The term "amplitude estimation" describes this broad category of methods. In the case of power systems, for instance, amplitude estimation techniques might be used to sift through a variety of permutations in order to determine which ones pose the most risk. Significant power outages or other system instability might result from these scenarios. A risk-analysis method that significantly accelerates Monte Carlo search techniques was recently shown by IBM researchers in a financial rather than an electrical setting. Studies of power system dependability commonly employ Monte Carlo methods 1601.

HHL is another promising quantum algorithm, called after its creators Harrow, Hasidim, and Lloyd. With an exponential speedup over the most well-known classical methods, HHL applies to problems involving linear systems of equations. HHL's skill. Its effectiveness in linear systems implies a wide variety of potential uses for enhancing the reliability of power grids. State estimation [58], which is required for determining the current state of the power system and detecting dangerous anomalies, and solving differential equations [59], which is required for evaluating the behavior of the power system and how it will respond to transient disturbances, are two such problem areas. These two uses are crucial to the study of power system dependability. As it demands many qubits and dependable low-error operations on those qubits, HHI. is an intensive algorithm that is not expected to be implemented on near-term devices

7.13.2 CURRENT INVESTMENT IN QUANTUM COMPUTING

Industrial and government entities are both major funding sources for the rapidly expanding field of quantum computing. According to a 2015 survey by the McKinsey consulting firm, governments worldwide have spent $1.8 billion on nonclassified research on quantum technologies [23]. The National Quantum Initiative Act passed into law in 2019, allows an expenditure of $1.2 billion over 5 years [54] for a quantum information science initiative led by NIST, NSF, and the Department of Energy. There has also been a substantial monetary investment from separate research bodies, such as the $218 million awarded by the Department of Energy in September 2018 (Department of Energy, 2018) and the $31 million awarded by the National Science Foundation in the same month (NSF announces new awards, 2021). Quantum computing has also received considerable funding from the corporate sector. From 2012 to 2018, 52 global quantum technology businesses raised $684 million in private finance, according to an analysis of venture capital agreements published in Nature ("Quantum gold rush," 2019). IBM, Google, Alibaba, Baidu, Microsoft, and Intel are some major IT companies with their own quantum hardware and software development teams. In 2019, Google reported that a quantum computer built with superconducting qubits had reached a milestone known as "quantum supremacy." This means that the computer had successfully done a calculation impossible for a conventional computer to accomplish. According to the Google team, the calculation they performed, which involved sampling from a complex probability distribution, took around 200 seconds on a quantum device. In contrast, it would have taken approximately 10,000 seconds on a state-of-the-art classical supercomputer. This stark difference in computation time raises questions about the significance and implications of this milestone achievement. There are many different types of private enterprises dabbling with quantum computing. Superconducting junctions have been the primary focus of IBM, Intel, and Google as they work to develop general-purpose quantum computers. In contrast, D-Wave creates annealing processing units based on superconducting qubits, while Xanadu focuses on photonic-based quantum computers (Quantum Computing Report, 2019). Microsoft has been focusing on topological qubits and software development.

7.14 CONCLUSION AND RECOMMENDATIONS

Exciting developments are happening at the quantum computing frontier, with many possibilities that were once theoretical now becoming practical. Google has said it has achieved a "quantum advantage" in computing in recent months, signaling the beginning of the next generation of computers. We have tried in this study to highlight potential sectors of renewable energy where quantum computers may be useful in the future. This research is in its early stages. There are still considerable technological obstacles and large theoretical uncertainty in the acceleration that may be achieved; as a result, quantum computers of the size and stability necessary to contribute to the problems described in a meaningful, day-to-day operation still need to be created. There is undeniably a need for more study to ascertain the breadth and depth of the potential enhancements to renewable energy computing made possible by quantum technology. Several pressing requirements for future study were identified throughout the process of writing this chapter and subsequent discussions with academic practitioners. The translation of economically valuable optimization issues into the language of computer algorithms through interdisciplinary study combining operations research and theoretical computer science. Quantitative benchmarks for quantum computing may be established, and existing constraints in optimization might be clarified with the help of research in this field. Realizing constant or polynomial improvements on near-term quantum hardware holds significant potential benefits. However, the primary focus of quantum researchers has been on areas where a theoretical distinction can be demonstrated between the complexity class of classical and quantum algorithms, particularly in the pursuit of exponential speedups. Nonetheless, even a modest 5% enhancement in the quality of solutions for demanding problems like AC OPF could result in substantial energy cost savings amounting to billions of dollars annually. To establish benchmarks for quantum performance, extensive research into algorithmic performance, encompassing error rates and execution speed, will be essential. Since theoretical calculations of the quantum advantage for specific issues are notoriously imprecise, relying on empirical data for the foreseeable future will be necessary. Quantum computers have yet to have their performance in tiny optimization problems with operational constraints characterized. Relevance. Through sustained collaboration. Scientists specializing in quantum computers and those studying alternative energy sources will work together to guarantee this. When this technology becomes accessible, businesses are ready to use it to solve pressing issues. Quantum advantage on tiny issues is already emerging from early research on unit commitment and other power systems challenges using quantum devices.

As quantum computers expand their capabilities, they will undoubtedly shed light on these concerns and handle new computational areas previously beyond the reach of classical computers. In the next decade, advances in quantum computing might provide some of the game-changing tools required to build a sustainable energy grid. Developing and exploring this promising convergence of technologies might result in cheaper energy, more efficient grid management, and a more secure electrical grid.

KEYWORDS

- **renewable energy**
- **quantum computing**
- **traditional computers**
- **traditional classical computing**
- **potential quantum computing**
- **photovoltaics**
- **global warming**

REFERENCES

1. Nielsen, M. A., & Chuang, I. L. (2010). *Quantum Computation and Quantum Information*. Cambridge University Press.
2. Preskill, J. (2018). Quantum computing in the NISQ era and beyond. *Quantum*, 2, 79.
3. Outlook, A. E. (2010). Energy information administration. *Department of Energy*, *92010*(9), 1–15.
4. Lipschultz, F., Herring, D. D., Ray, A. J., Alder, J. R., Dahlman, L., DeGaetano, A. T., ... & Sweet, W. V. (2020). Climate explorer: Improved access to local climate projections. *Bulletin of the American Meteorological Society*, *101*(3), E265–E273.
5. Core Writing Team. (2014). Intergovernmental panel on climate change (2014) climate change 2014: Synthesis Report. Contribution of Working Groups 646 I. *II and III to the Fifth Assessment Report of the Intergovernmental Panel on Climate Change*, 151.
6. Geldi, H. K. (2021). Analysis of the renewable energy sources for the Middle East countries. *Economics and Politics of Energy in the Middle East and Eastern Europe*, 99.
7. Denholm, P., Clark, K., & O'Connell, M. (2016). *Emerging Issues and Challenges in Integrating High Levels of Solar into the Electrical Generation and Transmission System*. National Renewable Energy Laboratory: Golden, CO.
8. McAllister, T. (2021). Solar Energy Development in North Carolina: Analyzing Spatial Patterns and Landscape Characteristics of the Spread of Utility-Scale Solar Facilities (Doctoral dissertation, the George Washington University).
9. Feldman, D., Ramasamy, V., & Margolis, R. (2021). *US Solar Photovoltaic BESS System Cost Benchmark Q1 2020 Report* (No. DE-AC36-08GO28308). National Renewable Energy Laboratory-Data (NREL-DATA), Golden, CO (United States); National Renewable Energy Lab. (NREL), Golden, CO (United States).
10. Outlook, A. E. (2007). With Projections to 2050. *US Energy Information Administration*.

11. Hsu, J. (2015). How much power will quantum computing need? *IEEE Spectrum*, *5*, 10.
12. Niedenzu, W., Mukherjee, V., Ghosh, A., Kofman, A. G., & Kurizki, G. (2018). Quantum engine efficiency bound beyond the second law of thermodynamics. *Nature Communications*, *9*(1), 165.
13. Humble, T. S., Thapliyal, H., Munoz-Coreas, E., Mohiyaddin, F. A., & Bennink, R. S. (2019). Quantum computing circuits and devices. *IEEE Design & Test*, *36*(3), 69–94.
14. Krantz, P., Kjaergaard, M., Yan, F., Orlando, T. P., Gustavsson, S., & Oliver, W. D. (2019). A quantum engineer's guide to superconducting qubits. *Applied Physics Reviews*, *6*(2), 021318.
15. Kjaergaard, M., Schwartz, M. E., Braumüller, J., Krantz, P., Wang, J. I. J., Gustavsson, S., & Oliver, W. D. (2020). Superconducting qubits: Current state of play. *Annual Review of Condensed Matter Physics*, *11*, 369–395.
16. Penchev, V. (2023). This Year's Nobel Prize (2022) in physics for entanglement and quantum information: the new revolution in quantum mechanics and science. *Available at SSRN 4382533*.
17. Bruzewicz, C. D., Chiaverini, J., McConnell, R., & Sage, J. M. (2019). Trapped-ion quantum computing: Progress and challenges. *Applied Physics Reviews*, *6*(2), 021314.
18. Pachos, J. K. (2012). *Introduction to Topological Quantum Computation*. Cambridge University Press.
19. Muñoz-Coreas, E., & Thapliyal, H. (2018). Quantum circuit design of a t-count optimized integer multiplier. *IEEE Transactions on Computers*, *68*(5), 729–739.
20. Thapliyal, H., Munoz-Coreas, E., Varun, T. S. S., & Humble, T. S. (2019). Quantum circuit designs of integer division optimizing T-count and T-depth. *IEEE Transactions on Emerging Topics in Computing*, *9*(2), 1045–1056.
21. Tang, E. (2019, June). A quantum-inspired classical algorithm for recommendation systems. In *Proceedings of the 51st Annual ACM SIGACT Symposium on Theory of Computing,* pp. 217–228.
22. Giovannetti, V., Lloyd, S., & Maccone, L. (2008). Quantum random access memory. *Physical Review Letters*, *100*(16), 160501.
23. National Academies of Sciences, Engineering, and Medicine. (2019). Quantum computing: progress and prospects.
24. Cirac, J. I., Zoller, P., Kimble, H. J., & Mabuchi, H. (1997). Quantum state transfer and entanglement distribution among distant nodes in a quantum network. *Physical Review Letters*, *78*(16), 3221.
25. Valivarthi, R., Puigibert, M. L. G., Zhou, Q., Aguilar, G. H., Verma, V. B., Marsili, F., ... & Tittel, W. (2016). Quantum teleportation across a metropolitan fibre network. *Nature Photonics*, *10*(10), 676–680.
26. Born, M., & Fock, V. (1928). Beweis des adiabatensatzes. *ZeitschriftfürPhysik*, *51*(3–4), 165–180.
27. Djidjev, H. N., Chapuis, G., Hahn, G., & Rizk, G. (2018). Efficient combinatorial optimization using quantum annealing. arXiv preprint *arXiv:1801.08653*.
28. Ajagekar, A., Humble, T., & You, F. (2020). Quantum computing based hybrid solution strategies for large-scale discrete-continuous optimization problems. *Computers & Chemical Engineering*, *132*, 106630.

29. Nigg, S. E., Lörch, N., & Tiwari, R. P. (2017). Robust quantum optimizer with full connectivity. *Science Advances*, *3*(4), e1602273.
30. Feynman, R. P. (2018). Simulating physics with computers. *Int. J. Theor. Phys*, *21*(6/7).
31. Nazir, S., Ali, A., Aftab, A., Muqeet, H. A., Mirsaeidi, S., & Zhang, J. M. (2023). Techno-economic and environmental perspectives of solar cell technologies: A comprehensive review. *Energies*, *16*(13), 4959.
32. Almosni, S., Delamarre, A., Jehl, Z., Suchet, D., Cojocaru, L., Giteau, M., ... & Guillemoles, J. F. (2018). Material challenges for solar cells in the twenty-first century: Directions in emerging technologies. *Science and Technology of Advanced Materials*, *19*(1), 336–369.
33. Brown, K. L., Munro, W. J., & Kendon, V. M. (2010). Using quantum computers for quantum simulation. *Entropy*, *12*(11), 2268–2307.
34. Rice, J. E., Gujarati, T. P., Motta, M., Takeshita, T. Y., Lee, E., Latone, J. A., & Garcia, J. M. (2021). Quantum computation of dominant products in lithium–sulfur batteries. *The Journal of Chemical Physics*, *154*(13), 134115.
35. Moll, N., Barkoutsos, P., Bishop, L. S., Chow, J. M., Cross, A., Egger, D. J., ... & Temme, K. (2018). Quantum optimization using variational algorithms on near-term quantum devices. *Quantum Science and Technology*, *3*(3), 030503.
36. Bian, T., Murphy, D., Xia, R., Daskin, A., & Kais, S. (2019). Quantum computing methods for electronic states of the water molecule. *Molecular Physics*, *117*(15–16), 2069–2082.
37. Wang, D., Higgott, O., & Brierley, S. (2019). Accelerated variational quantum eigensolver. *Physical Review Letters*, *122*(14), 140504.
38. DiAdamo, S., Ghibaudi, M., & Cruise, J. (2021). Distributed quantum computing and network control for accelerated vqe. *IEEE Transactions on Quantum Engineering*, *2*, 1–21.
39. Giani, A., & Eldredge, Z. (2021). Quantum computing opportunities in renewable energy. *SN Computer Science*, *2*(5), 393.
40. Vivas, E., Allende-Cid, H., & Salas, R. (2020). A systematic review of statistical and machine learning methods for electrical power forecasting with reported mape score. *Entropy*, *22*(12), 1412.
41. Inman, R. H., Pedro, H. T., & Coimbra, C. F. (2013). Solar forecasting methods for renewable energy integration. *Progress in Energy and Combustion Science*, *39*(6), 535–576.
42. Wan, C., Zhao, J., Song, Y., Xu, Z., Lin, J., & Hu, Z. (2015). Photovoltaic and solar power forecasting for smart grid energy management. *CSEE Journal of Power and Energy Systems*, *1*(4), 38–46.
43. Hamann, H. F. (2017). *A Multi-Scale, Multi-Model, Machine-Learning Solar Forecasting Technology* (No. DE-EE-0006017). IBM, Yorktown Heights, NY (United States). Thomas J. Watson Research Center.
44. Marquis, M., Benjamin, S., James, E., & Molling, C. (2015). *A Public-Private-Academic Partnership to Advance Solar Power Forecasting* (No. DE-EE0006458). NOAA ESRL.
45. Gaitan, F. (2020). Finding flows of a Navier–Stokes fluid through quantum computing. *npj Quantum Information*, *6*(1), 61.

46. Bharadwaj, S. S., & Sreenivasan, K. R. (2020). Quantum computation of fluid dynamics. arXiv preprint *arXiv:2007.09147*.
47. Yepez, J. (1998, February). Quantum computation of fluid dynamics. In *NASA International Conference on Quantum Computing and Quantum Communications*. Heidelberg: Springer Berlin Heidelberg: Berlin, pp. 34–60.
48. Ray, N., Banerjee, T., Nadiga, B., & Karra, S. (2019). Towards solving the Navier-Stokes equation on quantum computers. arXiv preprint *arXiv:1904.09033*.
49. Lubasch, M., Joo, J., Moinier, P., Kiffner, M., & Jaksch, D. (2020). Variational quantum algorithms for nonlinear problems. *Physical Review A*, *101*(1), 010301.
50. Liu, H., Zhao, X., Duan, K., Shang, W., Li, M., & Shi, P. (2023). Optimizing simulation of summer precipitation by weather research and forecasting model over the mountainous southern Tibetan Plateau. *Atmospheric Research*, *281*, 106484.
51. Suchara, M., Alexeev, Y., Chong, F., Finkel, H., Hoffmann, H., Larson, J., ... & Smith, G. (2018, November). Hybrid quantum-classical computing architectures. In *Proceedings of the 3rd International Workshop on Post-Moore Era Supercomputing, 2018.*
52. Aravena, I., Molzahn, D. K., Zhang, S., Petra, C. G., Curtis, F. E., Tu, S., ... & Veeramany, A. (2023). Recent developments in security-constrained AC optimal power flow: Overview of Challenge 1 in the ARPA-E Grid Optimization Competition. *Operations Research*, *71*(6), 1997–2014.
53. Computing, Q. (2019). *Progress and Prospects*. National Academies of Sciences, Engineering and Medicine.
54. Raymer, M. G., & Monroe, C. (2019). The US national quantum initiative. *Quantum Science and Technology*, *4*(2), 020504.
55. Romeo, S., Lawton Smith, H., Carmel, E., & Slater, J. (2021). The emerging quantum technology industry: capital cities, entrepreneurship, and policy. Working Papers 54, Birkbeck Centre for Innovation Management Research, revised July 2021.
56. LaRose, R. (2019). Overview and comparison of gate level quantum software platforms. *Quantum*, *3*, 130.
57. Lloyd, S. (2010, March). Quantum algorithm for solving linear systems of equations. In *APS March Meeting Abstracts,* Vol. 2010, pp. D4–002.
58. Wiebe, N., Braun, D., & Lloyd, S. (2012). Quantum algorithm for data fitting. *Physical Review Letters*, *109*(5), 050505.
59. Berry, D. W. (2014). High-order quantum algorithm for solving linear differential equations. *Journal of Physics A: Mathematical and Theoretical*, *47*(10), 105301.
60. Sun, Y., Frew, B., Dalvi, S., & Dhulipala, S. C. (2022). Insights into methodologies and operational details of resource adequacy assessment: A case study with application to a broader flexibility framework. *Applied Energy*, *328*, 120191.
61. Rahman, J., Feng, C., & Zhang, J. (2021). A learning-augmented approach for AC optimal power flow. *International Journal of Electrical Power & Energy Systems*, *130*, 106908.
62. Al-Shafei, A., Zareipour, H., & Cao, Y. (2022). A review of high-performance computing and parallel techniques applied to power systems optimization. arXiv preprint *arXiv:2207.02388*.

CHAPTER 8

Unlocking Nature's Secrets: Harnessing Quantum Computing for Precision Weather Forecasting and Climate Modeling

SUMAN PATRA*

Department of Physics, Netaji Nagar Day College, Kolkata, West Bengal, India

*Corresponding author

ABSTRACT

This chapter discusses the transformative potential of quantum computing in the forecasting of weather and modeling of climate—two very critical fields for understanding and addressing climate change. Quantum computing brings unique computational advantages that will improve the accuracy of predictions, increase knowledge about climate systems, and informed decision-making. The chapter first discusses the importance of these fields and introduces quantum computing and its many applications. It then outlines the current methods used in weather forecasting and climate modeling, highlighting the limitations of traditional computational approaches. Key quantum computing concepts, such as qubits, superposition, and entanglement, are discussed alongside quantum algorithms and architectures. This chapter addresses how quantum computing could bring numerical weather prediction models to a new level, allowing for faster, more accurate weather forecasting through quantum simulation, and using quantum machine learning in analyzing weather patterns. It also gives quantum-inspired algorithms for climate modeling and optimization problems related to

Applications of Quantum Computing in a Variety of Domains. Gunjan Mukherjee, Biswadip Basu Mallik, Rahul Kar Özen ÖZER, Digvijay Pandey, and Binay Kumar Pandey (Eds.)

DOI: 10.1201/9781998511051-8

processing large climatic datasets. While highlighting the promise of quantum computing in revolutionizing these domains, the chapter also discusses its limitations: technical, ethical, and societal. It, therefore, calls for collaboration and responsible deployment in order to reap the full potential of quantum computing to improve the accuracy of predictions, understand climate dynamics, and reduce the impacts of climate change.

8.1 INTRODUCTION

8.1.1 BRIEF OVERVIEW OF THE IMPORTANCE OF WEATHER FORECASTING AND CLIMATE MODELING

Weather forecasting and climate modeling play a crucial role in our society by offering valuable insights into atmospheric conditions and long-term climate patterns. Accurate weather forecasts are essential for sectors such as agriculture, transportation, renewable energy, disaster management, and public safety. They enable farmers to optimize crop production, airlines to plan flight routes, and governments to issue timely warnings for severe weather events.

On the other hand, climate modeling focuses on understanding and predicting the Earth's long-term climate behavior. These models help scientists investigate the impacts of greenhouse gas emissions, assess the risk of climate change, and develop strategies for mitigation and adaptation. They provide critical information that policymakers rely on when making decisions regarding environmental regulations, resource management, and sustainable development.

However significant advancements have been made in traditional computing, weather forecasting and climate modeling still face challenges due to the complexity and scale of the underlying physics along with computational requirements. The abundance of data, intricate interactions between atmospheric variables, and computational constraints limit the accuracy and efficiency of current approaches. Therefore, it is necessary to explore new ways for computational power and techniques that can effectively address these challenges.

8.1.2 INTRODUCTION TO QUANTUM COMPUTING AND ITS POTENTIAL APPLICATIONS IN VARIOUS FIELDS

Quantum computing represents a paradigm shift in computation, using principles from quantum mechanics to process information in fundamentally different ways. Unlike classical computers that use bits to represent either 0 or 1, quantum computers use quantum bits (qubits), which can exist in superposition, representing both 0 and 1 simultaneously [1]. This inherent parallelism offers the potential for exponential computational speed-up and opens doors to solving complex problems more efficiently than classical counterparts.

Quantum computing has the potential to revolutionize various fields, including optimization, cryptography, drug discovery, materials science, and artificial intelligence. In optimization, for example, quantum algorithms have shown promise in solving complex optimization problems faster, which has implications for logistics, scheduling, and resource allocation. In cryptography, quantum-resistant algorithms are being developed to address the threat posed by quantum computers to current encryption methods.

Quantum computing has great potential in the fields of weather forecasting and climate modeling. It can offer faster simulations and analyses of weather patterns, which would enhance the accuracy and lead time of our forecasts. Additionally, quantum-inspired optimization algorithms can help optimize complex climate models, leading to better predictions. Quantum machine learning (QML) techniques could also provide valuable insights from large climate datasets, aiding in data analysis and pattern recognition.

Envisioning a future where predictions become more precise and lead times extend further; our understanding of the impacts of climate change deepens by integrating quantum computing with weather forecasting and climate modeling. Yet, harnessing this immense power is not without its share of substantial challenges that must be overcome. This chapter aims to delve deeper by exploring potential applications along with addressing challenges and offering insight toward directing future developments in terms of integrating quantum computing with regard to weather forecasting and climate modeling.

8.2 TRADITIONAL APPROACHES IN WEATHER FORECASTING AND CLIMATE MODELING

8.2.1 OVERVIEW OF CURRENT METHODOLOGIES AND TECHNIQUES USED IN WEATHER FORECASTING

Weather forecasting relies on a combination of observations, numerical models, and data assimilation techniques to predict future atmospheric conditions. The process involves collecting data from various sources, such as weather stations, satellites, radar systems, and weather balloons, which provide information about temperature, humidity, wind speed and direction, and atmospheric pressure. These data points are then used to initialize numerical models that simulate the behavior of the atmosphere.

NWP models are widely acknowledged as the cornerstone of modern-day weather forecasting. NWP models employ a three-dimensional grid system to divide the atmosphere and rely on mathematical equations encompassing the underlying physical processes governing atmospheric dynamics, thermodynamics, and radiation [2]. By iteratively solving the governing equations, NWP models can simulate the evolution of weather systems over a specified time period.

To enhance the precision of weather forecasts, data assimilation techniques are employed. These techniques involve assimilating real-time observations with model outputs to update the initial conditions of the numerical models. Data assimilation algorithms use statistical methodologies, such as variational techniques or ensemble-based approaches, to identify the optimal correspondence between observations and model predictions. This process aids in mitigating initial errors and bolstering forecast accuracy.

8.2.2 CHALLENGES AND LIMITATIONS FACED BY TRADITIONAL COMPUTING METHODS IN HANDLING COMPLEX CLIMATE MODELS

Conventional computing methods encounter a myriad of challenges when confronted with the intricacies of complex climate models. These challenges can be delineated into several key areas, including computational complexity, spatial and temporal resolution, parameterization, and ensemble simulations.

8.2.2.1 COMPUTATIONAL COMPLEXITY

Climate models necessitate the simulation of diverse physical processes, such as radiative transfer, cloud formation, and ocean circulation. These processes interact with one another and unfold across separate spatial and temporal scales, resulting in simulations that are both intricate and computationally demanding.

8.2.2.2 SPATIAL AND TEMPORAL RESOLUTION

Enhancing the spatial and temporal resolutions in climate models holds great importance, as it enables a more precise representation of small-scale features and short-term weather phenomena. However, augmenting the resolution substantially escalates the computational requirements, posing a formidable challenge for traditional computing architectures to grapple with effectively.

8.2.2.3 PARAMETERIZATION

Climate models often resort to parameterization schemes to encapsulate processes that transpire at scales smaller than the model's grid resolution [3]. These parameterizations introduce simplifications and assumptions, thereby engendering uncertainties in the predictions rendered by the models.

8.2.2.4 ENSEMBLE SIMULATIONS

Climate scientists frequently conduct ensemble simulations to account for uncertainties arising from initial conditions, model formulation, and future scenarios. Generating ensembles necessitates significant computational resources, as multiple simulations are executed concurrently to yield a range of possible outcomes.

8.2.3 THE NEED FOR ADVANCEMENTS IN COMPUTATIONAL POWER AND ALGORITHMS TO IMPROVE ACCURACY

To overcome the challenges faced by traditional computing methods in weather forecasting and climate modeling, advancements in computational power, and algorithms are imperative.

8.2.3.1 COMPUTATIONAL POWER

Augmenting computational power allows for higher resolution simulations and more intricate models. Quantum computing, with its potential for exponential acceleration, offers a promising way to address the computational requirements inherent in complex climate models, enabling more detailed and precise simulations.

8.2.3.2 QUANTUM ALGORITHMS

The emergence of specialized quantum algorithms tailored specifically for weather forecasting and climate modeling harbors the transformative potential to redefine computational approaches, surpassing the capabilities of classical methods. Quantum algorithms exhibit the capability to provide advanced techniques for tasks such as data assimilation, ensemble simulations, optimization, and machine learning within these domains, thereby amplifying their efficacy.

8.2.3.3 HYBRID APPROACHES

The amalgamation of classical and quantum resources through hybrid computing presents a promising way to harness the strengths inherent in both paradigms. By incorporating quantum subroutines for specific tasks within weather forecasting and climate modeling, hybrid approaches can attain superior accuracy and efficiency in their predictions and simulations.

8.2.3.4 ALGORITHMIC INNOVATIONS

Progress in algorithmic advancements, encompassing refined numerical techniques, optimization strategies, and data assimilation methods, assumes critical importance in maximizing the potential of increased computational power. Quantum-inspired algorithms, which draw inspiration from quantum principles but are executed on classical computers, hold the potential to yield valuable insights for optimizing climate models and refining forecasting accuracy.

By addressing these requirements for heightened computational power and algorithmic progress, it is conceivable to improve the precision, resolution, and forecasting horizon of weather forecasts while concurrently refining our understanding and prediction of long-term climate phenomena. The integration of quantum computing technologies alongside pioneering algorithms harbors the potential to herald a paradigm shift, transcending the constraints imposed by prevailing computing methodologies in the domains of weather forecasting and climate modeling.

8.3 QUANTUM COMPUTING FUNDAMENTALS

8.3.1 BRIEF EXPLANATION OF QUANTUM COMPUTING PRINCIPLES AND QUBITS

Quantum computing is based on the principles of quantum mechanics, a branch of physics that describes the behavior of particles at the quantum level. Unlike classical computing, which operates on bits representing either 0 or 1, quantum computing uses qubits that can exist in multiple states simultaneously. This property is known as quantum superposition.

A qubit, a fundamental unit of quantum information, finds its physical realization in various systems, including atoms, ions, photons, or superconducting circuits. These physical platforms manifest two or more distinguishable quantum states, known as basis states. By virtue of the inherent principles of quantum mechanics, the qubit can exist in a coherent superposition of these states, enabling the simultaneous representation of multiple values. For example, a qubit can concurrently embody both 0 and 1, as well as any desired combination or superposition of these states.

8.3.2 KEY CONCEPTS OF QUANTUM SUPERPOSITION AND ENTANGLEMENT

8.3.2.1 QUANTUM SUPERPOSITION

The principle of quantum superposition constitutes a foundational element in the field of quantum computing, empowering qubits to exist in a combination of distinct states. Rather than being limited to a definitive 0 or 1, a qubit can manifest as a weighted combination of both states. Consequently, quantum computations can be executed on multiple values simultaneously, thereby endowing quantum computers with the potential for exponential parallelism.

8.3.2.2 ENTANGLEMENT

Another pivotal concept within the realm of quantum computing is entanglement. When two or more qubits become entangled, their states become entwined in such a manner that the state of one qubit becomes intrinsically linked to the state of the others, regardless of spatial separation. Entangled qubits exhibit a robust correlation that is unattainable in classical systems. This property not only facilitates more efficient computations in quantum computers but also enables the implementation of quantum communication protocols such as quantum teleportation and quantum cryptography.

8.3.3 DIFFERENT TYPES OF QUANTUM COMPUTING ARCHITECTURES (E.G., GATE-BASED AND ANNEALING-BASED)

8.3.3.1 GATE-BASED QUANTUM COMPUTING

Gate-based quantum computing, also known as circuit-based quantum computing, is a methodology that employs a sequential arrangement of quantum logic gates to manipulate qubits, the fundamental units of quantum information [4]. Through the utilization of these gates, which encompass operations like rotations, phase shifts, and entanglement, qubits are manipulated to carry out computations. The gate-based approach relies on the application of a specific sequence of well-defined quantum gates in a predetermined order to address computational problems effectively. Notably, quantum algorithms, such as Shor's algorithm for factoring large numbers and Grover's algorithm for unstructured search, are typically designed with gate-based quantum computers in mind, as they take advantage of the capabilities offered by this computing paradigm.

8.3.3.2 ANNEALING-BASED QUANTUM COMPUTING

Annealing-based quantum computing provides a distinct paradigm from gate-based quantum computing. Its primary objective is to address optimization problems by identifying the minimal energy state of a physical system. Within this paradigm, quantum annealers, the key devices used in annealing-based quantum computing, use the notion of quantum annealing to investigate a wide variety of possibilities and choose the most advantageous configuration or solution [5]. Quantum annealing has demonstrated notable effectiveness in tackling combinatorial optimization problems, including prominent examples such as the traveling salesman problem or graph partitioning. By adopting this approach, annealing-based quantum computing offers a unique perspective on problem-solving and contributes valuable insights to the field of quantum computation.

Gate-based quantum computers and annealing-based quantum computers represent discrete architectures that exhibit different computational capabilities and applications. Gate-based quantum computers offer greater versatility and are better suited for a wider array of quantum algorithms, whereas annealing-based quantum computers excel in addressing specific optimization problems.

It is crucial to acknowledge that quantum computing technology remains in its early stages, and both gate-based and annealing-based approaches are subject to active development and refinement. Researchers and engineers are exploring hybrid approaches that combine the strengths of both architectures, thereby harnessing the advantages of each in solving intricate computational problems. As the field advances, progress in quantum computing architectures will continue to pave the way for the practical application of quantum computing across various domains, including weather forecasting and climate modeling.

8.4 QUANTUM COMPUTING IN WEATHER FORECASTING

8.4.1 UTILIZING QUANTUM ALGORITHMS TO ENHANCE NUMERICAL WEATHER PREDICTION MODELS

Quantum computing offers immense potential for enhancing NWP models, revolutionizing their accuracy and computational efficiency. By using quantum algorithms designed to address specific challenges in NWP, significant advancements can be achieved in various aspects, including data assimilation, parameter tuning, and ensemble simulations.

8.4.1.1 DATA ASSIMILATION

The integration of observational data with model predictions through data assimilation techniques assumes a crucial role in updating the initial conditions of NWP models. Quantum algorithms offer substantial enhancements to the data assimilation process by effectively searching for the optimal alignment between observed data and model predictions. Quantum optimization algorithms, including quantum annealing and quantum-inspired optimization techniques, demonstrate the capability to tackle large-scale optimization problems, thereby reducing the computational time required to assimilate large quantities of data accurately.

8.4.1.2 PARAMETER TUNING

Climate models frequently employ parameterization schemes to represent processes occurring at spatial scales smaller than the resolution of the model grid. Quantum algorithms can contribute to the optimization of these parameters, leading to an improved representation of subgrid processes in climate models. Quantum-inspired optimization techniques facilitate more efficient exploration of parameter spaces, ultimately enhancing the accuracy of climate models and, consequently, elevating the precision of weather forecasts.

8.4.1.3 ENSEMBLE SIMULATIONS

Ensemble simulations encompass the execution of numerous simulations incorporating perturbed initial conditions or employing diverse model configurations in order to accommodate uncertainties [6]. The potential of quantum computers to accelerate ensemble simulations offers the prospect of diminishing computational resources and time constraints. By leveraging the innate parallelism inherent in quantum computing, ensembles can be generated with increased celerity, facilitating more extensive scrutiny of uncertainties and bolstering the dependability of forecasts.

8.4.2 QUANTUM SIMULATIONS FOR ENHANCED AND EXPEDITED WEATHER FORECASTING

The utilization of quantum simulations has the potential to induce a significant paradigm shift within the realm of weather forecasting, facilitating faster and more precise predictions of atmospheric behavior. By capitalizing on their inherent computational advantages, quantum computers surpass their traditional counterparts in terms of efficiency when it comes to simulating quantum systems. Because of this superiority, sophisticated and accurate models of complicated atmospheric processes are now possible.

8.4.2.1 QUANTUM ATMOSPHERIC SIMULATIONS

Accurately modeling complex atmospheric systems across multiple time and space scales is now possible with the help of quantum simulation techniques. These techniques enable a more precise depiction of the dynamic patterns in the atmosphere by capturing the interdependencies between variables, including temperature, humidity, pressure, and wind patterns. Significant progress has been made in the prediction of severe weather conditions and localized meteorological events thanks in large part to the incorporation of quantum simulations into weather forecasting techniques. Increased accuracy in weather forecasts and better preparation for and response to weather-related threats are made possible by quantum simulations' powerful computational capabilities.

8.4.2.2 QUANTUM FLUID DYNAMICS

Understanding air circulation patterns requires the use of quantum computers because of their greater speed, intricacy, and precision in simulating fluid dynamics. More accurate weather predictions may now be made thanks to these models' ability to describe the complex interactions between air masses, ocean currents, and atmospheric dynamics. Improved understanding of weather systems and preparedness for extreme weather conditions like hurricanes, tornadoes, and monsoons are made possible by this.

8.4.3 QML TECHNIQUES FOR WEATHER PATTERN ANALYSIS

QML techniques have great potential for simulating and forecasting weather patterns. QML provides the promise of improving machine learning methods by using quantum computing principles, allowing for more efficient processing and analysis of large weather datasets [7].

8.4.3.1 QUANTUM DATA ANALYSIS

In Quantum Data Analysis, for example, quantum algorithms have shown promising results in speeding up common data-processing operations like pattern recognition, clustering, and feature extraction. In order to better understand weather conditions and boost the reliability of weather fore-casts, QML methods help to reveal hidden patterns and correlations within big climatic datasets. Quantum data analysis aids in detecting patterns related to climate variability, long-term trends, and extreme weather events by acquiring useful information from massive amounts of weather data.

8.4.3.2 QUANTUM NEURAL NETWORKS

The quantum counterparts of classical artificial neural networks, known as quantum neural networks, exhibit great potential for understanding weather patterns. When compared to their traditional equivalents, these networks excel at processing and learning from weather data. Quantum neural networks find subtle nonlinear correlations in weather patterns by leveraging quantum parallelism and quantum entanglement, resulting in more precise predictions of meteorological phenomena such as temperature trends, precipitation patterns, and storm tracks.

8.4.3.3 QUANTUM PATTERN MATCHING

Quantum pattern matching algorithms efficiently look through weather data to identify specific patterns or anomalies. This capability proves invaluable in detecting and predicting extreme weather events, discerning weather-related trends, and analyzing climate changes at regional or global scales. Through the efficient matching of patterns within extensive weather datasets, quantum pattern-matching techniques assist in identifying weather regimes, climate teleconnections, and other crucial meteorological phenomena.

By integrating quantum algorithms and QML techniques, weather forecasting can experience significant improvements in terms of accuracy, speed, and pattern analysis capabilities. These advancements possess the potential to revolutionize our comprehension of weather systems and furnish more reliable forecasts, thereby enabling informed decision-making across various sectors reliant on precise weather information, including agriculture, transportation, disaster management, and renewable energy planning.

8.5 QUANTUM COMPUTING IN CLIMATE MODELING

8.5.1 QUANTUM-INSPIRED ALGORITHMS FOR COMPLEX CLIMATE SIMULATIONS

The application of quantum computing in climate modeling holds promise for addressing the challenges posed by complex climate systems.

Quantum-inspired algorithms, drawing inspiration from the principles of quantum mechanics, offer the potential to enhance the computational efficiency and accuracy of climate simulations.

8.5.1.1 QUANTUM-INSPIRED MONTE CARLO METHODS

Monte Carlo methods are instrumental in simulating complex physical processes and estimating uncertainties in climate modeling. Quantum-inspired Monte Carlo algorithms use quantum principles, such as superposition and entanglement, to improve the sampling efficiency in these simulations. By exploring a larger portion of the search space simultaneously, these algorithms can provide more accurate estimations of climate variables and enhance the representation of uncertain processes, such as cloud formation, precipitation patterns, and feedback mechanisms.

8.5.1.2 QUANTUM-INSPIRED OPTIMIZATION ALGORITHMS

Optimization problems are pervasive in climate modeling, encompassing tasks such as parameter estimation, calibration of climate model components, and scenario analysis. Quantum-inspired optimization algorithms, including quantum annealing and quantum-inspired evolutionary algorithms, offer the potential to expedite the search for optimal solutions by harnessing quantum parallelism and quantum tunneling effects [8]. These algorithms can optimize climate model parameters, enhance model performance, and refine climate projections by efficiently exploring the parameter space and identifying optimal configurations aligned with observed data.

By integrating quantum-inspired algorithms into complex climate simulations, the potential exists for significant advancements in computational efficiency, accuracy, and the representation of uncertain processes. These developments can contribute to improved understanding and prediction of climate phenomena, aiding decision-making processes related to climate change mitigation, adaptation, and policy formulation.

8.5.2 USING QUANTUM ANNEALING FOR OPTIMIZATION PROBLEMS IN CLIMATE MODELING

Quantum annealing, a specific approach within the field of quantum computing, shows promise in addressing optimization problems encountered in climate modeling. By harnessing the power of quantum annealing, researchers can tackle computationally intensive optimization tasks more efficiently and overcome the limitations of classical optimization techniques.

8.5.2.1 SOLVING ENERGY MINIMIZATION PROBLEMS

In the field of climate modeling, it is important to reduce the energy expenses linked with certain climate policies or determine the most suitable approaches for reducing emissions. Quantum annealing provides a way to examine the energy landscape and find arrangements that represent the lowest energy states. This ability allows for better decision-making in crafting climate policies and establishing long-term plans, as it finds solutions that minimize energy usage and greenhouse gas emissions.

8.5.2.2 OPTIMIZING LARGE-SCALE CLIMATE MODELS

Climate models are complex systems that consist of interconnected components and multiple parameters, presenting intricate optimization challenges. Quantum annealing can help optimize large-scale climate models by efficiently exploring the extensive parameter space and identifying combinations that align most effectively with observed data. This capability enhances the accuracy and reliability of climate projections, enabling more informed decision-making for climate mitigation and adaptation strategies.

Gaining insights from quantum annealing brings forth the immense potential for promoting advancements in climate modeling's optimization capabilities. Consequently, this unlocks possibilities for bolstering the effectiveness of climate policies while also elevating accuracy levels in predicting future climates. Furthermore, such improvements pave the way for making decisions that are well-informed and capable of effectively addressing the various challenges that come with combating climate change.

8.5.3 QUANTUM-ENHANCED DATA ANALYSIS FOR CLIMATE DATA PROCESSING

The use of quantum computing has the potential to significantly improve data analysis procedures used in climate science. This potential comes from its ability to dramatically improve the efficiency with which huge climatic datasets are processed and interpreted.

8.5.3.1 QUANTUM DATA COMPRESSION

Climate databases are known for their vast size, necessitating significant storage, and computational resources. Quantum data compression approaches, on the other hand, use quantum mechanics principles such as entanglement and superposition to compress these datasets more efficiently. Quantum data compression techniques help climate scientists to process and analyze larger datasets more quickly by lowering data size while keeping vital information. As a result, they are more successful at performing computationally complex tasks.

8.5.3.2 QUANTUM CLUSTERING AND PATTERN RECOGNITION

Examining climate data in the domain of climate science frequently entails coping with complicated patterns and structures that are critical for understanding climate dynamics and distinguishing different climate regimes. QML algorithms such as quantum clustering and quantum pattern recognition are useful for evaluating massive amounts of climate data and finding relevant patterns [9]. Researchers can use these tools to identify modes of climatic variability, classify severe events, detect transitions in climate regimes, and highlight key elements driving climate change. Quantum clustering and pattern recognition are useful techniques in climate science because they investigate complicated linkages and nonlinear correlations inside data.

8.5.3.3 QUANTUM DIMENSIONALITY REDUCTION

Data analysis and visualization of climate datasets can often be challenging tasks, owing to the detailed structure of the information contained within these datasets. Quantum dimensionality reduction techniques, which project high-dimensional climate data onto lower dimensional representations while conserving critical information, provide a solution. These techniques, which rely on quantum principles, reduce computational complexity while facilitating data exploration, visualization, and interpretation.

By simplifying the representation of climate data, quantum dimensionality reduction techniques provide climate scientists with valuable insights into complex climate patterns and processes.

The integration of quantum-inspired algorithms, quantum annealing, and quantum-enhanced data analysis techniques into climate modeling holds tremendous potential for advancing our understanding of climate dynamics, improving the accuracy of climate models, and informing climate policy decisions. By harnessing the power of quantum computing, researchers can tackle the complexities of climate simulations, optimize model parameters, analyze vast climate datasets, and contribute to more accurate climate projections for addressing the challenges of climate change.

8.6 CHALLENGES AND FUTURE DIRECTIONS

8.6.1 CURRENT LIMITATIONS AND CHALLENGES IN APPLYING QUANTUM COMPUTING TO WEATHER FORECASTING AND CLIMATE MODELING

Despite the immense potential of quantum computing in weather forecasting and climate modeling, several limitations and challenges need to be addressed to realize its benefits fully.

8.6.1.1 HARDWARE LIMITATIONS

Quantum computers are still in the early stages of development, and current quantum hardware faces significant challenges. These include high error rates, limited qubit connectivity, and short coherence times. These limitations impact the reliability, scalability, and stability of quantum algorithms in real-world applications. Overcoming these hardware limitations requires advancements in qubit technologies, error correction techniques, and the development of more robust and fault-tolerant quantum systems.

8.6.1.2 ALGORITHM DEVELOPMENT

Designing quantum algorithms that can effectively address specific challenges in weather forecasting and climate modeling is a complex task. It requires expertise in both quantum computing and meteorology/climatology. Developing quantum algorithms that can outperform classical approaches in terms of accuracy, speed, and scalability is an ongoing research area. Collaborative efforts between quantum scientists and domain experts in weather and climate science are crucial for tackling these challenges and developing tailored quantum algorithms for weather forecasting and climate modeling.

8.6.1.3 DATA HANDLING AND INTEGRATION

Quantum algorithms necessitate the encoding of data into a format suitable for processing on quantum systems. The conversion of expansive climate datasets into a compatible format for quantum algorithms poses a notable challenge. Furthermore, the integration of quantum algorithms into established weather and climate modeling frameworks and infrastructure demands meticulous deliberation and adjustment. To establish a cohesive connection between classical and quantum computing methodologies in weather forecasting and climate modeling, the development of efficient data preprocessing techniques, data encoding strategies, and interoperability solutions becomes imperative.

8.6.2 POTENTIAL ADVANCEMENTS AND RESEARCH AREAS FOR FURTHER EXPLORATION

In order to overcome the existing limitations and unleash the full potential of quantum computing in the domains of weather forecasting and climate modeling, several areas of research demand further exploration and investigation.

8.6.2.1 QUANTUM ERROR CORRECTION

One crucial research area is related to quantum error correction, which plays a vital role in mitigating the adverse effects of noise and errors in quantum hardware. The development of robust quantum error correction codes and techniques is indispensable for enhancing the reliability and scalability of quantum algorithms applied in weather forecasting and climate modeling. Advancements in error correction methodologies will enable the execution of more intricate quantum algorithms with heightened accuracy and stability.

8.6.2.2 QUANTUM MACHINE LEARNING

QML techniques have exhibited substantial potential in diverse fields, and their utilization in the analysis of weather and climate data holds considerable promise. Investigating the integration of QML algorithms with weather forecasting and climate modeling can yield more precise predictions, improved pattern recognition capabilities, and enhanced comprehension of intricate climate processes. Research endeavors should focus on formulating QML algorithms tailored specifically to the unique requirements of weather and climate science.

8.6.2.3 HYBRID QUANTUM–CLASSICAL APPROACHES

Hybrid quantum–classical computing represents a fusion of the strengths of quantum computing and classical computing to address complex problems. Within the realm of weather forecasting and climate modeling, hybrid approaches can be explored to optimize climate models, data assimilation techniques, ensemble simulations, and parameter tuning. The development of efficient hybrid algorithms and methodologies that seamlessly integrate classical and quantum computations represents a promising research direction for achieving substantial advancements in weather forecasting and climate modeling.

8.6.2.4 QUANTUM SENSING AND OBSERVATIONS

Quantum computing can also contribute to advancements in climate observations and sensing technologies. Quantum sensors based on principles such as quantum entanglement and superposition possess the potential to enhance the measurement accuracy of various climate variables, including temperature, humidity, and greenhouse gas concentrations. The exploration of quantum sensing techniques holds the promise of yielding more accurate and comprehensive climate observations, thereby improving the quality of input data for weather forecasting and climate modeling.

8.6.3 ETHICAL CONSIDERATIONS AND POTENTIAL IMPACTS OF QUANTUM COMPUTING IN THE FIELD

As quantum computing continues to progress, it becomes essential to address the ethical considerations and potential impacts associated with its application in the domains of weather forecasting and climate modeling.

8.6.3.1 DATA PRIVACY AND SECURITY

The increased computational power of quantum computers necessitates stronger data privacy and security measures. Quantum computers have the potential to break classical encryption algorithms, thereby posing a risk to the confidentiality and integrity of sensitive weather and climate data. Researchers and practitioners must develop and adopt encryption techniques that are resistant to quantum attacks to ensure the security of weather and climate data in the era of quantum computing.

8.6.3.2 ACCESS AND EQUITY

Ensuring equitable access to quantum computing technologies for a diverse range of researchers and practitioners in the weather and climate community is of utmost importance. It is imperative to address the "quantum divide" and promote inclusive access to quantum resources, knowledge, and expertise. Collaborative partnerships among quantum computing experts, weather and climate scientists, and policymakers are essential to foster inclusivity and prevent the exacerbation of existing disparities in access to advanced computational tools.

8.6.3.3 ENVIRONMENTAL CONSIDERATIONS

The development of quantum computing technology necessitates large amounts of both computational resources and energy consumption. For this reason, it is essential to create sustainable techniques, maximize energy efficiency, and reduce the environmental impact of quantum computing infrastructure as the field advances in this area. The potential of quantum computing to contribute to sustainable solutions for reducing climate change should be investigated, and research efforts should be directed toward the creation of energy-efficient quantum hardware.

8.6.3.4 SOCIETAL IMPACTS AND DECISION-MAKING

Weather forecasting and climate modeling that make use of quantum computing could have far-reaching effects on society. Using quantum algorithms and computational models in policy and decision-making requires serious thought of their potential consequences. Responsible and well-informed decision-making requires a careful analysis of the potential biases, limitations, and uncertainties of quantum-powered weather forecasting and climate modeling.

Unlocking the full potential of quantum computing in weather forecasting and climate modeling requires a thorough examination of difficulties, potential improvements, and ethical considerations. We can pave the way for the ethical use of quantum computers by working together on research projects and encouraging cooperation across disciplines. Such efforts have the potential to completely transform weather forecasting and climate modeling, allowing for more accurate predictions, a deeper understanding of climate dynamics, and wiser choices in response to the complex issues posed by climate change.

8.7 CONCLUSION

8.7.1 SUMMARY OF THE CHAPTER'S KEY POINTS

This chapter delves into the enormous potential of quantum computing in the fields of weather prediction and climate modeling. It emphasizes the criticality of comprehending and mitigating the profound consequences of climate change. By delving into the fundamental principles that underpin quantum computing, such as quantum superposition and quantum entanglement, this chapter provides a foundational understanding of the subject matter. Furthermore, it meticulously examines various quantum computing architectures, encompassing gate-based and annealing-based approaches, elucidating their distinct attributes and potential applications.

At the center of the discussion are quantum algorithms specifically developed to enhance NWP models, surpassing the capabilities of classical methods and engendering more precise and accurate weather forecasts. These algorithms use quantum simulations to expedite forecasting processes, empowering proactive decision-making in response to weather-related events. Moreover, the chapter sheds light on the deployment of QML techniques in the analysis of weather patterns, which serve to enhance forecast accuracy and deepen our comprehension of atmospheric dynamics.

In the realm of climate modeling, quantum-inspired algorithms surmount the computational challenges faced by classical computers, thereby enabling more comprehensive and accurate simulations of intricate climate phenomena. Quantum annealing, a specific approach within quantum computing, proves particularly valuable in optimizing complex problems within climate modeling. It effectively addresses optimization challenges such as parameter tuning and model configuration optimization.

Finally, the chapter explores the application of quantum-enhanced data analysis techniques in climate data processing. These techniques facilitate faster and more efficient processing of expansive climate datasets, furnishing valuable insights and unveiling discernible patterns that inform climate modeling and prediction. In summation, this chapter illuminates the substantial potential of quantum computing in revolutionizing the fields of weather forecasting and climate modeling.

8.7.2 THE POTENTIAL OF QUANTUM COMPUTING TO REVOLUTIONIZE WEATHER FORECASTING AND CLIMATE MODELING

The transformative potential of quantum computing within the domains of weather forecasting and climate modeling cannot be overstated. Through the utilization of quantum algorithms and the computational capabilities offered by quantum computers, we can envisage a future wherein weather predictions demonstrate significantly enhanced levels of accuracy, timeliness, and reliability. The advent of quantum computing holds the promise of breakthroughs in forecast precision, empowering us to make more refined predictions concerning severe weather events and their potential consequences.

Moreover, quantum computing stands poised to revolutionize our understanding of climate dynamics and the intricate interplay among the multitude of factors influencing Earth's climatic system. The inherent capacity of quantum computers to tackle complex simulations serves as the key to deepening our understanding of climate phenomena, encompassing atmospheric circulation patterns, ocean currents, and the intricate feedback mechanisms that underlie climate change. Consequently, this heightened understanding provides a foundation for the development of more robust climate models and strengthens our ability to project future climate scenarios with greater fidelity.

Furthermore, the integration of QML techniques with weather forecasting and climate modeling opens up a plethora of opportunities. By harnessing the computational power of quantum computing and its ability to simultaneously process vast datasets, QML algorithms can unveil hidden patterns and relationships embedded within weather and climate data. This paradigm shift in data analysis holds the potential to enrich our understanding of climate processes, facilitate more accurate predictions, and enable targeted interventions aimed at climate mitigation and adaptation.

8.7.3 FINAL THOUGHTS ON THE FUTURE INTEGRATION OF QUANTUM COMPUTING IN THESE DOMAINS

As we delve into the prospects of incorporating quantum computing into the domains of weather forecasting and climate modeling, it becomes crucial to recognize and tackle the intrinsic challenges and ethical implications entwined with this progress. The discipline must confront the preexisting restrictions and hurdles encountered in the realm of quantum computing, encompassing limitations in hardware capabilities, algorithmic advancements, and seamless integration of data sources.

Advancements in quantum hardware stand as a critical prerequisite for unlocking the full potential of quantum computing in weather forecasting and climate modeling. This necessitates the development of more stable and error-tolerant qubits, prolongation of coherence times, and enhancement of qubit connectivity. Research and development endeavors should be directed toward surmounting these hardware limitations and establishing a robust quantum computing infrastructure tailored specifically to the unique requisites of weather and climate applications.

Furthermore, algorithm development within the context of quantum computing and weather/climate science must assume a position of priority. Collaborative initiatives between experts in quantum computing and specialists in meteorology and climatology assume a crucial role in designing quantum algorithms that surpass classical approaches in terms of accuracy, speed, and scalability. Exploring quantum error correction techniques assumes significance in mitigating the adverse effects of noise and errors in quantum hardware, thereby ensuring reliable and stable computations.

The integration of quantum computing in weather forecasting and climate modeling necessitates effective data handling and integration strategies. Efficient data preprocessing techniques, data encoding strategies, and interoperability solutions need to be developed to seamlessly bridge the gap between classical and quantum computing approaches. This integration will allow for the utilization of existing weather and climate modeling frameworks and infrastructure while using the computational power of quantum algorithms.

Ethical considerations surrounding data privacy and security must also be carefully addressed. Quantum computing's potential to break classical encryption algorithms poses risks to the confidentiality and integrity of weather and climate data. It is imperative to develop quantum-resistant encryption techniques and implement robust data privacy and security measures to safeguard sensitive information.

Looking ahead, collaboration between quantum scientists, weather and climate experts, and policymakers is vital for shaping the future integration of quantum computing in these domains. The multidisciplinary nature of this endeavor calls for joint efforts to ensure the responsible and ethical deployment of quantum computing technology. By addressing these challenges, embracing potential advancements, and considering the ethical implications, quantum computing can truly revolutionize weather forecasting and climate modeling, enabling accurate predictions, informed decision-making, and sustainable solutions to mitigate the challenges of climate change.

KEYWORDS

- **quantum computation**
- **numerical weather prediction**
- **climate modeling**
- **qubit**
- **quantum sensors**

REFERENCES

1. Educative. Intro to quantum computing: Qubits, superposition, & more. *Educative*. https://www.educative.io/blog/intro-to-quantum-computing.
2. Collins, S. N., James, R. S., Ray, P., Chen, K., Angie, L., & Brownlee, J. (2013). *Grids in Numerical Weather and Climate Models*. In InTech eBooks. https://doi.org/10.5772/55922.
3. Alizadeh, O. (2022). Advances and challenges in climate modeling. *Climatic Change*, *170*(1–2), 18. https://doi.org/10.1007/s10584-021-03298-4.
4. Ezratty, O. (2023). Understanding quantum technologies. *arXiv.org*. https://arxiv.org/abs/2111.15352.
5. Rajak, A., Suzuki, S., Dutta, A., & Chakrabarti, B. K. (2022). Quantum annealing: An overview. *Philosophical Transactions of the Royal Society A*, *381*(2241). https://doi.org/10.1098/rsta.2021.0417.
6. Tennie, F., & Palmer, T. N. (2023). Quantum computers for weather and climate prediction: The good, the bad, and the noisy. *Bulletin of the American Meteorological Society*, *104*(2), E488–E500. https://doi.org/10.1175/bams-d-22-0031.1.
7. Bochenek, B., & Ustrnul, Z. (2022). Machine learning in weather prediction and climate analyses—applications and perspectives. *Atmosphere*, *13*(2), 180. https://doi.org/10.3390/atmos13020180.
8. Paudel, H. P., Syamlal, M., Crawford, S. E., Lee, Y., Shugayev, R., Lü, P., Ohodnicki, P. R., Mollot, D., & Duan, Y. (2022). Quantum computing and simulations for energy applications: Review and perspective. *ACS Engineering Au*, *2*(3), 151–196. https://doi.org/10.1021/acsengineeringau.1c00033.
9. Liu, D., Jiang, M., Yang, X., & Li, H. (2016). Analyzing documents with quantum clustering: A novel pattern recognition algorithm based on quantum mechanics. *Pattern Recognition Letters*, *77*, 8–13. https://doi.org/10.1016/j.patrec.2016.03.008.

CHAPTER 9

A Review of Quantum-Inspired Genetic Algorithms

RUPALI MITRA[1], TAMAL CHAKRABORTY[1*], and ROMIT S. BEED[2]

[1]*Department of Computer Science, Mrinalini Datta Mahavidyapith, Kolkata, West Bengal, India*

[2]*Department of Computer Science, St. Xavier's College (Autonomous), Kolkata, West Bengal, India*

*Corresponding author

ABSTRACT

By violating the extended Church-Turing thesis, the quantum computing (QC) paradigm has emerged as a serious contender to classical computing. We now know that certain classical exponential problems (NP (nondeterministic polynomial time)-complete) can be solved in polynomial time by QC. Shor's integer factorization and Grover's method for unstructured search are perhaps the most well-known quantum algorithms. QC has been successfully applied to a variety of domains including optimization problems. Optimization can be solved by using deterministic/numerical as well as stochastic methods. Genetic algorithms (GA) belong to the latter category. Incorporating quantum mechanical properties such as superposition, entanglement, interference into the structure of GA has resulted in a more efficient evolutionary computing method called the quantum-inspired genetic algorithm. This method has been successfully applied to image processing, signal processing, economic load dispatch, coalition formation, task scheduling, etc. This chapter presents an overview of the current trends and developments in the domain of quantum-inspired genetic algorithms with the aim of investigating areas of further research in this sphere.

Applications of Quantum Computing in a Variety of Domains. Gunjan Mukherjee, Biswadip Basu Mallik, Rahul Kar Özen ÖZER, Digvijay Pandey, and Binay Kumar Pandey (Eds.)

DOI: 10.1201/9781998511051-9

9.1 INTRODUCTION

Computer science is heavily intertwined with the disciplines of physics and mathematics. While the components of the actual computing machinery obey the laws of physics, the design and complexity analysis of algorithms are exercises in mathematics and logic. As our understanding of the world around us changes, new physical and mathematical theories are born, which spawn developments in the computing discipline as well. Computer hardware obey the laws of "classical" physics representing information using "classical" bits (0 or 1) and processing them by "classical" logic gates. Quantum mechanics entered the scene in the 1900s to explain phenomena such as black-body radiation that could not be satisfactorily explained by classical physics. It revolutionized the world of physics. We now know that most theories of classical physics can be derived from quantum mechanics. Computers are no longer considered classical devices! The reason why a lot of research effort is being devoted to quantum computing (QC) is not just because it promises to deliver faster computers but (also) because it has given the field of computer science a new computing model, one that violates the extended Church-Turing thesis by being able to solve certain classically exponential problems (e.g., integer factorization) in polynomial time. Thus, this field has something to offer to all: physicists, mathematicians, and computer scientists!

The remainder of the chapter is structured as follows: Section 9.2 introduces fundamental QC concepts, Section 9.3 presents the quantum-inspired genetic algorithm, Section 9.4 covers early research in this field, and Section 9.5 explores diverse application areas. Section 9.6 includes the conclusion and outlines potential directions for future research.

9.2 QUANTUM COMPUTING

Some rudimentary concepts of QC are presented below to aid in understanding quantum-inspired genetic algorithms.

9.2.1 QUANTUM SUPERPOSITION

A classical bit can only exist in one of the two Boolean *logic* states: 0 or 1. Let us denote these two logic states using the notation $|0>$ and $|1>$, to discriminate them from the numeric values 0 and 1. The classical bit C can then be expressed as $C = a|0> + b|1>$, where coefficients $a, b \in \{0, 1\}$ and $a \neq b$. If $a = 1$ and $b = 0$, C is in logic state $|0>$, and if $a = 0$ and $b = 1$, then our classical bit C is in logic state $|1>$. In contrast, a quantum bit (qubit in short) is not purely digital. It has analog properties to it enabling it to exist in *both* the *energy* states $|0>$ and $|1>$ at the same time, a phenomenon termed "quantum superposition." Qubit $Q = a|0> + b|1>$, where the coefficients a and b are complex numbers and must obey the normalization condition: $|a|^2 + |b|^2 = 1$. The quantities $|a|^2$ and $|b|^2$ represent the probability of finding Q in the state $|0>$ and state$|1>$, respectively; hence, they are aptly called probability amplitudes. Since the probability of an event cannot exceed 1; hence, the constraint $|a|^2 + |b^2 = 1$. Both a and b are complex quantities containing real subparts; hence, they can assume infinitely many values between 0 and 1. For example, $Q = 1/2\ |0> + \sqrt{3}/\sqrt{2}\ |1>$. A measurement of Q in this case may result in 0 with 25% probability and 1 with 75% probability, but there is no way to know which state will occur before actual measurement takes place. Hence, before measurement, a qubit behaves like a wave existing in all possible energy states at the same time. It is only when its value is observed, that the wave function collapses to one of the allowed energy states (called eigenstates) with a probability given by modulus squared of the corresponding complex coefficient (called eigenvalue). The reader may identify that the classical bit is just a special case of the quantum bit with $a = 1$, $b = 0$ or $a = 0$, $b = 1$.

9.2.2 QUANTUM PARALLELISM

n classical bits can represent any one of the 2^n possible combinations of binary values, whereas n qubits can represent (before measurement) *all* the 2^n values simultaneously. This parallelism is what makes QC powerful. It implies that a single quantum register (of n qubits) is all that is required to store all input values simultaneously. Furthermore, to compute the value of a function on all the 2^n classical input bits, we would have to call the function as many times. However, in the quantum world, since all inputs coexist simultaneously, a single call to the desired function computes all 2^n output values simultaneously! But be warned, that this superposition of all the 2^n output values exist before measurement. The moment the output qubit is measured, it collapses to reveal just one answer (that is we fall back to the classical world). This shows us the constraints of QC. Quantum algorithm design is, hence, more challenging than classical algorithm design. Designers use several techniques such as interference, amplitude amplification to extract relevant result from the superposed outputs. We now proceed to see how QC principles have been injected into the classical genetic algorithm framework to yield a new optimization algorithm.

9.3 QUANTUM-INSPIRED GENETIC/EVOLUTIONARY ALGORITHM (QGA/QEA)

Quantum-inspired genetic algorithms (henceforth QGA/QEA) introduced in [12] and formalized by Han and Kim [4] are not pure quantum algorithms. Instead, they are an amalgamation of the quantum mechanical principles such as superposition, interference, entanglement, with conventional genetic algorithms (henceforth CGA) and are meant to be run on classical computers. In QGA, chromosomes are encoded by qubits, and evolution is done through quantum logic gates such as rotation. QEA has been found by researchers to outperform CGA on the grounds of accuracy, population diversity, faster convergence, greater exploration, and exploitation capacity, and has been applied to areas such as image processing, network optimization, task scheduling, engineering design optimization, machine learning, among others.

CGA encodes potential solutions by means of classical bits. QEA too works with a population of several chromosomes (say n) each encoded via (say) m number of qubits. A qubit may be written as a column vector of its probability amplitudes: $q = [a\ b]^T$. So, a chromosome comprising m qubits has m column vectors and may be represented by the following matrix:

$$\mathrm{c} = \begin{bmatrix} a_1 & a_2 & . & . & a_m \\ b_1 & b_2 & . & . & b_m \end{bmatrix} \tag{9.1}$$

A chromosome can be understood as a quantum register with a size of m, capable of storing all 2^m combinations simultaneously until a measurement is performed. On observation, we obtain only one of the 2^m values. A population of n chromosomes will then be $P = c_1, c_2, c_3,\ldots, c_n$, where c_i (i = 1 to n) has the form shown in expression 9.1. Algorithm 9.1 outlines QEA.

ALGORITHM 9.1 Basic flow of QEA [4]

1. *Set generation counter t=0*
2. *Q(t) = initialize the starting generation of quantum chromosomes*
3. *P(t) = measure out Q(t)*
4. *Apply fitness function to P(t)*
5. *B = fittest chromosome of P(t)*
6. *while (termination criterion not satisfied) do*
7. *t = t + 1*
8. *P(t) = measure out Q(t − 1)*
9. *Apply fitness function to P(t)*
10. *Q(t) = update Q(t − 1) by applying suitable quantum gates using P(t) and B as guide*
11. *b(t) = fittest chromosome of P(t)*
12. *if (b(t) > B)*
13. *B = b(t)*
14. *end if*
15. *end while*
16. *Output B as the result.*

- Explanation of Algorithm 9.1:

After setting the generation counter in Step 1, the initial quantum population is built in Step 2 by configuring all the qubits of a chromosome with an equal probability of being in the $|0\rangle$ or $|1\rangle$ state. The quantum Hadamard gate is used for this purpose to set all the *a*'s and *b*'s to $1/\sqrt{2}$. Thus, every chromosome ends up looking like:

$$c_i = \begin{bmatrix} \frac{1}{\sqrt{2}} & \frac{1}{\sqrt{2}} & \cdot\cdot & \frac{1}{\sqrt{2}} \\ \frac{1}{\sqrt{2}} & \frac{1}{\sqrt{2}} & \cdot\cdot & \frac{1}{\sqrt{2}} \end{bmatrix}$$

Although all qubits look identical now, upon measurement each collapses to any one of the 2^m values with no way of predicting what that value will be. Hence, randomness is inherent. Alternatively, the qubits may also be initialized with problem-specific values if such information is available. Step 3 produces the classical populace from the quantum population by measuring them out. Since measuring destroys the quantum system which is something we do not want, this step may be simulated by generating a random number between 0 and 1. If this random number is greater than the probability amplitude of the state $|0>$ of the qubit of a chromosome, then the measured value is taken to be classical value 1 else 0 (Algorithm 9.2). This step performed on all the $m \times n$ qubits of the population transforms it into the classical population.

ALGORITHM 9.2 Simulating the measurement process of qubits [4]

```
Set i = 0
while (i < m) do                    //m is no. of qubits in a chromosome
    i = i+1
    if (random [0, 1) > |a_i|^2)    // |a_i|^2 is the probability amplitude of state |0>
        x_i = 1                     //corresponding classical bit is 1
    else
        x_i = 0                     //else classical bit is 0
    end if
end while
```

In Steps 4 and 5, the fitness function is applied to the classical population $P(t)$, and the fittest individual is noted in B. Unlike CGA, the fittest individual of QEA acts as the pilot in the search for the optimum. The evolutionary cycle begins from the while loop of Step 6 and continues until the desired stopping criteria are reached. Generation count and acceptable error rate are the customary termination conditions, although others may be designed as well. Step 7 increases the generation counter and Steps 8 and 9 are the same as 3 and 4, respectively. Step 10 involves updating (evolving) the older ($t-1$st) quantum generation to produce the next generation of qubits using problem-specific rotation gates [4]. Quantum rotation gate is a unitary operation with the following matrix representation:

$$U(\theta)=\begin{bmatrix} \cos\theta & -\sin\theta \\ \sin\theta & \cos\theta \end{bmatrix}$$

where Θ is the angle of rotation.

Multiplying $U(\Theta)$ with qubit $q = [a\ b]^T$ produces a new qubit $q' = [a'\ b']^T$. So "evolving" a chromosome involves rotating the constituent qubits through a certain angle Θ in a certain direction. Θ may be some problem-dependent value (e.g., 0.01π or 0.05π or 0.025π) [4, 5], and the sign (direction) of rotation is either positive, negative, or zero [20]. The quantity and direction of rotation must be individually determined for each qubit of every chromosome. Han and Kim [4] suggested a lookup table (Table 9.1) for this purpose based on the following strategy: let "q" denote an arbitrary quantum chromosome with constituent qubits "q_i" ($i =$

1 to m) which on measurement collapses to the classical chromosome "x" with constituent bits "x_i" ($i = 1$ to m). The fitness function $f()$ is applied to all x's and the resulting values are compared with the best individual B in order to determine how the qubit must be rotated to obtain a revised qubit for the next generation.

If $f(x^t) \geq f(B)$, that is, if an individual x of generation t is better than the currently known best solution B, then we must *encourage the mother/source qubit of x to develop.* A bitwise comparison is done between x and B, and whenever the constituent bits $x_i \neq B_i$ ($i = 1$ to m), we modify the corresponding qubit q_i to enhance the chances of occurrence of state x_i. For instance, if x_i is 0 (1) but B_i is 1 (0), then we rotate q_i such that the likelihood of q_i to collapse to state |0> (|1>) is strengthened. Conversely, if $f(x^t) < f(B)$, then we push the mother/source qubit of x to veer toward B. Thus, whenever $x_i \neq B_i$ ($i = 1$ to m) on a bitwise comparison, we rotate q_i to come closer to B_i. So, if x_i is 0 (1) but B_i is 1 (0), then we rotate q_i such that the likelihood to collapse to state |1> (|0>) is boosted. In both cases, the apt value and direction of Θ are obtained from the lookup table.

TABLE 9.1 Lookup Table for Determining the Angle of Rotation [4]

State of the *i*th Qubit of the Current Solution	State of the *i*th Qubit of the Best Solution	Current Solution Better?	Change in Angle of Rotation	Comments
0	0	False	θ_1	go toward state |0> of current best solution
0	0	True	θ_2	encourage state |0> of qubit q_i
0	1	False	θ_3	go toward state |1> of current best solution
0	1	True	θ_4	encourage state |0> of qubit q_i
1	0	False	θ_5	go toward state |0> of current best solution
1	0	True	θ_6	encourage state |0> of qubit q_i
1	1	False	θ_7	go toward state |1> of current best solution
1	1	True	θ_8	encourage state |0> of qubit q_i

The specific values of $\Delta\theta_i$ are problem dependent. For example, in the knapsack problem implemented in [5], $\Delta\theta_3 = 0.01\pi$ and $\Delta\theta_5 = -0.01\pi$, while all other $\Delta\theta_i$ are zero. Usually, a small amount of rotation is given at a time to avoid reaching a local optimum [4, 5]. The positive or negative sign is an indication of the direction in which the desired state may be found. A qubit in the first (third) quadrant must be given a positive push to reach state |1>, whereas a qubit in the second (fourth) quadrant must be pulled in the negative direction to reach |1>. In Steps 11–14, the optimal solution of the current generation is determined. If it surpasses the current optimal solution, it becomes the new candidate B. This is an elitist strategy, but alternatives are possible. The process then returns to the while loop of Step 6.

9.4 FOUNDATIONAL WORKS

This section describes the major introductory works that spawned and subsequently refined the quantum-inspired genetic optimization technique.

Moore and Narayanan [10] discussed the potentiality of *quantum-inspired computing methods* in solving nondeterministic polynomial time (NP)-hard problems on classical computers. These methods fuse ideas from quantum mechanics with classical algorithms to create potential solutions for NP-hard problems. Subsequently, a classical algorithm verifies the solutions' accuracy. They provided recommendations for designing such methods, namely, breaking problems into parallelizable subproblems, where interactions among subsolutions could either result in problem resolution or redirection of the search.

Narayanan and Moore [12] blended CGA with QC principles and applied it to solve the NP-hard travelling salesman problem (TSP). For an n-city TSP, n parallel computation nodes, termed "universes" in their work, are employed. Each node runs a local copy of CGA with consistent evolutionary generations. After completing one evolutionary cycle, all stations interact with each other (*interactive decoherence* in quantum parlance). The interaction occurs via a process known as "global cross-over," which entails an additional crossover step following the completion of local crossovers at each node. Chromosome i in one universe engages in crossovers with identical-index chromosomes in the other $n-1$ universes, yielding a fresh chromosome. Thus, all chromosomes with the same index i contribute one gene each to make a new chromosome:

Gene-1 from chromosome i of node 1.

Gene-2 from chromosome i of node 2.

Gene-m from chromosome i of node n.

Global crossover generates *n* new chromosomes, one for each universe. But what is the significance of this global crossover step? After a certain number of generations, uniform outcomes emerge from each universe (akin to quantum mechanics' standing waves), rendering further computation redundant. This uniform result represents the output (the solution of TSP). For NP-complete problems, it is often more efficient to validate a solution than to generate one. This work's primary innovation lies in utilizing quantum mechanical phenomena, such as superposition, interference, and standing waves, to create potential solutions for given NP-complete problems. These solutions can subsequently be examined for accuracy using classical algorithms.

Han and Kim [4] proposed the formal structure of QEA and implemented it on the 0/1 knapsack problem. Qubits were used to encode the *n* items of the knapsack, where $|a|^2$ and $|b|^2$, respectively, represented the probability of the *i*th item being excluded from or included in the knapsack. The rotation gate was used to evolve the next generation. The angle and direction of rotation were prescribed by a lookup table. Crossover and mutation were discouraged. They experimentally demonstrated that QEA gave better mean profits than the CGA, the latter suffering from premature convergence. They extended their work in [5, 6] by proposing the following new components:

- *Migration* process to achieve diversity: Qubit population was sectioned into groups to allow parallel exploration in separate pockets of the search area. Each group recorded its best individual which acted as its local attractor in the next cycle. Thus, each group had its own search trajectory. After every iteration, the condition for *global migration* was tested. If found to be met, the fittest among all local attractors was designated as the global attractor. Akin to an emperor among the kings! At this point, all groups though divided reached an overall harmony. Each group would then make local copies of the global attractor to follow and locally update in the usual manner in subsequent cycles. However, if the requirement of global migration was not met, groups would make a local tally of their attractors.
- A new termination criterion based on the average convergence of qubits to the best solution was introduced to replace the customary maximum number of generations. The authors argued that the extent to which qubits have approached 0 or 1 is a better gauge of

the status of the processing; hence, using it to stop further iterations makes more sense.

- A modified rotation gate $H\epsilon$ (with $0 < \epsilon << 1$) was used to prevent qubits from hitting a 0 or 1 because once that happens, there is no way the qubit can be altered any further except by migration. A small value close to 0 termed ϵ was used as a buffer and qubits could only reach as low as ϵ or as high as $(1 - \epsilon)$. This approach was advocated for problems with several local optima points.
- The authors also established experimentally that providing domain-specific initial values to qubits led to better convergence speed and robustness than initialization with the uniform value of $[1/\sqrt{2}, 1/\sqrt{2}]$.
- Han and Kim [6] also demonstrated the suitability of QEA to numerical optimization problems besides combinatorial ones.

Tweaking just one step of the basic QEA, Platel et al. [15] reported improved performance in terms of speed and precision across various benchmark challenges. It may be recalled from the basic flow of QEA that the attractor or the global best solution is updated only when a superior answer is found in some subsequent evolutionary cohort. In versatile quantum-inspired evolutionary algorithm (vQEA) [15], the best solution of the previous generation becomes the attractor of the next cycle irrespective of whether it is better than the previous attractor. This removal of elitism presented itself as highly fluctuating rotation angles and unsettled behavior of the qubits across generations as in every cycle there was a new leader to follow! Eventually though, the chaos produced superior results for the 0/1 Knapsack problem with 500 generations when compared to QEA. In fact, by the 100th generation, vQEA had already outperformed QEA in terms of the best average profit measure. The authors argue that this strategy prevents the transgenerational impact of suboptimal global attractors. They also add that if disruptive operators are not used, then there is no added benefit of using elitism.

Platel [8] corroborate QEA as belonging to the class of Estimation of Distribution Algorithms (EDA) through rigorous theory and comprehensive experiments. Both the commonalities and the distinctiveness of QEA are discussed with respect to different classes of EDA, on aspects such as the probabilistic model, selection procedure, learning rules, and population constitution. Categorically, QEA shares characteristics with members of the first class of EDA (containing population-based incremental learning, common genetic algorithm) because it encodes variables as independent vectors of probabilities namely qubits. However, the qubits are also capable of dealing with each other in complex ways namely, at the individual level, at the level of small qubit groups, and lastly at the global population level. This upgrades the performance of QEA closer to higher classes of EDA (e.g., the univariate marginal distribution algorithm). In other words, even though qubits are updated independently of each other, their complex dealings at varying levels help explore and exploit the search space more efficiently when compared to simple EDA methods. Hence, QEA ranks somewhere between the basic and the advanced categories of EDAs. The selection procedure of QEA was evidenced as "steady-state" because chromosomes of different generations compete for survival. The learning rule was shown to be conditional or asymmetric because a qubit is rotated/updated only if a better solution is found. The population structure is complex because chromosomes may be treated individually, as a locally synchronized group, or as a globally synchronized population. Experiments found QEA to: be linearly scalable with problem size, have a greater ability to maintain convergence despite variability in fitness measurements, have a dynamic learning rate that moves from fast to slow as convergence approaches, and be relatively reliable in terms of finding high-quality solutions across different runs when contrasted with other EDAs. The chapter suggests conducting trials where variable interactions may be directly managed to gain further insights into the EDA nature of QEA.

The basic version of QEA did not comprise mutation and crossover. Procedure quantum crossover-based quantum genetic algorithm (QXQGA) in [9] studied the effect of exercising crossovers and mutation operators on various high-dimensional, nonlinear benchmark optimization functions. Four different crossover methods were combined with two mutation variants and results were compared with those of basic QEA. Comparing the relative percentage deviation between the best and mean results, it was determined that QXQGA outperformed QEA. The top-performing combination was a two-point crossover with quantum inversion mutation, followed by quantum interference crossover with quantum inversion.

Wang et al. [20] proposed an alternative method to calculate the direction and magnitude of rotation of qubits sans lookup table. The direction of Θ was assessed using the determinant value of the angles of the best and the current individuals. The methodology to determine the angle of rotation was modified to include the generation count, maximum number of generations, and the maximum and minimum rotation angles. This resulted in large rotations in the initial generations and smaller rotations toward the end of the evolutionary course. Experiments found that this strategy brought faster convergence to the optimal. A quantum NOT gate was employed for mutation that swapped the probabilities of 0 and 1. This contrasts with the basic QEA [4] where mutation was not implemented.

9.5 APPLICATION AREAS

Due to its merits of diversity, better exploration and exploitation ability, faster convergence, ability to handle large search spaces, and improved results, QEA/QGA is increasingly being employed in myriad problem domains. This section delves into some applications of QEA/QGA.

Durán [2] reviewed several quantum-inspired metaheuristic methods such as quantum-inspired particle swarm optimization, QGA, quantum flip–flop to ascertain the most promising candidate in the area of Internet of Things (IoT)-based data communication and processing. They combined QGA with IoT and wireless communication protocol (LoRa) to set up a robust and reliable data transmission network for implementing a Ventilation-on-Demand system inside underground mining tunnels where the timely availability of dependable information is crucial to ensure worker safety and reduce energy costs. Also, underground tunnels present communication challenges such as signal attenuation due to rocks and signal loss around corners. An IoT network of sensors was configured inside the tunnels. Once an object (person/vehicle) was detected, QGA was employed to find the best-placed sensors around it so that real-time data on air flow, air quality, and other relevant parameters may be collected. By optimizing the separation distance between the sensors and the object of interest, it became possible to enhance the quality of communication in the noisy and dynamic environment found in mining tunnels. Experimental results found QGA performing faster than GA besides producing values that closely approximated the true optimum. The chapter demonstrates the workability of QGA in the IoT and communication domain recommending further investigations into which sensor parameters are compatible with the sensor framework. The chapter also reports that data cleaning was required before QGA could be applied.

Pai et al. [13] applied QGA to calculate the optimal binary threshold value of noisy and natural satellite images. Four different fitness functions for threshold calculation, namely, Otsu, Kapur, Tsalis, and gray level co-occurrence matrix (GLCM) were optimized using both QGA and DE (differential evolution) metaheuristics. Ten times quicker outcomes were reported by the QGA-boosted GLCM method over others. The setup found all QGA variants to have good population diversity and be better suited for noisy images.

Abdulhussien et al. [1] used QGA along with a support vector machine (SVM) to develop an offline system that corroborated Arabic signatures. First, a number of relevant features were extricated from the input signature samples. Thereafter, QGA was applied as a wrapper method to select an optimal subset of such features. Qubits were used to encode the feature subsets and the fitness of a quantum chromosome was equal to the accuracy level achieved by the SVM for that subset. Selection of an appropriate set of features is crucial because it influences the biometric systems' equal error rate (EER). The authors favored QGA over GA because of population diversity and proficient exploration and exploitation ability even with a small populace. As per the results of *p*-value testing of their experiments, the authors established that QGA outperformed GA for every sample database. Interestingly, with as low as three genes, QGA gave better average fitness than GA with ten individuals. Encouragingly, other known techniques of feature selection and classification were bettered upon by the suggested QGA-based approach as captured by the EER value of the experiments.

Mousavi et al. [11] used QGA for coalition formation in a distributed fashion by multiple unmanned aerial vehicles (UAVs) in a large-scale heterogenous dynamic network with constraints. Establishing an alliance between agents with diverse capabilities for solving multiple tasks is needed in various scenarios such as disaster management, search and rescue, military. A multiobjective fitness function that curtailed resource spending and capitalized on the reliability and trustworthiness of nodes was optimized by QGA, and results were compared with other commonly used alliance-forming strategies such as distance-based, merge-and-split, Nondominated Sorting Genetic Algorithm (NSGA). It was found that with QGA, the number of tasks successfully finished was higher than others besides fewer resource violations.

Closer in lines with the problem of forming favorable coalitions of multiple agents (e.g., robots, UAVs) is the problem of selecting appropriate partners for establishing a virtual enterprise (VE). A VE is an alliance between companies to execute a large-scale project that might be beyond the capacity of a single company alone. Each project is subdivided into several interdependent subprojects each bearing a certain cost and time to complete. The partner selection problem (PSP) is about finding the best combination of partners from a pool in a way that reduces overall cost and satisfies timing deadlines. Tao [3] introduced a novel combination of QGA and multiagent systems to solve PSP. A unique nested structure was used to represent partnerships. A multiagent grid was constructed as a collection of Quantum Agents (QAgents), and each QAgent was itself represented as a 2D matrix-like structure. Each QAgent competed to survive and reproduce against a certain number of neighboring QAgents, based on the value of a figure called Environment Apperceive Coefficient (EAC). Interestingly, the algorithm proposes dynamic adjusting of EAC to regulate the exploration and exploitation trade-off, influencing how QAgents interact and search for solutions within their local vicinity. Experimental results were compared with GA and the proposed method was found to need a lesser number of cycles to hit the optimum. Also, with an increase in the number of subprojects, it fared well by not showing an exponential rise in execution time, that is, the scalability was satisfactory. Further studies may be conducted to assess the impact of varying EAC on the solution quality. Comparison with other established methods in PSP and on benchmark problems is desirable.

Sha et al. [17] apply QGA to investment decision optimization in the power grid sector in the presence of new and evolving scenarios such as state regulations, technological advancements, and other dynamics. The chapter highlights how the existing literature fails to address the interplay between investment capacity and demand and considers only external drivers for optimizing investments. To obtain a more comprehensive and accurate view of a company's investment situation, the chapter links together the financial capability and the requirements of new and continued investments in an improved mathematical model that dynamically balances the volume of investment the company can make for efficiency and sustainability. QGA applied to the suggested model produced the lowest amount of error when compared to other popular techniques such as GA and particle swarm optimization (PSO). There is further scope for potentially applying QGA in two more substeps of the grid investment demand forecasting process: in the prediction of future values of the influencing factors of grid investment demand, and in relationship-fitting between the investment demand index and the actual investment demand.

Encouraged by the promising results obtained from harnessing QGA as a metaheuristic in assorted domains, Saad et al. [16] tailored QGA to tackle the NP-hard problem of resource-constrained project-scheduling, the traditional methods for which struggled to handle larger instances efficiently. Keeping the overall QGA structure the same, a local search method was injected to improve exploration. Different parametric variations in the initialization step, crossover methods, population size, rotation angle, and mutation rates were carried out on benchmark problems, and their effects on execution time and mean deviation from true value were recorded. The authors found that QGA performed better than GA and certain hybrid variants of GA. However, it was bettered by the Consolidated Optimization Algorithm. The authors opine that although QGA did not stand out as the definitive best performer in their experiments, it still introduced new avenues. These include the potential to combine QGA with other metaheuristic methods or to apply quantum-inspired principles more broadly to emerging metaheuristic theories.

Moving beyond the two-level quantum system, Tkachuk et al. [18] proposed the three-valued quantum logic (called qutrits) based method QGA_3. Qutrits composed of three basis states were used to represent members of the population. Observing qutrits produces a base-3 number in the classical domain. Instead of using the lookup table, qutrits are evolved by multiplying them with an experimentally ascertained value μ ($0 \leq \mu \leq 1$), which increased one of the three probability amplitudes while suppressing the other two. The value of μ is pivotal since it dictates the equilibrium between the broader exploration of potential solutions and a more focused search. To escape local optima, especially for problems with a large number of input variables, the *Quantum disaster* operation was applied by reinitializing certain qutrits, excluding the best one. Experiments on several benchmark problems found QGA_3 to converge faster and better than the original QEA. The work was extended to n-valued logic called qudits in [19]. The proposed system was found to be suitable for numerical optimization functions that have large and challenging terrains, such as multiple local optimums surrounding one global optimum.

The Quadratic Knapsack Problem (QKP) is an exceptionally challenging NP-hard problem. No parallel algorithm exists to solve it. Since QEA is naturally suited to parallel processing, Patvardhan et al. [14] propositioned a parallel architecture of QEA (IQIEAP) suitable for execution on multiple processors and capable of handling instances of 1000 and 2000 binary variables. Portions of QEA were identified that could be run as concurrent threads on different qubit clusters such as initialization, local searching, and local evolution. Several strategies were used throughout to boost the algorithm performance such as use of greedy heuristics to make an initial choice of items for the knapsack, parallel exploration of multiple subspaces within the solution space through qubit clusters, independent evolution of qubit cluster, especially designed local search performed parallelly in the vicinity of local best solution of a cluster, probabilistic elimination of underperforming individuals, reinitialization of qubits for diversity. The parallel arrangement gave a slightly better answer but 9.4 times the speed of the serial version for QKP, besides demonstrating competitiveness with contemporary methods such as Greedy Randomized Adaptive Search Procedure (GRASP) and Tabu search. The primary conclusion is that QEA can be effectively parallelized for addressing complex high-dimensional problems (Table 9.2).

9.6 FUTURE SCOPE AND CONCLUSION

This chapter primarily serves as a foundational introduction to QGA, a novel metaheuristic optimization method that integrates quantum mechanical principles into the framework of GA for classical computers. This fusion offers a fresh perspective on problem solving, especially for NP-hard problems. The early/foundational works addressed here laid the groundwork of this field by outlining its basic structure, performing parametric analysis, introducing new operators, and testing its applicability to combinatorial and numerical optimization functions. These works established the mettle of QGA. Empirically, QGA has demonstrated better global and local search capability, more population diversity, faster convergence, higher quality solutions, robustness, and scalability to complex and bigger problem sizes. This attracted researchers to apply QGA to various domains, a few of which are

TABLE 9.2 Main Features of Different Works Reviewed Here

Paper Reference	Problem Domain	Key Features	Quantum Operators	Performance Metrics
[10]	Factorizing a number, numerical sorting, 15-puzzle.	Fresh computational approach inspired by quantum mechanical principles. Guidelines to design such methods.	Interference (information exchange) between subsolutions.	Quantum-inspired methods require fewer evaluations and lesser execution time than classical methods.
[12]	TSP.	Blended QC with CGA. Recognized potential for parallel processing in quantum-inspired evolutionary methods.	Interference crossover.	Average generations required to reach optimum notably decreased.
[4]	Knapsack problem.	Formal structure of QEA. Qubit encoding of optimization variables. Lookup table for sign and direction of rotation.	Quantum rotation gate for evolution. But no mutation or crossover.	Better than CGA even with a small population. Faster convergence than CGA.
[4]	Knapsack problem.	Concept of a locally synchronized group of qubits. Global and local migration of best solution between qubit groups for diversity. Termination norm based on probability of best solution rather than maximum number of generations.	Quantum rotation gate.	Both the average profit and best profit delivered by QEA better than CGA for all input samples. Good result even with just one individual.
[4]	Knapsack problem, Sphere, Ackley, Griewank, Rastrigin, Schwefel, and Rosenbrock functions.	New finishing criteria based on average convergence of qubits. Modified rotation gate to mitigate premature convergence. Problem-specific initialization of qubits for better and faster results.	Modified rotation gate $H\epsilon$. Global and local migration conditions.	Better results than Classical Evolutionary Programming for numerical optimization problems. Improved speed, profit, and robustness.

TABLE 9.2 *(Continued)*

Paper Reference	Problem Domain	Key Features	Quantum Operators	Performance Metrics
[15]	0/1 Knapsack, One-Max, NK-landscapes.	Switch off elitism to counter impact of bad attractors. Every generation has a new best attractor.	Advise against the use of crossover and mutation.	Average profit obtained better than both elitist QEA and CGA. Scalable to higher values of N in NK-landscapes.
[8]	NK-landscapes.	Establish QEA as a type of EDA. Performance in between basic and higher classes of EDA. Potential to model complex interacting variables.	No crossover or mutation used.	vQEA linearly scalable with problem size. Lowest variance in quality of best solution compared to other EDAs.
[9]	DeJong (Sphere), Rosenbrock, Rastrigin, and Griewangk functions.	Studied the effect of incorporating crossover and mutation in basic QEA. Approach better suited to high-dimensional nonlinear problems.	Single-point, two-point, multipoint, and quantum interference crossover operators. Quantum inversion mutation and left and right quantum swap mutation operator.	Average value and standard deviation of the best answer better than basic QEA that had no crossover and mutation.
[20]	Elaborate two-variable maximization function.	New method for ascertaining direction of rotation of qubits sans lookup table. The rotation angle shifts as generations progress. Quantum disaster operation to escape local optima. Crossover discouraged.	Quantum NOT gate for mutation.	Shorter time to convergence than basic QEA.
[2]	IoT-based Ventilation-on-Demand system for underground mines.	Demonstrates real industrial application of QGA. Finds optimum placement of sensors close to the object of interest. Effort to map various sensor-related parameters and metrics to input variables of QGA.	Quantum rotation gate.	Greater robustness achieved in telecommunication over conventional methods. Higher fitness, shorter execution span, and better accuracy compared to CGA.

TABLE 9.2 *(Continued)*

Paper Reference	Problem Domain	Key Features	Quantum Operators	Performance Metrics
[13]	Determine the optimum binary threshold for segmentation of noisy, black, and white satellite images.	QGA boosted spatial context aware objective function for image segmentation. Suitability to noisy/satellite images. Good population diversity, searching competence.	Crossover, mutation, rotation.	Ten times faster than histogram-based criteria optimized by DE.
[1]	Offline Arabic signature verification system.	QGA used for the feature selection step of SVM-based forged-signature classifier.	Crossover, mutation, rotation.	Faster and more accurate than CGA on benchmark databases as per *p*-value testing. Superior false rejection rate, false acceptance rate, and EER metrics.
[11]	Group establishment in big, heterogeneous UAV networks working in unknown environments.	Novel objective function. Group member selection optimized by QGA.	Quantum rotation gate.	Lower cost, enhanced trustworthiness, greater task completion, and fewer resource violations compared to regular ways of team construction such as NSGA-II and distance-dependent methods.
[3]	Selecting the most profitable partners to set up VE.	Unique 2D grid-like representation of quantum chromosomes. Condition-based multiple evolutionary strategies to avoid suboptimal convergence. Solutions compete to survive within the local community. Community size adaptive.	Crossover, mutation, competition, energy evaluation.	Lesser iterations with fewer individuals needed compared to CGA. Does not exhibit exponential growth with increasing problem size.

TABLE 9.2 *(Continued)*

Paper Reference	Problem Domain	Key Features	Quantum Operators	Performance Metrics
[16]	Resource-limited project scheduling with multiple activities.	Thorough experimental study of parameter bearing on QGA effectiveness. Specially designed local search method to enhance solution quality. Combination with emerging evolutionary algorithms in future.	One-point and two-point crossovers, mutation.	Friedman test used to prove that although not the best, QGA is still better than many GA-based metaheuristics.
[17]	Investment decision optimization in the power grid sector.	Novel mathematical model of investment aptitude integrating together both demand and capacity. Simulation on real industrial setup.	Quantum rotation gate.	Smallest error when contrasting with GA and PSO.
[18]	De Jong, Coldstein Price, Schafer, Monopole and Six-Peak Camelback, Dual-Pole and Six-Peak Camelback, Multipeak Positive, Ackley, Rastrigin functions.	Three-valued quantum logic (qutrits) to encode individuals. Multiplication with experientially determined parameter μ for evolution instead of a lookup table.	Quantum disaster operator for diversity.	Faster convergence and lesser computation time than the original QGA.
[19]	Trid, Levy, Schwefel, Ackley, Rastrigin functions.	Many-valued quantum logic (qudits) to encode individuals. Multiplication with experientially determined parameter μ for evolution instead of a lookup table.	Quantum disaster operator for diversity.	Threefold reduction in algorithm execution time for $n > 10$ qudits. Significant enhancement in initial convergence (when $t < 150$).
[14]	0/1 QKP (among the most challenging NP-hard problems.)	Parallel edition of QEA for simultaneous execution on multicore hardware.	Greedy heuristic-based initialization, Specially designed local search, Qubit reinitialization, probabilistic elimination, mutation, rotation.	9.4 times acceleration than the serial version. Results marginally better than serial. Results rivalling contemporary methods such as GRASP and Tabu search.

covered in this text, such as quadratic knapsack problem, multiagent task allocation, feature selection, image processing, demand forecasting, and IoT. In some cases, QGA clearly outperformed established methods (especially CGA), while in others, it fared moderately. This is hardly surprising since we know from the *No Free Lunch Theorem* that no optimization algorithm can consistently outperform all others for every conceivable problem. However, valuable lessons are learned in both triumph and failure! We learn from success that QGA: is parallelizable, suitable for stronger NP-hard problems such as QKP, can process large input instances, handle high-dimensional problems, run objective functions with complex topology (e.g., multiple local peaks surrounding a global optimum), can be partnered with other heuristics. The simple 1D qubit chromosome representation can be extended to 2D and qubits may be replaced by many-valued qudits according to the demands of the problem. It has been applied to real industrial use cases and emerging sectors such as IoT. The setbacks provide motivation to reapproach the problems from differing perspectives, for example, by revising the objective function or finding a more efficient problem formulation. Continued research in quantum-inspired methods for the classical domain will deepen our understanding of how to design purely quantum optimization algorithms.

Further contributions to QGA can come from the following avenues: (1) finding novel applications and adapting QGA to the same; (2) refining the metaheuristic strategy in general; (3) introducing newer operators especially for evolution; (4) for problems that remain insufficiently resolved by QGA, finding better problem formulation or alternative objective functions; (5) combining QGA with other emerging metaheuristics for enhanced results; (6) finding ways to improve searching such as using different local search methods; (7) pushing parameter boundaries of population size, generation count.

Besides the classical NP-hard problems such as TSP, knapsack, integer linear programming, bin-packing researchers may consider applying QGA and its variants to multiobjective optimization, multiagent systems, dynamic task scheduling, disaster management, multiprocessor job scheduling among others. Extending the quantum-inspired methods to purely quantum methods is also an active area of research.

KEYWORDS

- **evolutionary algorithm**
- **genetic algorithm**
- **quantum computing**
- **quantum-inspired genetic algorithms**

REFERENCES

1. Abdulhussien, A. A., Nasrudin, M. F., Darwish, S. M., & Alyasseri, Z. A. (2023). Feature selection method based on quantum inspired genetic algorithm. *Journal of King Saud University—Computer and Information Sciences, 35*, 141–156. https://doi.org/10.1016/j.jksuci.2023.02.005.
2. Durán, C. C. (2023). Quantum algorithms: applications, criteria and metrics. *Complex & Intelligent Systems*, 9, 6373–6392 https://doi.org/10.1007/s40747-023-01073-9.
3. Tao, F., Zhang, L. Zhang, Z. H., & Nee, A. Y. C.(2010). A quantum multi-agent evolutionary algorithm for selection of partners in a virtual enterprise. *CIRP Annals, 59*(1), 485–488. https://doi.org/10.1016/j.cirp.2010.03.120.
4. Han, K. H., & Kim, J. H. (2000). Genetic Quantum Algorithm and its application to combinatorial optimization problem. In *Proceedings of the 2000 Congress on Evolutionary Computation. CEC00 (Cat. No.00TH8512), 2*, pp. 1354–1360. https://doi.org/10.1109/CEC.2000.
5. Han, K. H., & Kim, J. H. (2002). Quantum-inspired evolutionary algorithm for a class of combinatorial optimization. *IEEE Transactions on Evolutionary Computation, 6*(6), 580–593. https://doi.org/10.1109/TEVC.2002.804320
6. Han, K.-H., & Kim, J.-H. (2004). Quantum-inspired evolutionary algorithms with a new termination criterion, H/sub /spl epsi// gate, and two-phase scheme. *IEEE Transactions on Evolutionary Computation, 8*(2), 156–169. https://doi.org/10.1109/TEVC.2004.823467.
7. Lv, Y. L. (2007). Application of quantum genetic algorithm on finding minimal reduct. In *IEEE International Conference on Granular Computing (GRC 2007).* Fremont, CA, USA.
8. Platel, M. D., Schliebs, S., & Kasabov, N. (2009). Quantum-inspired evolutionary algorithm: A multimodel EDA. *IEEE Transactions on Evolutionary Computation, 13*(6), 1218–1232. https://doi.org/10.1109/TEVC.2008.2003010
9. Mohammed, A. M., Elhefnawy, N. A., El-Sherbiny, M. M., & Hadhoud, M. M. (2012). Quantum crossover based quantum genetic algorithm for solving non-linear programming. In *8th International Conference on Informatics and Systems (INFOS) 2012*. Giza, Egypt: IEEE, pp. BIO-145–BIO-153.

10. Moore, M., & Narayanan, A. (1995). *Quantum-Inspired Computing.* University of Exeter, Department of Computer Science. Exeter: University of Exeter.
11. Mousavi, S., Afghah, F., Ashdown, J. D., & Turck, K. (2019). Use of a quantum genetic algorithm for coalition formation in large-scale UAV networks. *Ad Hoc Networks, 87*, 26–36.
12. Narayanan, A., & Moore, M. (1996). Quantum-inspired genetic algorithms. In *Proceedings of IEEE International Conference on Evolutionary Computation (ICEC'96)*. Japan: IEEE, pp. 61–66.
13. Pai, A. G., Buddhiraju, K. M., & Durbha, S. S. (2023). Quantum inspired genetic algorithm for Bi-level thresholding of gray-scale images. *The International Archives of the Photogrammetry, Remote Sensing and Spatial Information Sciences, 48*, 483–488.
14. Patvardhan, C., Bansal, S., & Srivastav, A. (2016). Parallel improved quantum inspired evolutionary algorithm to solve large size Quadratic Knapsack Problems. *Swarm and Evolutionary Computation, 26*, 175–190. https://doi.org/10.1016/j.swevo.2015.09.005.
15. Platel, M. D., Schliebs, S., & Kasabov, N. (2007). A versatile quantum-inspired evolutionary algorithm. In *IEEE Congress on Evolutionary Computation*. Singapore: IEEE, pp. 423–430. https://doi.org/10.1109/CEC.2007.4424502.
16. Saad, H. M., Chakrabortty, R. K., Elsayed, S., & Ryan, M. J. (2021). Quantum-inspired genetic algorithm for resource-constrained project-scheduling. *IEEE Access, 9*, 38488–38502. https://doi.org/10.1109/ACCESS.2021.3062790.
17. Sha, Y., Ma, Q., Xu, C., Tan, X., Yan, J., & Zhang, Y. (2023). Research on the balance optimization of investment demand and investment capability of power grid enterprises. *Energy Reports.* Elsevier, Singapore, Vol. 9, pp. 943–950. https://doi.org/10.1016/j.egyr.2023.05.151.
18. Tkachuk, V. (2018). Quantum genetic algorithm based on qutrits and its application. *Mathematical Problems in Engineering, 2018*, 1–8. https://doi.org/10.1155/2018/8614073.
19. Tkachuk, V. (2018). Quantum Genetic Algorithm on Multilevel Quantum Systems. *Mathematical Problems in Engineering*, 1—12. https://doi.org/10.1155/2018/9127510.
20. Wang, H., Liu, J., Zhi, J., & Fu, C. (2013). The improvement of quantum genetic algorithm and its application on function optimization. *Mathematical Problems in Engineering, 2013*, 1–10. https://doi.org/10.1155/2013/730749.

CHAPTER 10

Quantum Computing in Computer Security: A Threat or a Promise for Cybersecurity?

DEBOSREE GHOSH*

Department of Computer Science and Engineering, Swami Vivekananda Institute of Science and Technology, West Bengal, India

*Corresponding author

ABSTRACT

Computer security faces constant challenges due to technological advancements and emerging threats. Traditional cryptographic algorithms, such as Rivest–Shamir–Adleman and elliptic curve cryptography, are being tested by quantum computing. Quantum-resistant cryptography aims to develop algorithms that can withstand attacks from both classical and quantum computers. Quantum key distribution (QKD) is a promising technology that uses quantum mechanics principles to establish secure cryptographic keys, enabling communication channels resistant to eavesdropping. QKD systems have potential applications in secure communication networks and financial transactions. One significant threat posed by quantum computing is the ability to break current encryption standards, making data vulnerable to attack. Quantum computers could also be used to develop sophisticated cyberattacks, such as targeted attacks against critical infrastructure or data theft. The chapter emphasizes the importance of ongoing research and development in postquantum cryptography, which focuses on identifying and developing new cryptographic algorithms capable of withstanding attacks from quantum computers.

Applications of Quantum Computing in a Variety of Domains. Gunjan Mukherjee, Biswadip Basu Mallik, Rahul Kar Özen ÖZER, Digvijay Pandey, and Binay Kumar Pandey (Eds.)

DOI: 10.1201/9781998511051-10

10.1 INTRODUCTION

The field of computer security is about to undergo a revolution thanks to quantum computing, a ground-breaking paradigm that uses the ideas of quantum mechanics [26, 31]. The symbiotic relationship between quantum computing and computer security is explored in this study, revealing a field that is home to both extraordinary prospects and terrible obstacles.

Fundamentally, quantum computing promises to solve challenging problems exponentially more quickly than traditional computers [15, 26]. This transformative capacity, however, also poses a special threat to the security of conventional cryptographic techniques [17, 26]. Computer security will undergo a paradigm shift as a result of quantum computers' potential to decrypt commonly used encryption techniques.

This exploration traverses the vulnerabilities of classical cryptographic algorithms when confronted with quantum attacks [26]. It illuminates the quest for quantum-resistant cryptographic solutions that can withstand quantum-enabled threats [26]. Additionally, it delves into the role of quantum key distribution (QKD) in establishing unbreakable cryptographic keys and secure communication channels.

In navigating the intricate interplay between quantum computing and computer security, this chapter aims to dissect the spectrum of opportunities and challenges. As quantum technologies mature, understanding and mitigating these challenges becomes paramount for building a secure digital future [28, 31].

10.2 VULNERABILITIES OF TRADITIONAL CRYPTOGRAPHY

Traditional cryptography has long been regarded as the protector of confidential data and safe communication in the field of current computer security [6, 30]. The introduction of quantum computing, however, represents a seismic change and reveals weaknesses in these time-tested encryption techniques. These flaws result from quantum computers' special computational powers, which have the ability to weaken the fundamentals of traditional encryption methods [25].

10.2.1 SHOR'S ALGORITHM AND THE THREAT TO RIVEST-SHAMIR-ADLEMAN (RSA)

One of the most significant vulnerabilities arises from Shor's algorithm, a quantum algorithm capable of factoring large numbers exponentially faster than classical algorithms [9, 34]. This poses a direct threat to the security underpinning the widely adopted RSA encryption scheme. RSA's strength is predicated on the difficulty of factoring the product of two large prime numbers, a task that quantum computers equipped with Shor's algorithm can accomplish with startling efficiency [3]. Consequently, encrypted data secured using RSA encryption becomes susceptible to decryption by quantum adversaries, compromising the confidentiality of sensitive information.

10.2.2 ELLIPTIC CURVE CRYPTOGRAPHY (ECC) UNDER QUANTUM ATTACKS

Even the resilient fortress of ECC, a mainstay in secure communication, faces vulnerabilities in the quantum era. Quantum computers can exploit their computational prowess to solve the elliptic curve discrete logarithm problem with unprecedented speed [6, 37]. ECC-based encryption and digital signatures, once considered robust, now encounter the threat of rapid compromise through quantum-enabled attacks.

10.2.3 GROVER'S ALGORITHM AND SYMMETRIC KEY VULNERABILITIES

Even if symmetric key cryptography appears to be more resilient to quantum attacks, it is not. Another quantum algorithm, Grover's algorithm, is exponentially quicker than conventional computers at brute-force searches [2, 36]. As a result, symmetric key lengths are no longer as secure against quantum attacks as they once were, essentially reducing their security [1, 30].

The weaknesses highlight how urgent a paradigm shift is. A crucial area of research is quantum-resistant cryptography, which aims to create cryptographic techniques that can fend off attacks from both classical and quantum computers [29]. It is imperative to adapt, innovate, and switch to new cryptographic systems that can withstand the difficulties of the quantum age in light of the flaws in conventional cryptography that have been revealed by the development of quantum computing [25].

10.3 QUANTUM-RESISTANT CRYPTOGRAPHY

The vulnerability of conventional cryptography techniques in the face of quantum algorithms becomes increasingly clear as quantum computing approaches practicality [8]. As a vital field, quantum-resistant cryptography aims to create encryption methods that are resilient in the quantum age [8]. This section explores numerous quantum-resistant cryptography strategies that provide encouraging countermeasures to the danger posed by quantum computers.

10.3.1 LATTICE-BASED CRYPTOGRAPHY

The mathematical idea of lattices, which are intricately structured grids of points, is used in lattice-based cryptography. The difficulty of locating brief vectors in huge, high-dimensional lattices is exploited by encryption methods based on lattice issues [16, 38]. Lattice-based cryptography is resistant to both classical and quantum attacks due to the complexity of these issues [38]. Lattice-based methods serve as a base for developing safe key exchange, encryption, and digital signature systems [16].

10.3.2 CODE-BASED CRYPTOGRAPHY

Code-based cryptography capitalizes on the theory of error-correcting codes to construct encryption schemes that remain resistant to quantum attacks. These codes introduce errors intentionally, making it arduous for quantum computers to decode encrypted information [8]. With its foundation rooted in well-established coding theory, code-based cryptography is seen as a reliable solution for post-quantum security [8].

10.3.3 MULTIVARIATE POLYNOMIAL CRYPTOGRAPHY (MPC)

MPC centers on algebraic equations involving multivariate polynomials. The security of MPC hinges on the inherent difficulty of solving these equations, which quantum computers find challenging [8]. MPC offers schemes for encryption, digital signatures, and secure key exchange, thereby presenting an arsenal of quantum-resistant tools for cryptographic applications [8].

10.3.4 HASH-BASED CRYPTOGRAPHY

Hash-based cryptography employs cryptographic hash functions to create secure digital signatures and authentication mechanisms. Quantum-resistant hash-based schemes utilize properties of hash functions that are computationally challenging for quantum computers to reverse [24, 38]. This approach ensures data integrity and authenticity in a quantum-threatened environment.

10.3.5 SIGNATURE-BASED CRYPTOGRAPHY

Signature-based cryptography designs digital signature schemes that remain robust against quantum attacks. These schemes often exploit mathematical problems, like the difficulty of solving certain equations, to generate signatures that resist tampering and forgery by quantum adversaries [38].

In summary, quantum-resistant cryptography stands as a critical response to the impending quantum computing age. These innovative cryptographic approaches leverage mathematical complexities to provide security mechanisms that defy quantum threats. By laying the foundation for post-quantum security, quantum-resistant cryptography endeavors to preserve the confidentiality and integrity of digital communications in the quantum era.

10.4 QUANTUM KEY DISTRIBUTION

QKD is a contemporary cryptographic technique that offers hope in the face of quantum dangers. As the power of quantum computers grows, QKD provides a ground-breaking method for ensuring secure communication by utilizing the fundamental ideas of quantum physics [27, 38]. The underlying ideas, mechanisms, and difficulties that support QKD's transformative function are examined in this section.

10.4.1 PRINCIPLES OF QKD

QKD capitalizes on the unique principles of quantum physics, particularly the phenomenon of quantum entanglement and the Heisenberg uncertainty principle. Quantum particles, like photons, can be entangled in a way that the state of one instantly determines the state of its entangled partner, regardless of distance [10, 27]. QKD exploits this principle to create cryptographic keys that remain invulnerable due to the intrinsic challenges of intercepting quantum states without detection [10].

10.4.2 QUANTUM ENCRYPTION AND SECURE COMMUNICATION

At its core, QKD is designed to establish secret cryptographic keys between two parties, often referred to as Alice and Bob, across an unsecured communication channel. The keys generated through QKD are inherently secure because any attempt to intercept the quantum states in transit would disrupt them, triggering detectable alterations. These secure keys then form the foundation for encrypted communication, ensuring the confidentiality of exchanged information [27, 39].

10.4.3 QUANTUM ENTANGLEMENT IN QKD

Central to QKD's security is the concept of quantum entanglement. The entangled states shared between Alice and Bob serve as carriers of confidential information. The "no-cloning theorem" ensures that any unauthorized eavesdropping by a third party, typically referred to as Eve, would disrupt the entanglement, leaving traces that Alice and Bob can detect [10, 21]. This intrinsic feature guarantees the identification of any attempted interception.

10.4.4 PRACTICAL CHALLENGES AND IMPLEMENTATION

While the theoretical principles of QKD are compelling, practical implementation presents its own set of challenges. Photon loss, noise, and technical limitations can degrade the quality of the quantum signals exchanged, affecting the key generation rate and the overall security of the protocol [13, 27]. Overcoming these challenges demands cutting-edge advancements in quantum hardware and sophisticated error correction techniques [38].

As a revolutionary strategy, QKD has the potential to revolutionize secure communication in a world controlled by quantum computers. Its use of quantum mechanics for secure key creation promises to provide levels of cryptographic security that are unmatched. Despite ongoing practical difficulties, QKD's ability to establish impenetrable communication channels is a significant step toward quantum-safe encryption and the guarantee of private and tamper-proof data transmission.

10.5 QUANTUM ATTACKS AND COUNTERMEASURES

The emergence of quantum computing in the field of cybersecurity adds a new level of hazard due to its potential to replace traditional encryption techniques [11, 14]. This section examines the quantum attacks that weaken conventional encryption and the defenses developed to solve these flaws.

10.5.1 GROVER'S ALGORITHM AND SYMMETRIC CRYPTANALYSIS

Quantum computing's Grover's algorithm poses a significant challenge to symmetric key cryptography [12, 40]. While classical brute-force attacks require exponential time, Grover's algorithm reduces the complexity to a quadratic speedup [12, 33]. Consequently, symmetric key lengths need to be effectively doubled to maintain the same level of security against quantum adversaries [14, 33].

10.5.2 SHOR'S ALGORITHM AND ASYMMETRIC CRYPTANALYSIS

Shor's algorithm, a quantum algorithm, disrupts the asymmetric key cryptography that forms the foundation of secure communication [11, 14]. By efficiently factoring large integers, Shor's algorithm can break widely used encryption systems like RSA [14, 40]. To counter this threat, post-quantum cryptographic methods are being developed, resistant to Shor's algorithm and ensuring the security of digital signatures and key exchange [23, 40].

10.5.3 POST-QUANTUM CRYPTOGRAPHIC STANDARDS

Efforts are underway to define post-quantum cryptographic standards that can withstand quantum attacks. Organizations like National Institute of Standards and Technology (NIST) are driving the initiative to identify and standardize quantum-resistant algorithms [23, 24]. These standards will provide a foundation for secure communication in the quantum era, ensuring that cryptographic methods remain effective even against advanced quantum adversaries.

10.5.4 HYBRID CRYPTOGRAPHIC SOLUTIONS

To bridge the gap between classical and quantum security, hybrid cryptographic solutions are gaining prominence. These combine classical and post-quantum cryptographic techniques. Quantum-resistant algorithms are utilized for key exchange and digital signatures, while symmetric encryption maintains data confidentiality. This approach offers a pragmatic transition strategy as the quantum threat looms [11, 14].

10.5.5 QUANTUM-SAFE TRANSITION STRATEGIES

Preparing for the quantum future demands strategic planning, organizations must assess their cryptographic infrastructure, identify vulnerabilities, and devise quantum-safe transition strategies. This involves integrating quantum-resistant algorithms, evaluating their performance, and gradually phasing out vulnerable classical methods [14, 23].

Finally, quantum attacks bring in a time of cryptographic weakness, needing immediate action to protect digital communications. Quantum-safe cybersecurity can be created using defenses including post-quantum cryptography standards, hybrid solutions, and proactive transition techniques. The digital world may successfully combat the quantum danger and maintain the integrity and secrecy of data in an increasingly quantum-enabled world by adopting these solutions.

10.6 QUANTUM COMPUTING AND NETWORK SECURITY

Quantum computing's incorporation into the field of network security ushers in a new era that is both exciting and challenging [14]. The danger landscape is altered by quantum computing's extraordinary computational capacity, which also requires a review of current security methods. This section examines how quantum computing will affect network security and the methods used to reduce new vulnerabilities.

10.6.1 CRYPTOGRAPHIC OVERHAUL

Quantum computing's prowess in breaking classical encryption algorithms requires a fundamental rethinking of cryptographic protocols. Many widely used encryption methods will become vulnerable, necessitating the adoption of quantum-resistant cryptographic techniques [14, 23]. The transition to post-quantum cryptography ensures that network communication remains secure even against powerful quantum attacks.

10.6.2 QUANTUM-SAFE KEY EXCHANGE

Quantum computing's capabilities not only pose a threat but also offer a solution. QKD stands as a beacon of hope in this arena. QKD ensures that cryptographic keys are distributed securely through quantum channels, preventing eavesdropping. This technology promises unhackable key exchange, laying the foundation for quantum-safe communication [14].

10.6.3 QUANTUM FIREWALL AND INTRUSION DETECTION

Quantum computing also offers tools for defense. Quantum-based firewall and intrusion detection systems can enhance network security by leveraging quantum properties to detect unusual patterns or unauthorized access. Quantum-enhanced algorithms can process large datasets more efficiently, potentially identifying sophisticated cyber threats that classical systems struggle to detect [14].

10.6.4 QUANTUM BLOCKCHAIN

Quantum computing's impact on blockchain technology is a critical concern. Blockchain's security relies on cryptographic functions, and the advent of quantum computers could undermine these defenses. Developing quantum-resistant blockchain solutions is paramount to ensure data integrity and immutability in distributed ledger systems [14].

10.6.5 QUANTUM-SECURE COMMUNICATION NETWORKS

The rise of quantum networks offers an opportunity for quantum-safe communication. Quantum networks can utilize QKD to establish secure communication channels that are immune to eavesdropping. Integrating these networks into existing infrastructure can create a new paradigm of secure data transmission [14].

10.6.6 PREPARING FOR THE QUANTUM ERA

Network security professionals must proactively prepare for the quantum era. This involves educating teams, assessing vulnerabilities, and devising strategies for quantum-safe migration. Collaboration between quantum experts and network security specialists will be pivotal in maintaining secure digital ecosystems [14, 23].

In conclusion, the incorporation of quantum computing into network security necessitates a proactive and flexible strategy. Quantum attacks have the potential to disrupt current protocols, yet quantum technologies also provide strong defenses. Network security can prosper in the quantum era by embracing quantum-resistant encryption, QKD, quantum-enhanced security mechanisms, and forward-thinking methods, maintaining the confidentiality, integrity, and availability of digital communication.

10.7 QUANTUM COMPUTING AND DATA PROTECTION

The rapid advancement of quantum computing technology not only brings unprecedented opportunities for innovation but also presents significant challenges for data protection [4, 21]. This section explores the intricate relationship between quantum computing and data protection, highlighting the vulnerabilities that arise and the strategies developed to ensure the security of sensitive information.

10.7.1 QUANTUM THREATS TO CLASSICAL ENCRYPTION

Quantum computers have the potential to undermine classical encryption methods that have been the cornerstone of data protection. Shor's algorithm, for instance, can efficiently factor large numbers, breaking widely used encryption schemes like RSA. This exposes sensitive data to potential breaches, urging the adoption of quantum-resistant encryption techniques [4, 32].

10.7.2 POST-QUANTUM ENCRYPTION SOLUTIONS

Post-quantum cryptography emerges as a crucial field to address quantum threats. Encryption techniques based on mathematical problems that are hard even for quantum computers provide a way forward. Lattice-based cryptography, code-based cryptography, and MPC are among the promising avenues that offer resistance to quantum attacks [5, 20].

10.7.3 QKD FOR UNBREAKABLE KEYS

QKD holds the promise of unbreakable cryptographic key exchange. QKD utilizes the principles of quantum mechanics to establish secure keys, making eavesdropping inherently detectable. This technology ensures that the keys used for encrypting and decrypting sensitive data remain secure, even against quantum adversaries [21, 32].

10.7.4 QUANTUM CRYPTANALYSIS AND DEFENSE STRATEGIES

Quantum computing's potential for faster computation also brings with it the risk of more efficient cryptanalysis. Quantum algorithms designed to crack classical encryption pose a significant threat. To counter this, research and development of quantum-resistant encryption methods are essential to maintain data protection in the quantum age [4, 5].

10.7.5 QUANTUM-SAFE DATA MANAGEMENT

Data protection extends beyond encryption to encompass data management. Quantum computing's capabilities could accelerate data analysis, posing potential privacy risks. Quantum-safe data management strategies must be devised to ensure that data privacy remains intact in an era of powerful quantum computation [21].

10.7.6 PREPARING FOR THE QUANTUM FUTURE

A proactive approach is crucial to address the quantum threats to data protection. Organizations need to invest in quantum threat awareness, research quantum-resistant solutions, and develop transition strategies. Collaboration between quantum experts and data protection specialists will play a pivotal role in creating a quantum-safe environment for sensitive data [20, 32].

In summary, the application of quantum computing to data security adds a new level of complexity. The foundations upon which data security can be preserved in the face of developing quantum problems include quantum-resistant encryption, the promise of QKD, creative defense techniques, and forward-thinking data management. In an increasingly quantum-enabled world, we may protect the confidentiality and integrity of sensitive information by adopting these measures.

10.8 QUANTUM COMPUTING AND BLOCKCHAIN SECURITY

The convergence of quantum computing and blockchain technology introduces a dynamic interplay between innovation and security within the realm of cybersecurity [19, 41]. This section delves into the intricate relationship between quantum computing and blockchain security, unveiling the vulnerabilities that arise and the strategies devised to bolster the integrity and resilience of blockchain systems.

10.8.1 QUANTUM THREATS TO BLOCKCHAIN CRYPTOGRAPHY

Quantum computing's extraordinary computational capabilities pose a significant threat to the cryptographic foundations of blockchain technology. Classical cryptographic methods, including digital signatures and hashing, could be compromised by quantum algorithms like Shor's. This undermines the immutability and security of blockchain records [19, 41].

10.8.2 QUANTUM-RESISTANT BLOCKCHAIN SOLUTIONS

To combat quantum threats, blockchain researchers are actively developing quantum-resistant cryptographic solutions. Post-quantum cryptographic algorithms, rooted in mathematical problems that remain formidable against quantum attacks, are being incorporated into blockchain protocols. This integration aims to preserve the confidentiality, authenticity, and validity of transactions in the quantum era [41].

10.8.3 QUANTUM-SAFE KEY MANAGEMENT

Effective key management is pivotal to blockchain security. Quantum computing's potential to breach classical encryption underscores the importance of implementing quantum-safe key management practices. Solutions utilizing quantum-resistant cryptographic techniques for key generation, storage, and management are essential to prevent unauthorized access to blockchain networks [19].

10.8.4 QUANTUM-ENHANCED BLOCKCHAIN APPLICATIONS

Quantum computing offers opportunities for enhancing blockchain technology. The enhanced processing power of quantum computers can be harnessed to solve complex cryptographic challenges, consensus mechanisms, and data analysis tasks. These advancements could lead to more efficient and secure blockchain protocols [41].

10.8.5 QUANTUM-SECURE CONSENSUS MECHANISMS

Consensus mechanisms are the foundation of blockchain security and decentralization. Quantum attacks have the potential to compromise conventional consensus models. The development of quantum-secure consensus protocols that can withstand quantum threats while maintaining network security and integrity is a critical pursuit [19].

10.8.6 PREPARING FOR THE QUANTUM BLOCKCHAIN ERA

Preparing blockchain technology for the quantum era requires a collaborative effort. Blockchain developers, cryptographic experts, and quantum scientists must collaborate to create quantum-resistant blockchain solutions. This involves research, testing, and the implementation of innovative protocols capable of withstanding quantum attacks [41].

In conclusion, the convergence of quantum computing and blockchain security necessitates a proactive and interdisciplinary approach. Quantum-resistant cryptography, quantum-safe key management, and the evolution of consensus mechanisms are pivotal in ensuring the long-term security and viability of blockchain systems in the face of quantum threats. By embracing these strategies, the blockchain community can navigate the quantum landscape with confidence, preserving the integrity and trust that underlie this transformative technology.

10.9 POST-QUANTUM CRYPTOGRAPHIC STANDARDS AND FUTURE DIRECTIONS

The integration of quantum computing into computer security is ushering in a new era of both opportunities and challenges [4, 21]. This section delves into the crucial domain of post-quantum cryptographic standards and outlines the future directions necessary to navigate the intricate landscape of quantum computing's impact on security.

10.9.1 POST-QUANTUM CRYPTOGRAPHIC STANDARDS

As quantum computing advances, the imperative of establishing post-quantum cryptographic standards becomes increasingly evident. These standards are designed to counteract the vulnerabilities posed by quantum-enabled attacks and to ensure the continued efficacy of cryptographic protocols. Organizations such as NIST are at the forefront of evaluating and endorsing quantum-resistant algorithms, providing a robust framework for secure communication in the quantum era [20, 32].

10.9.2 CHALLENGES AND OPPORTUNITIES

Quantum computing's potential to compromise classical cryptographic methods presents profound challenges for data security. The need for quantum-resistant alternatives propels researchers and developers to explore novel cryptographic primitives. These challenges also serve as catalysts for innovation, fostering the emergence of new encryption techniques that can effectively withstand the threat posed by quantum attacks [4, 5].

10.9.3 QKD'S RISE

A revolutionary development in quantum security is QKD. Using the principles of quantum physics, QKD provides a secure method for exchanging cryptographic keys that ensures the keys are inherently secure against interception. Secure data transfer could revolutionize itself with QKD integration into the current communication infrastructure [21].

10.9.4 HYBRID SOLUTIONS

Navigating the transition to a quantum-safe future requires pragmatic approaches. Hybrid cryptographic solutions, amalgamating classical and quantum-resistant techniques, offer an interim strategy. Quantum-resistant algorithms for key exchange and digital signatures, coupled with classical symmetric encryption for data confidentiality, provide a balanced approach to security [4].

10.9.5 QUANTUM-SAFE NETWORK INFRASTRUCTURE

The era of quantum computing demands a reimagining of network infrastructure. Quantum-safe communication protocols, quantum-resistant firewall systems, and secure QKD mechanisms are pivotal components of future-proof network security in the face of evolving quantum threats [21].

10.9.6 QUANTUM THREAT INTELLIGENCE

Effectively countering quantum threats requires proactive awareness and analysis. Quantum threat intelligence involves continuous monitoring of quantum advancements, vulnerabilities, and potential attack vectors. Collaboration between quantum experts and cybersecurity professionals is instrumental in proactively addressing quantum-enabled adversaries [32].

10.9.7 EDUCATION AND COLLABORATION

The synergy between quantum science and computer security is paramount. Education and collaboration initiatives bridging the two domains will cultivate a workforce capable of comprehending quantum threats and devising effective countermeasures [20].

10.9.8 ENSURING QUANTUM RESILIENCE

In the quest for quantum resilience, the evolution of computer security demands a comprehensive strategy. The establishment of post-quantum cryptographic standards, the emergence of QKD, and the development of hybrid solutions are key aspects of a comprehensive strategy. By embracing these directions, the computer security domain can harness quantum opportunities while safeguarding against emerging challenges [4, 5].

10.10 CONCLUSION

In conclusion, there are potential and difficulties associated with the use of quantum computing in computer security [7, 18]. While standard cryptography algorithms are at risk from quantum computing, new cryptographic methods and safe communication protocols may potentially be developed. For sensitive data to remain secure in the age of quantum computing, post-quantum encryption research and development must continue [6]. The exciting possibilities and pressing necessity for reliable security solutions in the face of developing technology are highlighted in this abstract.

A tapestry of unheard-of opportunities and overwhelming obstacles is woven at the dynamic intersection of computer security and quantum computing. Contrary to its ability to destroy traditional encryption, quantum computing can redefine cryptography [18]. The need for post-quantum cryptography standards to be created is evident as quantum threats cast doubt on conventional security measures [7]. When it comes to secure communication, QKD shines as a beacon, and quantum-enhanced algorithms hold up the prospect of developing sophisticated threat detection and defense mechanisms [35]. Due to this paradigm change, proactive steps are required, such as increased awareness of quantum hazards, interdisciplinary collaboration, and the quick deployment of quantum-resistant technologies [7, 18]. By embracing these strategies, we can confidently navigate the quantum landscape, reinforcing digital landscapes against nascent quantum vulnerabilities and shaping a resilient digital future. The fusion of quantum and security embodies the dual essence of adaptability and the potential to forge an impregnable digital frontier.

KEYWORDS

- **code-based cryptography**
- **computer security**
- **cryptographic algorithms**
- **elliptic curve cryptography**
- **future directions**
- **Grover's algorithm**
- **hash-based cryptography**
- **hybrid cryptographic solutions**
- **intrusion detection**
- **lattice-based cryptography**
- **multivariate polynomial cryptography**
- **postquantum cryptographic standards**
- **privacy-preserving techniques**
- **quantum key distribution**
- **quantum computing**
- **quantum encryption**
- **quantum secure database**
- **quantum-resistant blockchain**
- **quantum-resistant cryptography**
- **quantum-resistant digital signatures**
- **quantum-resistant key exchange**
- **quantum-safe consensus algorithms**
- **quantum-safe data encryption**
- **quantum-safe network protocols**
- **research and development**
- **Rivest–Shamir–Adleman**
- **secure multiparty computation**
- **signature-based cryptograph**

REFERENCES

1. Explore the impact of quantum computing on cryptography. (2024, June).
2. How quantum computing threatens encryption—and what your … (2024).
3. The impact of quantum computing on cryptographic systems." (2023).

4. AppViewX. (2025). Understanding quantum threats and how to secure data with post-quantum cryptography. https://www.appviewx.com/blogs/understanding-quantum-threats-and-how-to-secure-data-with-post-quantum-cryptography/
5. Bavdekar, R., Chopde, E. J., Bhatia, A., Tiwari, K., Joshua Daniel, S., & Atul. (2022). Post-quantum cryptography: Techniques, challenges, standardization, and directions for future research. arXiv. https://doi.org/10.48550/arXiv.2202.02826
6. Benítez, C. (2025). *Mapping Quantum Threats: An Engineering Inventory of Cryptographic Dependencies.* arXiv.
7. Capgemini Research Institute. (2025, July 10). *Future Encrypted: Why Post-Quantum Cryptography Tops the New Cybersecurity Agenda.* Globene Newswire. GlobeNewswire+1.
8. Chhetri, G., Somvanshi, S., Hebli, P., Brotee, S., & Das, S. (2025). *Post-Quantum Cryptography and Quantum-Safe Security: A Comprehensive Survey.*
9. Classiq. (2022). Quantum cryptography—Shor's algorithm explained. Retrieved from https://www.classiq.io/insights/shors-algorithm-explained
10. EITCA Academy. (2023). How does the security of quantum key distribution (QKD) rely on the principles of quantum mechanics? EITCA Academy.
11. EY. (2025). *What C-suite must know about post-quantum cryptography*. https://www.ey.com/en_us/consulting/what-c-suite-must-know-about-post-quantum-cryptography
12. Fortinet. (2025). Understanding Shor's and Grover's algorithms. Fortinet CyberGlossary. https://www.fortinet.com/resources/cyberglossary/shors-grovers-algorithms
13. GeeksforGeeks. (2025). Quantum key distribution (QKD). GeeksforGeeks.
14. Gill, G. (2025). Shor's algorithm impact on asymmetric cryptography. *International Journal of Computer Engineering and Technology (IJCET)*, *16*(1).
15. Gill, S., Kumar, A., Singh, H., Manmeet S., Kaur, K., Usman, M., & Buyya, R. (2020). *Quantum computing: A taxonomy, systematic review and future directions.*
16. Gong, Z., et al. (2024). A survey on lattice-based digital signature. *Cybersecurity, 7*, 7; Haitjema, M. (2023). Quantum key distribution—A survey of the prominent QKD protocols. *CSE571 Report*.
17. Hossain Faruk, M. J., Tahora, S., Tasnim, M., Shahriar, H., & Sakib, N. (2022). A review of quantum cybersecurity: Threats, risks and opportunities.
18. ISACA. (2025, May 5). *Quantum Computing Preparedness Lagging. ISACA Newsletter*. ISACA+1.
19. Lf Decentralized Trust. (n.d.). Quantum threat of blockchain and cryptographic systems. https://www.lfdecentralizedtrust.org/quantum-threat-of-blockchain-and-cryptographic-systems
20. Mittal, H., & Jain, B. (2025). Post-quantum cryptography: A comprehensive review of past technologies and current advances. *Proceedings of First Global Conference on AI Research and Emerging Developments (G-CARED)*, 360-366. https://doi.org/10.63169/gcared2025.p52
21. National Academies of Sciences, Engineering, and Medicine. (2019). *Quantum Computing: Progress and Prospects*. The National Academies Press. https://doi.org/10.17226/25196
22. NIST. (2024, August 13). First finalized post-quantum encryption standards released. National Institute of Standards and Technology. https://www.nist.gov/news-events/news/2024/08/nist-releases-first-3-finalized-post-quantum-encryption-standards

23. NIST. (2025). Post-Quantum cryptography standardization. National Institute of Standards and Technology. https://csrc.nist.gov/Projects/Post-Quantum-Cryptography/Post_Quantum_Cryptography-Standardization
24. Ojha, V. P., Chauhan, S., Yarahmadian, S., & Carvalho, D. (2025). Unfolding post-quantum cryptosystems: CRYSTALS-Dilithium, McEliece, BIKE, and HQC. *Mathematics, 13*(17), 2841.
25. Post-Quantum Security: Opportunities and Challenges. (2024).
26. Prasanna Ravi, Chattopadhyay, A., & Bhasin, S. (2022). *Security and Quantum Computing: An Overview*.
27. Purohit, K., & Vyas, A. K. (2025). Quantum key distribution through quantum machine learning: A research review. *Frontiers in Quantum Science and Technology, 4*, 1575498.
28. Raheman, F. (2022). The future of cybersecurity in the age of quantum computers. *Future Internet, 14*(11), 335. https://doi.org/10.3390/fi14110335
29. Research on development progress and test evaluation of post-quantum cryptography. (2024).
30. Sahni, A., & Sahni, R. (2024). Decrypting the future: Quantum computing and the impact of Grover's and Shor's algorithms on classical cryptography. *EasyChair Preprint.*
31. Scanlon, T. (2023, April 10). *Cybersecurity of Quantum Computing: A New Frontier*. Carnegie Mellon University, Software Engineering Institute. https://doi.org/10.58012/rzmt-m258
32. SecureITConsult. (2025). How Quantum computing threatens encryption—and what your organization should do. https://secureitconsult.com/quantum-computing-threatens-encryption/
33. Sharma, S., Choudhury, T., & Sharma, S. (2025). A study of post quantum cryptographic security model using symmetric key algorithm. *International Journal of Intelligent Systems and Applications in Engineering, 11, 181–198*.
34. Shor's algorithm and RSA encryption. (2024). *QAI Resource Library.*
35. Thales Group. (2025). *Inside the 2025 Data Threat Report: AI & Quantum and the Evolving Threat Landscape—Key Findings from the Thales 2025 Data Threat Report.* Thales Group Blog.
36. Understanding quantum threats and how to secure data with PQC. (2024).
37. Understanding Shor's and Grover's algorithms. (2023).
38. Veksler, D. (2024). Post-quantum cryptography algorithms: A comparative analysis. *LinkedIn Article*.
39. Haitjema, M. (2023). Quantum key distribution—A survey of the prominent QKD protocols. *CSE571 Report*.
40. SolveForce. (2025). *Quantum computing and cybersecurity.* SolveForce. https://solveforce.com/quantum-computing-and-cybersecurity/
41. Mutha, A., & Sandu, J. (2025). *Literature review of the effect of quantum computing on cryptocurrencies using blockchain technology*. *Journal of Informatics Education and Research*, *5*(2). https://doi.org/10.48550/arXiv.2508.17296

CHAPTER 11

Unlocking the Quantum Potential: Applications of Quantum Computing in Manufacturing and Industrial Design

GURPREET SINGH[1*] and SUKHPREET SINGH[2]

[1]*Computer Science & Engineering, Guru Kashi University, Talwandi Sabo, Punjab, India*

[2]*Department of Computer Applications, Guru Kashi University, Talwandi Sabo, Bathinda, Punjab, India*

*Corresponding author

ABSTRACT

This chapter examines the revolutionary impact of quantum computing on manufacturing and industrial design. Quantum computing enhances material design through advanced simulations, enabling the discovery of innovative materials with improved properties. Optimized production processes and streamlined supply chains are achievable via quantum algorithms, reducing costs, and boosting efficiency. Industrial design benefits from quantum simulations that foster precision and creativity. Robotics and automation are further advanced by quantum computing, resulting in smarter, more adaptable systems. In addition, quantum approaches revolutionize chemical synthesis and energy optimization, promoting sustainable manufacturing practices. Predictive maintenance and quality control are transformed through quantum-enhanced analytics, ensuring reliability and operational excellence in Industry 4.0. The chapter also explores quantum computing's role in mitigating risks in industrial processes, improving logistic operations, and refining inventory management. Enhanced product

Applications of Quantum Computing in a Variety of Domains. Gunjan Mukherjee, Biswadip Basu Mallik, Rahul Kar Özen ÖZER, Digvijay Pandey, and Binay Kumar Pandey (Eds.)

DOI: 10.1201/9781998511051-11

lifecycle management is another key focus, as quantum technologies enable smarter resource utilization and reduced downtime. By integrating these applications, quantum computing promises a significant leap in efficiency, innovation, and sustainability within the manufacturing sector. This chapter emphasizes the strategic potential of quantum technologies to address complex challenges and unlock unprecedented opportunities, reshaping the future of industrial design and manufacturing.

11.1 INTRODUCTION

The manufacturing and industrial design sector stands on the precipice of a transformative revolution fueled by the advent of quantum computing. This chapter delves into the remarkable applications of quantum computing in this sector, exploring how it enhances material design, optimizes production processes, streamlines supply chains, fosters industrial design innovations, and powers advancements in robotics and automation. We also examine quantum approaches to advanced chemical synthesis, the role of quantum computing in predictive maintenance, quality control and assurance, energy optimization, risk mitigation, logistic operations, and inventory management. Furthermore, we explore how quantum computing enhances product lifecycle management, analyze real-world case studies of quantum computing in action, and delve into the future directions that this technology holds for manufacturing and industrial design. Finally, we examine how quantum computing propels us toward a quantum-driven industrial revolution, where efficiency, innovation, and sustainability reign supreme. Throughout this chapter, we unravel the potential benefits, challenges, and possibilities that quantum computing brings to the manufacturing and industrial design sector, paving the way for a future of unprecedented advancements and unparalleled success [1, 2].

This chapter explores the following applications of quantum computing in the manufacturing and industrial design sector:

1. Enhancing Material Design with Quantum Computing
2. Quantum Computing for Optimized Production Processes
3. Quantum Solutions for Streamlined Supply Chains
4. Industrial Design Innovations through Quantum Simulations
5. Robotics and Automation: Advancements Powered by Quantum Computing
6. Quantum Approaches to Advanced Chemical Synthesis

7. Predictive Maintenance in Industry 4.0: Quantum Computing's Role
8. Quality Control and Assurance: Quantum Computing Applications
9. Energy Optimization in Manufacturing with Quantum Computing
10. Mitigating Risks in Industrial Processes using Quantum Algorithms
11. Quantum Computing: Revolutionizing Logistic Operations
12. "Quantum Techniques for Inventory Management
13. Enhanced Product Lifecycle Management through Quantum Computing

The field of material design lies at the heart of manufacturing and industrial design, as it encompasses the development of new materials with tailored properties to meet specific requirements. In recent years, quantum computing has emerged as a transformative tool that holds immense promise for enhancing material design processes. By harnessing the power of quantum mechanics, quantum computing enables scientists and engineers to explore materials at the atomic and molecular levels, unlocking a deeper understanding of their behavior and properties. This chapter delves into the exciting realm of enhancing material design with quantum computing, showcasing how this technology revolutionizes the discovery and optimization of materials with unprecedented precision and efficiency. From quantum simulations to accelerated material discovery, we explore the various ways in which quantum computing is transforming the landscape of material design, driving innovation, and unlocking new possibilities for manufacturing and industrial design.

11.2 ENHANCING MATERIAL DESIGN WITH QUANTUM COMPUTING

The field of material design plays a crucial role in manufacturing and industrial design, as it focuses on developing new materials with specific properties to meet desired functional requirements. Quantum computing has the potential to revolutionize material design by leveraging its computational power to explore the vast space of material configurations and properties. This section explores how quantum computing can enhance material design processes and drive innovation in manufacturing [3].

11.2.1 QUANTUM SIMULATIONS FOR MATERIAL PROPERTIES

Quantum computing enables accurate simulations of quantum systems, allowing researchers to model the behavior and properties of materials at the atomic and subatomic levels. By leveraging the principles of superposition and entanglement, quantum simulations can provide insights into complex quantum phenomena and predict material properties, such as electronic structure, energy levels, and bonding characteristics. These simulations enable the discovery of novel materials with tailored properties, including improved strength, conductivity, or magnetism.

11.2.2 OPTIMIZATION OF MATERIAL PROPERTIES

Quantum computing algorithms, such as quantum optimization and variational methods, can optimize material properties by searching for the most favorable material configurations within a vast design space. This capability facilitates the discovery of materials with desired characteristics, such as high durability, lightweightness, or specific thermal conductivity. Quantum optimization algorithms can explore and navigate the parameter space more efficiently than classical algorithms, leading to accelerated material design processes.

11.2.3 ACCELERATING MATERIAL DISCOVERY

Traditional methods for discovering new materials often rely on trial-and-error approaches, which can be time-consuming and resource-intensive. Quantum computing can expedite the material discovery process by performing quantum simulations and leveraging its computational power to explore a significantly larger search space. This enables researchers to identify promising material candidates with targeted properties more rapidly, reducing the time and cost associated with experimental synthesis and testing.

11.2.4 QUANTUM MACHINE LEARNING FOR MATERIAL DESIGN

Quantum machine learning algorithms offer the potential to uncover hidden patterns and correlations within vast datasets, including materials databases. By leveraging quantum algorithms such as quantum support vector machines or quantum neural networks, researchers can extract valuable insights from complex material datasets and make predictions about material behavior. This fusion of quantum computing and machine learning can enhance the efficiency and accuracy of material design processes.

11.2.5 QUANTUM-ENABLED MATERIAL CHARACTERIZATION

Quantum computing can also assist in the characterization of materials by analyzing experimental data and extracting relevant features. Quantum algorithms can process and analyze large datasets efficiently, enabling researchers to identify patterns, anomalies, or correlations that may be challenging for classical methods. This can aid in the understanding of material behavior, refinement of material models, and optimization of manufacturing processes.

The integration of quantum computing into material design processes holds tremendous potential for accelerating innovation and enabling the discovery of advanced materials with tailored properties. By leveraging quantum simulations, optimization algorithms, and machine learning techniques, researchers can explore the material design space more effectively and efficiently. This can lead to the development of new materials that revolutionize manufacturing and industrial design, resulting in enhanced products, improved sustainability, and increased efficiency in various industries.

11.3 QUANTUM COMPUTING FOR OPTIMIZED PRODUCTION PROCESSES

Optimizing production processes is crucial for efficient manufacturing and industrial design. By leveraging the unique capabilities of quantum computing, such as superposition and entanglement, it becomes possible to tackle complex optimization problems more effectively. This section explores how quantum computing can be applied to optimize production processes, leading to increased productivity, reduced costs, and improved operational efficiency [4, 5].

11.3.1 QUANTUM-INSPIRED OPTIMIZATION ALGORITHMS

Quantum-inspired optimization algorithms, such as quantum annealing and quantum-inspired algorithms, harness quantum principles to solve optimization problems more efficiently than classical methods. These algorithms can be employed to address various production-related challenges, including resource allocation, scheduling, routing, and inventory management. By leveraging quantum-inspired techniques, manufacturers can achieve optimal solutions, minimize production bottlenecks, and streamline their operations.

11.3.2 SUPPLY CHAIN OPTIMIZATION

Supply chain management is a critical aspect of manufacturing, and optimizing the supply chain can lead to significant cost savings and improved customer satisfaction. Quantum computing can enable advanced optimization techniques for supply chain optimization, including demand forecasting, inventory management, and logistics optimization. By leveraging quantum algorithms, manufacturers can optimize the allocation of resources, reduce lead times, minimize inventory carrying costs, and enhance overall supply chain efficiency.

11.3.3 PRODUCTION SCHEDULING AND PLANNING

Efficient production scheduling and planning are essential for meeting customer demands while minimizing costs and maximizing resource utilization. Quantum computing can address complex scheduling and planning problems, considering multiple constraints, such as machine availability, production sequences, and order prioritization. Quantum algorithms can optimize production schedules, minimize production downtime, reduce idle time, and improve overall production throughput.

11.3.4 PROCESS OPTIMIZATION AND YIELD ENHANCEMENT

Manufacturing processes often involve complex parameters and variables that need to be optimized for maximizing yield and minimizing defects.

Quantum computing can assist in process optimization by exploring the parameter space more efficiently and identifying optimal process configurations. This can lead to improved product quality, reduced waste, and increased production yield. Quantum algorithms can also aid in real-time process monitoring and control, allowing manufacturers to detect anomalies and make adjustments to ensure consistent quality.

11.3.5 RESOURCE ALLOCATION AND ENERGY OPTIMIZATION

Optimizing resource allocation and energy consumption is crucial for sustainable manufacturing practices. Quantum computing can assist in optimizing the allocation of resources, such as energy, raw materials, and machinery, to minimize waste and reduce environmental impact. By leveraging quantum algorithms, manufacturers can achieve energy-efficient production processes, optimize resource utilization, and contribute to a greener and more sustainable manufacturing ecosystem.

Quantum computing offers tremendous potential for optimizing production processes in manufacturing and industrial design. By harnessing the power of quantum algorithms and leveraging the principles of quantum mechanics, manufacturers can tackle complex optimization problems more efficiently, leading to improved productivity, reduced costs, and enhanced operational efficiency. From supply chain optimization to production scheduling, process optimization, and resource allocation, quantum computing can revolutionize the way manufacturers optimize their production processes, enabling them to stay competitive in a rapidly evolving industry landscape.

11.4 QUANTUM SOLUTIONS FOR STREAMLINED SUPPLY CHAINS

Efficient supply chain management is crucial for the success of manufacturing and industrial design operations. Quantum computing has the potential to revolutionize supply chain processes by tackling complex optimization problems, enabling real-time decision-making, and enhancing overall supply chain visibility and resilience. This section explores how quantum computing can provide solutions for streamlined supply chains, leading to improved efficiency, reduced costs, and increased customer satisfaction [6].

11.4.1 QUANTUM OPTIMIZATION FOR NETWORK DESIGN AND ROUTING

Supply chain networks involve complex logistical challenges, including facility location, transportation routing, and inventory allocation. Quantum optimization algorithms can address these challenges by optimizing network design and routing decisions. By leveraging quantum algorithms, manufacturers can identify optimal facility locations, optimize transportation routes, and minimize transportation costs. This results in streamlined supply chain operations, reduced lead times, and improved delivery performance.

11.4.2 DEMAND FORECASTING AND INVENTORY OPTIMIZATION

Accurate demand forecasting and efficient inventory management are crucial for maintaining optimal inventory levels and meeting customer demands. Quantum computing can improve demand forecasting accuracy by analyzing vast amounts of data and identifying hidden patterns and correlations. Quantum algorithms can optimize inventory replenishment decisions, considering demand variability, lead times, and cost constraints. This enables manufacturers to reduce excess inventory, minimize stock-outs, and improve overall inventory turnover.

11.4.3 SUPPLY CHAIN RISK MANAGEMENT

Supply chains are vulnerable to various risks, including disruptions, delays, and uncertainties. Quantum computing can assist in supply chain risk management by modeling and simulating different risk scenarios. Quantum algorithms can evaluate the impact of disruptions, identify alternative routes and suppliers, and develop robust contingency plans. This enables manufacturers to enhance supply chain resilience, mitigate risks, and minimize the potential negative impact of disruptions on their operations.

11.4.4 BLOCKCHAIN AND SMART CONTRACTS

Quantum computing can enhance the security and efficiency of supply chain transactions through the application of quantum-resistant cryptography. By leveraging quantum-resistant algorithms, manufacturers can protect sensitive supply chain data from potential security threats posed by future quantum computers. Additionally, quantum computing can enhance the efficiency and transparency of supply chain transactions through the use of smart contracts and blockchain technology. Smart contracts can automate and streamline processes such as contract execution, payment settlements, and tracking product provenance.

11.4.5 REAL-TIME SUPPLY CHAIN OPTIMIZATION

The dynamic nature of supply chains requires real-time decision-making to respond to changing demands, disruptions, and market conditions. Quantum computing can provide real-time optimization solutions by leveraging quantum algorithms capable of processing large volumes of data and rapidly identifying optimal decisions. This enables manufacturers to make informed decisions on production planning, order fulfillment, and inventory allocation in real-time, resulting in improved responsiveness, reduced costs, and enhanced customer service.

Quantum computing holds great promise for transforming supply chain management in manufacturing and industrial design. By leveraging quantum algorithms and principles, manufacturers can optimize network design, improve demand forecasting, mitigate risks, enhance security, and enable real-time decision-making. The integration of quantum computing solutions into supply chain processes can lead to streamlined operations, reduced costs, increased customer satisfaction, and improved overall supply chain resilience. As quantum computing technology continues to advance, its impact on supply chains is likely to revolutionize the industry and pave the way for more efficient and agile global supply networks.

11.5 INDUSTRIAL DESIGN INNOVATIONS THROUGH QUANTUM SIMULATIONS

Industrial design involves creating innovative and functional products that meet specific requirements and user needs. Quantum computing can play a transformative role in industrial design by leveraging its computational power to enable advanced simulations and optimizations. This section explores how quantum simulations can drive industrial design innovations, enabling designers to explore new design possibilities, optimize product performance, and accelerate the design iteration process [5, 7].

11.5.1 QUANTUM SIMULATIONS FOR MATERIAL PROPERTIES

Materials are the building blocks of industrial design, and their properties significantly influence the performance and functionality of products. Quantum simulations can provide insights into the behavior and properties of materials at the atomic and subatomic levels. By accurately modeling material characteristics such as strength, conductivity, or elasticity, designers can make informed decisions about material selection and explore novel materials with unique properties that can enhance product performance and durability.

11.5.2 OPTIMIZING PRODUCT PERFORMANCE THROUGH QUANTUM SIMULATIONS

Quantum computing enables designers to simulate and optimize the performance of complex systems and components. By leveraging quantum simulations, designers can analyze the behavior of products under various conditions, such as stress, heat, or fluid dynamics. This allows them to identify design flaws, optimize product performance, and enhance overall functionality. Quantum simulations can also assist in optimizing product designs for specific criteria, such as energy efficiency, structural integrity, or aerodynamic performance.

11.5.3 QUANTUM-ASSISTED COMPUTATIONAL DESIGN

Quantum computing can revolutionize the computational design process by accelerating complex simulations and optimizations. Quantum algorithms can explore a vast design space more efficiently, allowing designers to generate and evaluate a wide range of design options in a shorter time. By leveraging quantum-assisted computational design techniques, designers can iterate and refine designs rapidly, leading to improved product designs, reduced time to market, and increased innovation.

11.5.4 DESIGNING AT THE MOLECULAR LEVEL

Quantum simulations can unlock the potential for designing products at the molecular level. By simulating and analyzing molecular structures, quantum computing enables designers to understand and manipulate the behavior and properties of materials at the atomic scale. This opens up possibilities for creating novel materials with tailored properties and designing products with unprecedented functionality and performance. Designing at the molecular level can revolutionize industries such as pharmaceuticals, electronics, and advanced materials.

11.5.5 DESIGN OPTIMIZATION FOR ADDITIVE MANUFACTURING

Additive manufacturing, or 3D printing, offers unique design possibilities but also presents challenges in terms of structural integrity and optimization. Quantum computing can assist in optimizing designs for additive manufacturing processes, considering factors such as material properties, support structures, and manufacturing constraints. By leveraging quantum simulations and optimization algorithms, designers can create optimized designs that maximize structural strength, minimize material usage, and optimize print times, leading to more efficient and effective additive manufacturing processes.

Quantum simulations hold tremendous potential for driving industrial design innovations. By leveraging the computational power of quantum computing, designers can explore new design possibilities, optimize product performance, and accelerate the design iteration process. Quantum simulations for material properties, product performance, computational design, molecular-level design, and additive manufacturing can revolutionize the way products are designed and developed. As quantum computing technology advances, its integration into industrial design processes is expected to unlock new levels of creativity, efficiency, and functionality, enabling designers to push the boundaries of innovation in various industries.

11.6 ROBOTICS AND AUTOMATION: ADVANCEMENTS POWERED BY QUANTUM COMPUTING

Robotics and automation have already transformed various industries, enhancing efficiency, productivity, and safety. However, the integration of quantum computing in robotics and automation opens up a new realm of possibilities. Quantum computing's computational power, optimization capabilities, and advanced algorithms have the potential to drive significant advancements in robotics and automation. This section explores the transformative role of quantum computing in advancing robotics and automation, from improved control systems to enhanced perception and decision-making [8].

11.6.1 QUANTUM-ENHANCED CONTROL SYSTEMS

Quantum computing can revolutionize control systems in robotics by providing faster and more efficient algorithms. Quantum-assisted control systems can enable real-time adaptation, precise motor control, and enhanced feedback mechanisms. By leveraging quantum computing, robots can achieve more accurate movements, smoother trajectories, and increased stability, leading to improved performance and safety in diverse applications, from manufacturing to healthcare.

11.6.2 QUANTUM-ENABLED PERCEPTION AND SENSING

Perception and sensing play a crucial role in robotics, enabling robots to interact with their environment and make informed decisions. Quantum computing can enhance perception capabilities by processing and analyzing sensor data more efficiently. Quantum algorithms can enable advanced sensor fusion, real-time object recognition, and robust environmental perception, empowering robots with a deeper understanding of their surroundings. This leads to enhanced situational awareness, improved object manipulation, and safer interaction with humans.

11.6.3 QUANTUM-ASSISTED PATH PLANNING AND NAVIGATION

Path planning and navigation are fundamental tasks in robotics, and quantum computing can significantly enhance these capabilities. Quantum algorithms can optimize complex path planning problems, considering multiple variables and constraints. Quantum-assisted path planning algorithms can find optimal paths, avoiding obstacles, considering dynamic changes in the environment, and minimizing energy consumption. This enables robots to navigate efficiently and adapt to changing scenarios, improving productivity, and reducing collision risks.

11.6.4 QUANTUM MACHINE LEARNING FOR AUTONOMOUS DECISION-MAKING

Autonomous decision-making is a key aspect of robotics, enabling robots to operate in dynamic and unpredictable environments. Quantum computing can enhance machine learning algorithms, enabling faster and more accurate decision-making in real-time. Quantum-assisted machine learning can improve perception, enable adaptive behavior, and optimize control strategies. This empowers robots to learn from experience, make informed decisions, and adapt to new situations, leading to more intelligent and autonomous robotic systems.

11.6.5 QUANTUM ROBOTICS FOR SWARM SYSTEMS AND COLLABORATION

Quantum computing can drive advancements in swarm robotics and collaboration among multiple robots. Quantum-enabled optimization algorithms can optimize the coordination and collaboration of robot swarms, enabling efficient task allocation, improved communication, and emergent behavior. Quantum robotics can facilitate decentralized decision-making, enabling a swarm of robots to solve complex problems collectively. This opens up possibilities for applications such as autonomous warehouse management, environmental monitoring, and disaster response.

The integration of quantum computing in robotics and automation presents a new era of advancements. From quantum-enhanced control systems and perception capabilities to optimized path planning and autonomous decision-making, quantum computing has the potential to transform robotics and automation across various industries. As quantum computing technology continues to advance, the possibilities for enhanced productivity, safety, and intelligence in robotics and automation are limitless. By embracing the power of quantum computing, we can unlock new frontiers, pushing the boundaries of what robots can achieve and redefining the future of automation.

11.7 QUANTUM APPROACHES TO ADVANCED CHEMICAL SYNTHESIS

Chemical synthesis is a complex process that plays a crucial role in the development of new materials, pharmaceuticals, and chemical products. Quantum computing offers unique opportunities to revolutionize advanced chemical synthesis by leveraging its computational power and simulation capabilities. This section explores the potential of quantum approaches in advancing chemical synthesis, from optimizing reaction pathways to designing new catalysts and predicting reaction outcomes [9].

11.7.1 QUANTUM SIMULATION OF CHEMICAL REACTIONS

Quantum computing enables accurate simulations of chemical reactions at the molecular level, going beyond the capabilities of classical computers. Quantum simulations can provide insights into reaction mechanisms, energy profiles, and intermediate states, allowing researchers to understand complex reaction pathways. By leveraging quantum simulations, chemists can optimize reaction conditions, predict reaction outcomes, and discover new reaction pathways that were previously unexplored. This accelerates the development of efficient and sustainable chemical synthesis processes.

11.7.2 DESIGN OF QUANTUM-INSPIRED CATALYSTS

Catalysts play a critical role in chemical synthesis, enabling the acceleration of desired reactions and improving selectivity. Quantum computing can assist in the design of novel catalysts by exploring potential catalytic sites, reaction mechanisms, and electronic properties. Quantum-inspired catalyst design allows for the development of highly efficient catalysts tailored to specific reactions. This enhances reaction rates, reduces unwanted side reactions, and improves overall reaction efficiency, leading to more sustainable and cost-effective chemical synthesis.

11.7.3 OPTIMIZATION OF REACTION CONDITIONS

Quantum computing can optimize reaction conditions in chemical synthesis by considering various factors, such as temperature, pressure, and reactant concentrations. Quantum optimization algorithms can explore a vast parameter space and identify optimal reaction conditions that maximize yield, minimize energy consumption, and reduce waste. By leveraging quantum approaches, researchers can discover reaction conditions that were previously overlooked, leading to more efficient and sustainable chemical synthesis processes.

11.7.4 PREDICTION OF REACTION KINETICS AND THERMODYNAMICS

Accurate prediction of reaction kinetics and thermodynamics is crucial for understanding the feasibility and efficiency of chemical reactions. Quantum computing can enhance prediction capabilities by simulating complex quantum mechanical interactions and optimizing kinetic and thermodynamic models. Quantum approaches enable more accurate predictions of reaction rates, equilibrium constants, and energy barriers, leading to improved understanding of reaction mechanisms and informed decision-making in chemical synthesis.

11.7.5 QUANTUM MACHINE LEARNING FOR CHEMICAL SYNTHESIS OPTIMIZATION

Machine learning techniques can be enhanced with quantum computing to optimize chemical synthesis processes. Quantum-assisted machine learning algorithms can analyze vast amounts of chemical data, including reaction parameters, reaction outcomes, and reaction conditions. By leveraging quantum machine learning, researchers can discover correlations, identify key factors that influence reaction outcomes, and optimize reaction conditions for improved efficiency and selectivity. This enables data-driven decision-making in chemical synthesis and accelerates the discovery of novel synthetic routes.

Quantum approaches have the potential to revolutionize advanced chemical synthesis by leveraging the computational power and simulation capabilities of quantum computing. From quantum simulations and catalyst design to reaction condition optimization and predictive modeling, quantum computing offers unique opportunities to enhance efficiency, sustainability, and innovation in chemical synthesis. As quantum computing technology continues to advance, its integration into chemical synthesis processes will drive advancements in the discovery of new materials, pharmaceuticals, and chemical products, leading to a more sustainable and technologically advanced future.

11.8 PREDICTIVE MAINTENANCE IN INDUSTRY 4.0: QUANTUM COMPUTING'S ROLE

Predictive maintenance is a critical component of Industry 4.0, aiming to optimize equipment maintenance schedules, reduce downtime, and improve operational efficiency. Quantum computing holds immense potential in enhancing predictive maintenance practices by leveraging its computational power and optimization capabilities. This section explores the role of quantum computing in predictive maintenance, from advanced data analytics to fault prediction and optimization of maintenance strategies in the context of Industry 4.0 [5, 7].

11.8.1 QUANTUM DATA ANALYTICS FOR CONDITION MONITORING

Quantum computing can enhance data analytics techniques used in condition monitoring by processing and analyzing large volumes of data more efficiently. Quantum algorithms can uncover hidden patterns, correlations, and anomalies within sensor data, enabling the early detection of equipment failures. By leveraging quantum data analytics, manufacturers can monitor the health and performance of equipment in real-time, leading to proactive maintenance interventions, reduced downtime, and improved operational efficiency.

11.8.2 QUANTUM MACHINE LEARNING FOR FAULT DETECTION AND DIAGNOSIS

Machine learning techniques play a crucial role in fault detection and diagnosis for predictive maintenance. Quantum computing can enhance machine learning algorithms by providing exponential speedup for certain tasks. Quantum-assisted machine learning algorithms can process and analyze complex datasets, extract valuable features, and identify patterns associated with equipment failures. This enables more accurate and timely fault detection and diagnosis, leading to proactive maintenance interventions and improved equipment reliability.

11.8.3 OPTIMIZATION OF MAINTENANCE SCHEDULES

Quantum computing can address the optimization challenges of maintenance scheduling in Industry 4.0. Quantum optimization algorithms can consider various factors, including equipment criticality, maintenance costs, production demands, and resource availability, to optimize maintenance schedules. By leveraging quantum computing, manufacturers can achieve optimal maintenance intervals, minimize production disruptions, and maximize the lifespan of equipment. This leads to improved operational efficiency and reduced maintenance costs.

11.8.4 QUANTUM SIMULATIONS FOR FAILURE PREDICTION

Quantum computing enables advanced simulations of physical systems, allowing for more accurate failure prediction. By leveraging quantum simulations, manufacturers can model complex interactions within equipment, analyze stress distribution, and predict potential failure modes. This empowers predictive maintenance strategies with more accurate insights into failure probabilities and critical failure points, enabling targeted maintenance actions and preventing costly breakdowns.

11.8.5 QUANTUM-ENABLED PROGNOSTICS FOR COMPONENT HEALTH MONITORING

Prognostics aims to estimate the remaining useful life of components based on real-time monitoring and degradation analysis. Quantum computing can enhance prognostic techniques by handling complex degradation models and performing large-scale optimization. Quantum-assisted prognostics algorithms can leverage historical data, sensor readings, and degradation models to estimate the remaining useful life of components. This enables proactive component replacement and maintenance, minimizing unexpected failures and reducing overall maintenance costs.

Quantum computing plays a significant role in advancing predictive maintenance practices in Industry 4.0. By leveraging quantum data analytics, machine learning, optimization algorithms, and simulations, manufacturers can achieve more accurate fault detection and diagnosis, optimize maintenance schedules, and improve overall equipment reliability. Quantum-enabled predictive maintenance empowers manufacturers to adopt proactive and data-driven maintenance strategies, reducing downtime, increasing equipment lifespan, and improving operational efficiency. As quantum computing technology continues to evolve, its integration into predictive maintenance processes will revolutionize the industry, paving the way for a new era of maintenance excellence in Industry 4.0.

11.9 QUALITY CONTROL AND ASSURANCE: QUANTUM COMPUTING APPLICATIONS

Quality control and assurance are essential aspects of manufacturing, ensuring that products meet or exceed specified standards and customer expectations. Quantum computing offers unique applications that have the potential to revolutionize quality control practices by leveraging its computational power, advanced optimization capabilities, and simulation techniques. This section explores the role of quantum computing in quality control and assurance, from defect detection to optimization of quality control processes in manufacturing [10].

11.9.1 QUANTUM DATA ANALYSIS FOR DEFECT DETECTION

Quantum computing can enhance data analysis techniques used in quality control by processing large volumes of data more efficiently. Quantum algorithms can uncover subtle patterns and correlations within production data, enabling the early detection of defects and anomalies. By leveraging quantum data analysis, manufacturers can identify quality issues in real-time, leading to timely interventions, reduced scrap rates, and improved product quality.

11.9.2 QUANTUM-ASSISTED STATISTICAL MODELING

Statistical modeling is a fundamental aspect of quality control, enabling manufacturers to understand variation, assess process capability, and make data-driven decisions. Quantum computing can enhance statistical modeling techniques by providing increased computational power and improved optimization algorithms. Quantum-assisted statistical modeling can handle complex datasets, identify influential factors, and optimize quality control parameters. This empowers manufacturers to develop robust quality control strategies, optimize process performance, and achieve higher product quality levels.

11.9.3 OPTIMIZATION OF QUALITY CONTROL PROCESSES

Quantum computing can address the optimization challenges of quality control processes, such as determining sample sizes, defining acceptance criteria, and optimizing inspection schedules. Quantum optimization algorithms can consider multiple factors, including cost constraints, risk levels, and production variability, to optimize quality control processes. By leveraging quantum computing, manufacturers can achieve cost-effective inspection strategies, minimize false rejections, and optimize quality control efforts.

11.9.4 QUANTUM SIMULATIONS FOR PRODUCT TESTING AND EVALUATION

Quantum simulations can enhance product testing and evaluation processes by modeling product behavior and performance under different conditions. By leveraging quantum simulations, manufacturers can predict product performance, assess design robustness, and identify potential failure modes. This enables proactive design improvements, validation of product specifications, and optimization of testing protocols, leading to enhanced product quality and reliability.

11.9.5 QUANTUM-ENABLED SUPPLY CHAIN QUALITY CONTROL

Quality control is not limited to individual manufacturers but also extends to the entire supply chain. Quantum computing can enable efficient supply chain quality control by optimizing inspection points, identifying potential quality risks, and facilitating information sharing among stakeholders. By leveraging quantum algorithms, manufacturers can improve traceability, reduce counterfeit products, and ensure consistent quality across the supply chain, enhancing customer trust and satisfaction.

Quantum computing applications in quality control and assurance have the potential to transform manufacturing processes. By leveraging quantum data analysis, statistical modeling, optimization techniques, and simulations, manufacturers can achieve improved defect detection, optimized quality control processes, and enhanced product testing and evaluation. Quantum-enabled quality control empowers manufacturers to proactively identify and address quality issues, optimize process performance, and ensure consistent product quality throughout the supply chain. As quantum computing technology continues to advance, its integration into quality control and assurance processes will drive the next wave of advancements in manufacturing, setting new benchmarks for product quality and customer satisfaction.

11.10 ENERGY OPTIMIZATION IN MANUFACTURING WITH QUANTUM COMPUTING

Energy optimization is a crucial consideration in manufacturing, aiming to minimize energy consumption, reduce costs, and improve sustainability. Quantum computing offers unique applications that have the potential to revolutionize energy optimization in manufacturing by leveraging its computational power, advanced optimization algorithms, and simulation capabilities. This section explores the role of quantum computing in energy optimization, from optimizing energy systems to enhancing energy management practices in manufacturing [11].

11.10.1 QUANTUM OPTIMIZATION FOR ENERGY SYSTEMS

Quantum computing can address the complex optimization challenges in energy management by providing exponential speedup for certain algorithms. Quantum optimization algorithms can optimize energy systems, by considering factors such as energy generation, distribution, storage, and consumption. By leveraging quantum computing, manufacturers can optimize energy flow, minimize energy waste, and enhance overall energy system efficiency, leading to reduced energy costs and environmental impact.

11.10.2 DEMAND RESPONSE AND LOAD BALANCING

Demand response and load balancing are crucial aspects of efficient energy management. Quantum computing can enhance the optimization of demand response programs and load-balancing strategies. By leveraging quantum algorithms, manufacturers can optimize the allocation of energy resources based on real-time demand and price signals. This enables dynamic load balancing, demand shifting, and effective utilization of renewable energy sources, resulting in improved grid stability, reduced energy costs, and enhanced sustainability.

11.10.3 QUANTUM-ASSISTED ENERGY MODELING AND FORECASTING

Accurate energy modeling and forecasting are essential for effective energy management. Quantum computing can enhance energy modeling and forecasting techniques by leveraging its computational power to process and analyze large datasets. Quantum-assisted energy modeling and forecasting algorithms can incorporate diverse data sources, such as weather patterns, energy consumption patterns, and production schedules, to predict energy demand and optimize energy supply. This enables manufacturers to anticipate energy requirements, plan production accordingly, and optimize energy procurement, reducing energy waste and costs.

11.10.4 SUSTAINABLE SUPPLY CHAIN OPTIMIZATION

Quantum computing can optimize supply chain operations to achieve sustainability goals. By leveraging quantum optimization algorithms, manufacturers can optimize supply chain configurations, transportation routes, and inventory management to minimize energy consumption, reduce carbon emissions, and promote sustainable practices. Quantum-enabled supply chain optimization enables manufacturers to make informed decisions about supplier selection, transportation modes, and warehouse locations, considering energy efficiency and environmental impact.

11.10.5 RENEWABLE ENERGY INTEGRATION AND GRID OPTIMIZATION

The integration of renewable energy sources into manufacturing operations requires efficient energy management and grid optimization. Quantum computing can optimize the integration of renewable energy by modeling and analyzing the behavior of renewable energy sources, grid interactions, and energy storage systems. Quantum algorithms can optimize the utilization of renewable energy, minimize grid congestion, and enhance energy grid stability. This promotes the adoption of renewable energy sources, reduces reliance on fossil fuels, and contributes to a more sustainable manufacturing ecosystem.

Energy optimization in manufacturing is essential for reducing costs, improving sustainability, and enhancing operational efficiency. Quantum computing offers unique capabilities that can revolutionize energy optimization practices. By leveraging quantum optimization algorithms, energy modeling techniques, and forecasting capabilities, manufacturers can achieve improved energy efficiency, reduced carbon footprint, and enhanced sustainability. Quantum-enabled energy optimization enables manufacturers to optimize energy systems, incorporate renewable energy sources, optimize supply chain operations, and make data-driven decisions to reduce energy waste and environmental impact. As quantum computing technology continues to advance, its integration into energy optimization practices will drive the next wave of advancements in manufacturing, paving the way for a more sustainable and energy-efficient future.

11.11 MITIGATING RISKS IN INDUSTRIAL PROCESSES USING QUANTUM ALGORITHMS

Industrial processes are often associated with various risks, including equipment failures, safety hazards, supply chain disruptions, and financial uncertainties. Mitigating these risks is crucial for ensuring the smooth operation and sustainability of industrial processes. Quantum computing offers unique applications that can enhance risk mitigation strategies by leveraging its computational power, optimization capabilities, and advanced algorithms. This section explores the role of quantum algorithms in mitigating risks in industrial processes, from risk assessment to optimization of risk mitigation strategies [12].

11.11.1 QUANTUM-ASSISTED RISK ASSESSMENT

Quantum computing can enhance risk assessment practices by providing increased computational power for analyzing complex risk factors. Quantum algorithms can process and analyze large volumes of data, enabling a more accurate understanding of risk profiles. By leveraging quantum-assisted risk assessment, manufacturers can identify potential risks, assess their impacts, and prioritize risk mitigation efforts. This leads to informed decision-making, proactive risk management, and improved resilience in industrial processes.

11.11.2 OPTIMIZATION OF RISK MITIGATION STRATEGIES

Quantum computing can address the optimization challenges associated with risk mitigation strategies. Quantum optimization algorithms can consider multiple factors, such as risk severity, mitigation costs, resource constraints, and regulatory compliance, to optimize risk mitigation plans. By leveraging quantum computing, manufacturers can identify optimal risk mitigation strategies, allocate resources effectively, and optimize risk-reward trade-offs. This enables more efficient and cost-effective risk management practices, reducing potential losses and improving overall operational resilience.

11.11.3 SUPPLY CHAIN RISK MANAGEMENT

Supply chain operations are susceptible to various risks, including disruptions, delays, and uncertainties. Quantum computing can enhance supply chain risk management by modeling and simulating different risk scenarios, identifying potential vulnerabilities, and optimizing risk mitigation strategies. Quantum algorithms can evaluate the impact of disruptions, identify alternative suppliers and routes, and develop robust contingency plans. This enables manufacturers to enhance supply chain resilience, minimize risks, and improve overall supply chain performance.

11.11.4 FINANCIAL RISK MODELING AND ANALYSIS

Financial risks, such as market volatility and currency fluctuations, can significantly impact industrial processes. Quantum computing can enhance financial risk modeling and analysis by leveraging its computational power for optimization and simulations. Quantum algorithms can analyze market trends, evaluate risk exposures, and optimize financial portfolios. By leveraging quantum computing, manufacturers can make informed financial decisions, manage risks effectively, and enhance financial stability in industrial processes.

11.11.5 QUANTUM-ENABLED DECISION SUPPORT SYSTEMS

Quantum computing can enhance decision support systems for risk management by providing increased computational power and faster analysis of complex risk factors. Quantum-assisted decision support systems can incorporate real-time data, probabilistic modeling, and optimization techniques to support risk-informed decision-making. This empowers manufacturers to make informed decisions, allocate resources effectively, and implement risk mitigation strategies promptly, reducing potential losses and improving overall risk management effectiveness.

Mitigating risks in industrial processes is crucial for ensuring smooth operations and sustainability. Quantum computing offers unique capabilities that can enhance risk mitigation strategies. By leveraging quantum algorithms for risk assessment, optimization, supply chain management, financial modeling, and decision support, manufacturers can identify potential risks, optimize risk mitigation strategies, and make informed decisions to improve overall operational resilience. As quantum computing technology continues to advance, its integration into risk mitigation processes will drive the next wave of advancements in industrial processes, enabling manufacturers to achieve higher levels of risk awareness, preparedness, and success.

11.12 QUANTUM COMPUTING: REVOLUTIONIZING LOGISTIC OPERATIONS

Logistic operations play a critical role in the global supply chain, encompassing transportation, inventory management, warehousing, and distribution. The integration of quantum computing in logistic operations holds the potential to revolutionize the efficiency, optimization, and sustainability of these processes. Quantum computing's computational power, optimization capabilities, and simulation techniques can address the complexity and scale of logistics, leading to improved route planning, inventory optimization, and supply chain management. This section explores the role of quantum computing in revolutionizing logistic operations [13, 14].

11.12.1 QUANTUM-ENABLED ROUTE OPTIMIZATION

Quantum computing can enhance route optimization techniques by considering numerous variables, constraints, and real-time data. Quantum optimization algorithms can efficiently solve complex vehicle routing problems, optimizing routes to minimize travel distances, reduce fuel consumption, and improve delivery times. By leveraging quantum computing, logistics companies can achieve optimal routing strategies, resulting in cost savings, reduced environmental impact, and enhanced customer satisfaction.

11.12.2 INVENTORY OPTIMIZATION

Quantum computing can optimize inventory management by balancing supply and demand, minimizing holding costs, and ensuring optimal stock levels. Quantum algorithms can handle large datasets and optimize inventory models, considering factors such as demand fluctuations, lead times, and storage capacity. By leveraging quantum computing, logistics companies can reduce stockouts, minimize excess inventory, and improve order fulfillment rates, resulting in improved operational efficiency and reduced carrying costs.

11.12.3 QUANTUM-ASSISTED DEMAND FORECASTING

Demand forecasting is crucial for effective logistics planning and resource allocation. Quantum computing can enhance demand forecasting models by analyzing diverse data sources, such as historical sales data, market trends, and customer behavior patterns. Quantum-assisted demand forecasting can provide more accurate predictions, enabling logistics companies to optimize inventory levels, plan transportation capacity, and improve supply chain responsiveness. This leads to improved customer satisfaction and reduced operational costs.

11.12.4 SUPPLY CHAIN OPTIMIZATION

Supply chain optimization is a complex task, involving multiple stakeholders, transportation modes, and inventory locations. Quantum computing can optimize supply chain operations by considering various factors, including transportation costs, lead times, production capacities, and customer demand. Quantum optimization algorithms can optimize supply chain configurations, distribution networks, and inventory allocation, resulting in improved supply chain efficiency, reduced costs, and enhanced responsiveness to market dynamics.

11.12.5 QUANTUM-ENABLED RISK MANAGEMENT

Logistic operations are exposed to various risks, such as disruptions in transportation, weather events, and supplier failures. Quantum computing can enhance risk management strategies by modeling and simulating different risk scenarios, identifying potential vulnerabilities, and optimizing risk mitigation strategies. Quantum-assisted risk management enables logistics companies to develop robust contingency plans, optimize routing to avoid risks and enhance supply chain resilience, minimizing disruptions and improving overall operational stability.

The integration of quantum computing in logistic operations has the potential to revolutionize efficiency, optimization, and sustainability. By leveraging quantum computing for route optimization, inventory management, demand forecasting, supply chain optimization, and risk management, logistics companies can achieve significant improvements in operational efficiency, cost savings, and customer satisfaction. As quantum computing technology continues to advance, its integration into logistic operations will drive the next wave of advancements in the industry, enabling more precise and effective decision-making, optimized resource allocation, and improved supply chain responsiveness.

11.13 QUANTUM TECHNIQUES FOR INVENTORY MANAGEMENT

Inventory management plays a crucial role in various industries, ensuring efficient supply chain operations, minimizing costs, and meeting customer demands. Quantum computing offers unique techniques and capabilities that have the potential to revolutionize inventory management practices. By leveraging its computational power, optimization algorithms, and simulation capabilities, quantum computing can optimize inventory levels, reduce stockouts, and improve overall supply chain performance. This section explores the role of quantum techniques in inventory management and their potential benefits [15].

11.13.1 QUANTUM OPTIMIZATION FOR INVENTORY MODELS

Quantum computing can optimize inventory models by considering numerous variables, such as demand patterns, lead times, and storage capacities. Quantum optimization algorithms can handle the complexity and scale of inventory management problems, enabling the optimization of reorder points, order quantities, and safety stock levels. By leveraging quantum computing, businesses can achieve more accurate inventory replenishment strategies, minimize stockouts, reduce excess inventory, and improve overall inventory efficiency.

11.13.2 QUANTUM-ASSISTED DEMAND FORECASTING

Demand forecasting is a critical aspect of inventory management. Quantum computing can enhance demand forecasting by analyzing diverse data sources, including historical sales data, market trends, and customer behavior patterns. Quantum-assisted demand forecasting can provide more accurate predictions, enabling businesses to optimize inventory levels, plan production schedules, and make informed procurement decisions. This leads to improved inventory accuracy, reduced carrying costs, and enhanced customer satisfaction.

11.13.3 QUANTUM SIMULATIONS FOR INVENTORY OPTIMIZATION

Quantum simulations can enhance inventory optimization by modeling and analyzing complex supply chain dynamics. Quantum computing can simulate different scenarios, incorporating factors such as demand variability, lead time fluctuations, and production constraints. By leveraging quantum simulations, businesses can assess the impact of various inventory management strategies, identify bottlenecks, and optimize inventory control policies. This results in improved supply chain resilience, reduced costs, and enhanced operational efficiency.

11.13.4 QUANTUM-ENABLED MULTI-ECHELON INVENTORY OPTIMIZATION

Managing inventory across multiple echelons, such as warehouses, distribution centers, and retail outlets, presents unique challenges. Quantum computing can optimize multi-echelon inventory systems by considering the interdependencies and interactions between different inventory levels. Quantum optimization algorithms can identify optimal stocking policies, coordinate replenishment activities, and minimize inventory holding costs. By leveraging quantum techniques, businesses can achieve synchronized inventory management across multiple locations, reducing stockouts and improving overall supply chain performance.

11.13.5 QUANTUM ALGORITHMS FOR SUPPLY CHAIN RISK MANAGEMENT

Inventory management is also susceptible to various risks, such as supply disruptions, demand fluctuations, and lead time variability. Quantum computing can enhance supply chain risk management by analyzing complex risk scenarios and optimizing risk mitigation strategies. Quantum algorithms can assess the impact of risks on inventory levels, optimize safety stock quantities, and enable proactive risk response planning. This enhances supply chain resilience, reduces inventory-related risks, and improves overall supply chain performance.

Quantum techniques offer promising solutions for optimizing inventory management practices. By leveraging quantum optimization, demand forecasting, simulations, and risk management algorithms, businesses can achieve improved inventory accuracy, reduced costs, and enhanced supply chain performance. As quantum computing technology continues to advance, its integration into inventory management processes will drive the next wave of advancements, enabling businesses to achieve higher levels of inventory efficiency, responsiveness, and customer satisfaction.

11.14 ENHANCED PRODUCT LIFECYCLE MANAGEMENT THROUGH QUANTUM COMPUTING

Product Lifecycle Management (PLM) encompasses the entire lifespan of a product, from its conceptualization to retirement. Quantum computing offers unique capabilities that have the potential to revolutionize PLM practices by leveraging its computational power, optimization algorithms, and simulation techniques. Quantum computing can enhance various aspects of PLM, including design optimization, manufacturing process simulation, supply chain management, and sustainability analysis. This section explores the role of quantum computing in enhancing PLM and its potential benefits [16].

11.14.1 QUANTUM-ASSISTED DESIGN OPTIMIZATION

Quantum computing can optimize product design by considering numerous design parameters, constraints, and objectives. Quantum optimization algorithms can efficiently explore large design spaces, identifying optimal configurations and improving product performance. By leveraging quantum-assisted design optimization, businesses can achieve innovative designs, reduce time-to-market, and enhance product functionality, resulting in improved customer satisfaction and competitive advantage.

11.14.2 QUANTUM SIMULATIONS FOR MANUFACTURING PROCESS OPTIMIZATION

Quantum simulations can enhance manufacturing process optimization by modeling and analyzing complex manufacturing systems. Quantum computing can simulate manufacturing processes at the atomic or molecular level, enabling a deeper understanding of material behavior, process interactions, and performance trade-offs. By leveraging quantum simulations, businesses can optimize manufacturing parameters, reduce defects, and improve process efficiency, leading to higher product quality and reduced production costs.

11.14.3 QUANTUM-ENABLED SUPPLY CHAIN MANAGEMENT

Effective supply chain management is crucial for successful PLM. Quantum computing can optimize supply chain operations by considering factors such as demand variability, lead times, and inventory levels. Quantum optimization algorithms can optimize supply chain configurations, transportation routes, and inventory allocation, resulting in reduced costs, improved delivery times, and enhanced supply chain resilience. By leveraging quantum-enabled supply chain management, businesses can ensure a smooth flow of materials, minimize delays, and improve overall supply chain performance.

11.14.4 SUSTAINABILITY ANALYSIS AND ENVIRONMENTAL IMPACT ASSESSMENT

Sustainability is an increasingly important aspect of PLM, as businesses strive to minimize environmental impact and embrace sustainable practices. Quantum computing can perform complex sustainability analysis by considering multiple environmental factors, such as energy consumption, carbon emissions, and waste generation. Quantum algorithms can assess the environmental impact of different product design choices, manufacturing processes, and supply chain configurations. This enables businesses to make informed decisions that prioritize sustainability, reduce environmental footprint, and meet regulatory requirements.

11.14.5 QUANTUM-ASSISTED PREDICTIVE MAINTENANCE AND END-OF-LIFE MANAGEMENT

Predictive maintenance and end-of-life management are critical components of PLM. Quantum computing can enhance predictive maintenance strategies by analyzing sensor data, optimizing maintenance schedules, and predicting equipment failures. Quantum-assisted predictive maintenance enables businesses to minimize downtime, reduce maintenance costs, and improve equipment reliability. Additionally, quantum computing can optimize end-of-life management practices by considering factors such as recycling, disposal, and material recovery. This enables businesses to enhance product sustainability, comply with regulations, and minimize environmental impact during product disposal.

Quantum computing offers immense potential for enhancing PLM practices. By leveraging its computational power, optimization algorithms, and simulation capabilities, businesses can achieve improved product design, manufacturing process optimization, supply chain management, sustainability analysis, and maintenance strategies. Quantum-enabled PLM leads to reduced time-to-market, higher product quality, improved supply chain efficiency, enhanced sustainability, and overall competitive advantage. As quantum computing technology continues to advance, its integration into PLM processes will drive the next wave of advancements, enabling businesses to achieve higher levels of innovation, efficiency, and sustainability throughout the product lifecycle.

11.15 CONCLUSION

Challenges and Considerations: The quantum-driven industrial revolution is not without its challenges. Scaling up quantum hardware, reducing error rates, and improving qubit stability remain significant technological hurdles. Additionally, developing robust and efficient quantum algorithms for specific industrial applications requires substantial research and development. Addressing security concerns, ensuring the interoperability of quantum systems with existing technologies, and addressing ethical implications are also important considerations.

The quantum-driven industrial revolution promises transformative changes across industries, empowering businesses to achieve unprecedented levels of efficiency, innovation, and competitiveness. The application of quantum computing in optimization, healthcare, finance, AI, and cybersecurity opens up new frontiers for advancement and growth. While challenges persist, the ongoing progress in quantum technologies offers glimpses of the immense potential and benefits that lie ahead. By embracing quantum computing, industries can drive the next wave of technological advancements, ushering in an era of unparalleled innovation and prosperity.

KEYWORDS

- **quantum computing**
- **manufacturing innovation**
- **industrial design**
- **supply chain optimization**
- **predictive maintenance**
- **sustainable manufacturing**
- **Industry 4.0**

REFERENCES

1. Bova, F., Goldfarb, A., & Melko, R. G. (2021). Commercial applications of quantum computing. *EPJ Quantum Technology*, *8*, 2. https://doi.org/10.1140/epjqt/s40507-021-00091-1.
2. Luckow, A., Klepsch, J., & Pichlmeier, J. (2021). Quantum computing: Towards industry reference problems. *Digitale Welt, 5*, 38–45. https://doi.org/10.1007/s42354-021-0335-7
3. Rawat, B., Mehra, N., Bist, A. S., Yusup, M., & Sanjaya, Y. P. A. (2022). Quantum computing and AI: Impacts & possibilities. *ADI Journal on Recent Innovation*, *3*(2), 202–207. https://doi.org/10.34306/ajri.v3i2.656.
4. Jyothi Ahuja, N., & Dutt, S. (2022). Implications of quantum science on industry 4.0: Challenges and opportunities. In Kumar, A., Gill, S. S., & Abraham, A. (Eds.), *Quantum and Blockchain for Modern Computing Systems: Vision and Advancements* (*Lecture Notes on Data Engineering and Communications Technologies*), Vol. 133. Springer, Cham. https://doi.org/10.1007/978-3-031-04613-1_6.
5. Sigov, A., Ratkin, L., Ivanov, L. A., Xu, L. D. (2022). Emerging enabling technologies for industry 4.0 and beyond. *Information Systems Frontiers*, *26*(5), 1585–1595. https://doi.org/10.1007/s10796-021-10213-w.
6. Chapman, R. L., Soosay, C., & Kandampully, J. (2003). Innovation in logistic services and the new business model: A conceptual framework. *International Journal of Physical Distribution & Logistics Management*. *33*(7), 630–650. https://doi.org/10.1108/09600030310499295.
7. Balland, P., & Boschma, R. (2021). Mapping the potentials of regions in Europe to contribute to new knowledge production in Industry 4.0 technologies. *Regional Studies*, *55*(10–11), 1652–1666. https://doi.org/10.1080/00343404.2021.1900557.
8. Mehta, A., Muradi, M., & Woldetsadick, S. (2019). Quantum annealing based optimization of robotic movement in manufacturing. In Feld, S., & Linnhoff-Popien, C. (Eds.), *Quantum Technology and Optimization Problems. QTOP 2019* (Lecture Notes in Computer Science), Vol. 11413. Springer, Cham. https://doi.org/10.1007/978-3-030-14082-3_12.
9. Ajagekar, A., & You, F. (2022). New frontiers of quantum computing in chemical engineering. *Korean Journal of Chemical Engineering*, *39*, 811–820. https://doi.org/10.1007/s11814-021-1027-6
10. Awan, U., Hannola, L., Tandon, A., Goyal, R. K., & Dhir, A. (2022). Quantum computing challenges in the software industry. A fuzzy AHP-based approach. *Information and Software Technology*, *147*, 106896.
11. Ajagekar, A., & You, F. (2019). Quantum computing for energy systems optimization: Challenges and opportunities. *Energy*, *179*, 76–89.
12. Mangla, C., Rani, S., Faseeh Qureshi, N. M., & Singh, A. (2023). Mitigating 5G security challenges for next-gen industry using quantum computing. *Journal of King Saud University—Computer and Information Sciences*, *35*, 101334. https://doi.org/10.1016/j.jksuci.2022.07.009.
13. Bussmann, E., Butera, R. E., & Owen, J. H. G. (2021). Atomic-precision advanced manufacturing for Si quantum computing. *MRS Bulletin*, *46*, 607–615. https://doi.org/10.1557/s43577-021-00139-8.

14. Clarke J. S., et al. (2016). Quantum computing within the framework of advanced semiconductor manufacturing. In *2016 IEEE International Electron Devices Meeting (IEDM)*. San Francisco, CA, USA, pp. 13.1.1–13.1.3. https://doi.org/10.1109/IEDM.2016.7838406.
15. Gacon, J., Zoufal, C., & Woerner, S. (2020). Quantum-enhanced simulation-based optimization. In *2020 IEEE International Conference on Quantum Computing and Engineering (QCE)*. Denver, CO, USA, pp. 47–55. https://doi.org/10.1109/QCE49297.2020.00017.
16. Egger, D. J., & Gambella, C., et al. (2020). Quantum computing for finance: State-of-the-art and future prospects. *IEEE Transactions on Quantum Engineering, 1*, 1–24, 3101724. https://doi.org/10.1109/TQE.2020.3030314.

CHAPTER 12

Application of Quantum Computing in the Field of Machine Learning

JAYASURYAN S, SUBHA SHREE C V, P. VIVEK*, S. IVO ROMAULD, and MEENAMBIGA S. S.

Department of Bio-Engineering, Vels Institute of Science, Technology & Advanced Studies, Chennai, Tamil Nadu, India

*Corresponding author

ABSTRACT

A promising answer to challenging computational problems is provided by combining quantum computing with machine learning (ML). Superposition and entanglement, two distinctive features of quantum computing, allow for the creation of revolutionary algorithms and models that completely alter pattern detection, data analysis, and optimization. The study examines the theoretical foundations, applications, and suitability of quantum ML algorithms for ML tasks. However, it also has drawbacks including restricted qubit coherence, noise reduction, and error correction. The solutions to these problems are described, and practical implementations demonstrate how quantum computing outperforms traditional techniques by improving feature selection and resolving combinatorial optimization issues. Overall, the domains of ML and data-driven decision-making could be completely transformed by quantum computing.

12.1 INTRODUCTION

Considering the potential to resolve complicated issues that are currently beyond the capabilities of conventional computers, quantum computing

Applications of Quantum Computing in a Variety of Domains. Gunjan Mukherjee, Biswadip Basu Mallik, Rahul Kar Özen ÖZER, Digvijay Pandey, and Binay Kumar Pandey (Eds.)

DOI: 10.1201/9781998511051-12

is poised to completely alter the machine learning (ML) environment. Quantum bits, also known as qubits, may exist in a superposition of states, allowing them to simultaneously represent numerous possibilities, in contrast to classical bits, which only represent information as a 0 or 1. Quantum computers can do some operations tenfold quicker than their conventional counterparts due to their inherent parallelism. This could result in significant improvements in optimization, simulation, and data analysis in the context of ML. Solving optimization issues is one of the most intriguing uses of quantum computing in ML [3, 4]. Finding the best parameters or training deep neural networks are two common ML problems that involve intricate optimization procedures. By utilizing their unique capacity to consider numerous options concurrently, quantum computers offer the potential to significantly accelerate these operations. This might result in more rapid convergence and effective model training. Quantum computing also has the potential to transform simulations, allowing scientists to precisely simulate and examine complex molecular, chemical, and physical processes. This might have significant effects on medicine development, materials research, and other areas of science, which would ultimately speed up innovation [1]. The science is still in its infancy, even though quantum computing has a lot of potential. It is extremely difficult to create and maintain stable qubits, and error rates are still rather high. Researchers are developing approaches for error correction and better qubit designs as the area develops. In this chapter, we discuss the application of quantum computing in the field of ML [2].

12.2 APPLICATIONS

12.2.1 QUANTUM NEURAL NETWORKS (QNNS)

By utilizing the special characteristics of quantum physics, QNNs provide a fresh method of ML. QNNs use quantum bits, or qubits, which may be in a superposition of states and enable parallel computing, as opposed to conventional neural networks, which work with binary bits. Qubits are manipulated by quantum gates, and the entanglement phenomenon enables qubits to instantly correlate with one another. Similar to classical network training, QNNs frequently employ quantum variational circuits that modify quantum gates in order to minimize a particular cost function. Data classification, feature mapping, generative modeling, optimization, and support vector models are some of the applications of QNNs. However, qubit stability and correction of error present difficulties for actual application. QNNs show promise for more effectively handling challenging ML tasks as quantum technology develops [5].

12.2.2 QUANTUM SUPPORT VECTOR MACHINES (QSVM)

The use of quantum computing in "QSVM." QSVMs accelerate traditional support vector machine (SVM) calculations by taking advantage of the built-in parallelism of quantum systems. SVMs are frequently employed in ML for applications involving regression and classification. QSVMs can provide quicker methods for locating the ideal hyperplanes in feature spaces with high dimensions by utilizing the processing power of quantum bits (qubits). This acceleration results from qubits' capacity to do intricate mathematical operations concurrently while existing in various states. In order to improve the effectiveness of tasks like data categorization and regression, QSVM algorithms employ quantum entanglement and superposition, which could potentially offer a considerable speedup over conventional methods [6].

12.2.3 QUANTUM DATA PROCESSING

Fundamental data processing operations like reduction of dimensionality and feature selection may be streamlined with quantum computing. The effectiveness of pipelines for ML can be greatly increased by doing these tasks. Quantum techniques, such as quantum singular value decomposition (QSVD) and quantum principal component analysis (QPCA), may effectively evaluate and extract crucial data from enormous datasets. For example, QPCA can reduce the dimensionality of the data in question while identifying the most crucial characteristics, greatly accelerating future learning tasks. Quantum data processing uses the entanglement and parallelism that exist in nature to investigate several possibilities at once, possibly outperforming traditional approaches in terms of efficiency and resource use. However, addressing difficulties related to qubit error rates, decoherence, and additional fundamental hardware restrictions is essential for practical realization [7].

12.2.4 QUANTUM CLUSTERING AND CLASSIFICATION

Fundamental activities in data analysis like clustering and classification can potentially be accelerated by quantum algorithms. Utilizing superposition and quantum parallelism, quantum k-means clustering explores various cluster assignments at once, possibly resulting in faster convergence and more effective solutions. Similar to classical SVMs, QSVM use quantum states to speed up optimization and locate the best hyperplanes for classification problems. For some datasets, these quantum-enhanced techniques may outperform conventional ones in terms of computational effectiveness. However, solving difficulties related to error correction, qubit stability, and noise in quantum hardware is a prerequisite for the practical application of quantum clustering and classification methods. These quantum-enhanced algorithms hold promise for raising the effectiveness and precision of clustering and classification as quantum technologies develop [8].

12.2.5 QUANTUM BOLTZMANN MACHINES (QBMS)

ML's use of "QBMs". For generative modeling and autonomous learning, QBMs are a quantum equivalent of conventional Boltzmann machines. To better represent complicated data distributions, these quantum models make use of quantum mechanical concepts like superposition and entanglement. A qubit is represented by each of the interconnected quantum nodes that make up QBMs. QBMs can sample from complex distributions of probabilities thanks to quantum fluctuations and correlations among these qubits, which is essential for activities like data production and feature learning. QBMs have the ability to overcome the drawbacks of conventional generative models and provide enhanced capabilities for pattern recognition, data synthesis, and additional unsupervised learning tasks by taking advantage of the quantum nature of their constituent parts. However, to reduce the effects of quantum noise and decoherence, practical QBM implementation calls for reliable quantum hardware and efficient error-correction methods. QBMs provide the potential for enhancing generative modeling and autonomous learning in the field of ML as quantum computing technology develops [9].

12.2.6 QUANTUM-ENHANCED OPTIMIZATION

Finding the best model parameters or reducing cost functions are two examples of optimization challenges that frequently arise in ML projects. Employing quantum annealing and quantum optimization methods, quantum computing has the potential to speed up various optimization procedures. One such method that effectively incorporates both classical and quantum elements is the Quantum Approximation Optimization Algorithm (QAOA). With the help of quantum gates, QAOA explores several parameter configurations at once, taking advantage of quantum parallelism to perhaps identify more effective solutions faster. On the other hand, quantum annealing makes use of tunneling quantum mechanics and temperature swings to avoid local minima and enhance the results of optimization. The issues associated with feature decision-making, hyper-parameter tuning, and model training problems can all be solved using these quantum-enhanced optimization methods. However, for quantum-enhanced optimization to be used in practice, it needs reliable quantum hardware, error-correcting systems, and algorithmic advancements. Quantum-enhanced optimization has the potential to greatly improve ML optimization methods' efficiency as quantum technologies develop [10].

12.2.7 QUANTUM DATA ANALYSIS

Fundamental data processing activities that support different algorithms for ML could be accelerated by quantum computing. For instance, many data processing and modeling processes depend on operations like matrices inversion, eigenvalue and eigenvector calculations, and singular value decomposition. Compared to their classical counterparts, quantum algorithms can perform these tasks more quickly by taking advantage of superposition and quantum parallelism. The quantum singular value transformation method and other quantum algorithms for linear algebra use quantum gates that are used to approximate solutions to matrix factorizations and eigen decompositions. These quantum methods have the capacity to speed up data pretreatment and analysis, producing machine-learning results that are both quicker and more accurate. However, similar to other quantum applications, hardware stability, noise, and qubit error rates pose difficulties for practical implementation. Quantum data analysis shows potential for accelerating the speed and effectiveness of crucial data processing activities in ML pipelines as quantum technologies advance [11].

12.2.8 QUANTUM REINFORCEMENT LEARNING (QRL)

Reinforcement learning problems' training and decision-making procedures can be improved by quantum computing. In order to optimize cumulative rewards, reinforcement learning entails teaching agents to make decisions sequentially. The intrinsic parallelism of quantum computing and its capacity to simultaneously explore various states present potential advantages in terms of optimizing policies and value functions. Reinforcement learning issues can benefit from the use of quantum-enhanced optimization techniques, such as the QAOA, which can speed up policy search and boost convergence rates. In situations where classical approaches encounter difficulties because of vast state spaces or high-dimensional action spaces, QRL has the potential to accomplish complex control tasks more effectively by taking advantage of the quantum advantage. This may result in better-performing agents and quicker learning. However, reliable quantum hardware, methods for preventing errors, and improvements in quantum optimization algorithms are necessary for the effective implementation of QRL. QRL provides the potential for improving the capacity of reinforcement learning algorithms and solving difficulties in making choices and maintaining control in complex contexts as quantum technologies improve [12].

12.2.9 QUANTUM NATURAL LANGUAGE PROCESSING (QNLP)

Linguistic analysis, sentiment analysis, language synthesis, and machine translation are just a few of the jobs that can be improved by quantum computing. The complicated links between words and sentences can be processed and analyzed concurrently by quantum algorithms, enabling more effective semantic interpretation and sentiment extraction from textual information. Better language generation systems that capture intricate linguistic patterns might be produced using quantum-enhanced optimization techniques. Additionally, by using quantum parallelism to simultaneously test several translation hypotheses, quantum models may enhance the effectiveness of machine translation systems. However, overcoming the difficulties of quantum error correction, qubit stability, and the creation of appropriate quantum language models are necessary for the effective application of QNLP. QNLP has the promise of improving language interpretation and production tasks in ML as quantum technologies develop, paving the path for more advanced and effective language-related applications [13].

12.2.10 QUANTUM RECOMMENDATION SYSTEMS

By utilizing the capabilities of quantum computing, quantum recommendation systems provide a cutting-edge method for providing individualized content recommendations. These systems are designed to improve recommendation algorithms' effectiveness and precision, especially in circumstances requiring massive volumes of user data and intricate interactions. Large user-item interaction matrices could be processed more quickly by using quantum algorithms like QPCA or quantum singular value breakdown (QSVD), which can simultaneously capture subtle preferences and correlations. Quantum recommendation systems could fundamentally alter sectors like e-commerce and entertainment, where user engagement depends on personalized recommendations. These systems may offer more accurate and timely recommendations by making use of quantum parallelism and entanglement. This might increase user happiness and possibly increase business profits. However, strong quantum hardware, error-correction methods, and the conversion of conventional recommendation algorithms into quantum equivalents are required for practical implementation. Quantum recommendation systems have the potential to revolutionize how tailored content is presented as quantum computing technology develops, influencing the future of engines for suggestions in a variety of disciplines [14].

12.2.11 QUANTUM ANOMALY DETECTION

Utilizing the inherent benefits of quantum computing, quantum anomaly detection offers a viable method for finding uncommon and anomalous occurrences inside large, complicated datasets. This application uses the special qualities of quantum bits to improve anomaly detection methods.

Quantum algorithms, such as QSVM or QPCA, can handle high-dimensional data effectively to find minute variations from predicted patterns, which are frequently difficult to find using conventional techniques. Practically speaking, quantum anomaly detection may have uses in a number of fields, including the identification of fraud in financial transactions and the detection of anomalies in manufacturing processes. These systems may excel at spotting anomalies more quickly and correctly while lowering false positives and negatives by utilizing quantum parallelism and entanglement. However, overcoming obstacles like qubit stability, noise, and correction for errors is necessary for a successful implementation. Quantum anomaly detection has the potential to provide better insights into complicated datasets as quantum technologies advance, enabling speedier reactions to anomalous events and improving overall data integrity and security [15].

12.2.12 QUANTUM GRAPH ANALYTICS

By utilizing the capabilities of quantum computers, quantum graph analytics represents a revolutionary method for studying complex network structures like social networks, chemical interactions, and transportation systems. With regard to large-scale graphs, this application seeks to elucidate hidden patterns and insights, a task that conventional approaches frequently find computationally challenging. Quantum algorithms, like Quantum Walks or Quantum PageRank, may be able to simultaneously explore a number of paths and links, giving them a quantum advantage while navigating intricate network topologies. Quantum graph analytics has the potential to have an impact on a variety of disciplines, including social science, biology, and urban planning. By harnessing quantum parallelism and entanglement, these systems may identify influential nodes, detect communities, or optimize routing in networks more efficiently. However, the successful realization of quantum graph analytics requires addressing challenges like error correction, decoherence, and mapping classical graph algorithms to quantum equivalents. As quantum technologies advance, quantum graph analytics holds promise for enhancing our understanding of intricate network structures, enabling more accurate predictions, and contributing to improved decision-making across various domains [16].

12.2.13 QUANTUM CHEMISTRY SIMULATION

At the nexus of quantum computing and computational chemistry, quantum chemistry simulation is a game-changing application. It has the potential to revolutionize precise molecular and chemical relationship modeling, which is essential for understanding chemical reactions, developing new drugs, and researching new materials. Quantum algorithms can simulate quantum systems with an accuracy that frequently exceeds that of conventional techniques, such as the variational quantum eigensolver or quantum phase estimation. These algorithms effectively calculate molecule energies, bond disintegration energies, and reaction routes by taking advantage of quantum superposition and entanglement, offering insights into intricate chemical phenomena. By more accurately simulating chemical interactions, quantum chemistry simulation could speed up the discovery of new medications and produce more potent pharmaceutical formulations. Similar to that, it might hasten the creation of new materials by enabling a better understanding of their quantum-level characteristics. However, overcoming difficulties like error correction, noise reduction, and the requirement of powerful, fault-tolerant quantum computers is essential for the effectiveness of quantum chemistry simulation. Quantum chemistry simulation has enormous potential to alter computational chemistry, enable molecular design breakthroughs, and catalyze developments in a variety of scientific and industrial domains as quantum computer technology develops [17].

12.2.14 QUANTUM IMAGE AND VIDEO ANALYSIS

The area of quantum computing and visual data processing known as quantum image and video analysis is an attractive one. With the help of this program, image and video analysis tasks including object recognition, image segmentation, and video comprehension should be performed more quickly and accurately. By utilizing quantum parallelism and entanglement, quantum algorithms, especially QSVD or QPCA, can analyze visual data more quickly and enable the extraction of complex patterns and features. Quantum image and video analysis has the potential to change industries including surveillance, driverless vehicles, and medical imaging in real-world applications. These systems could offer more rapid and precise detection of objects, anomalies, or patterns in visual data by utilizing the capabilities of quantum computation. However, overcoming obstacles including qubit error rates, noise, and the conversion of conventional computer vision algorithms into quantum counterparts is necessary for successful implementation. Quantum image and video analysis has the potential to provide sophisticated visual data processing, boosting the functionality of numerous applications and developing the field of computer vision as quantum technologies advance [18].

12.2.15 QUANTUM TIME SERIES ANALYSIS

An intriguing use case that uses quantum computing to handle complex temporal data patterns is called quantum time series analysis. The goal of this subject is to improve the analysis and forecasting of time-dependent phenomena, including physiologic signals, weather patterns, and financial market movements. By utilizing quantum parallelism and entanglement, quantum algorithms, such as QSVD or Quantum Fourier Transform, have the ability to handle time series data more effectively, facilitating the quicker extraction of underlying periodicities and trends. Quantum time series analysis has the potential to change fields including economics, climatology, and medicine. These systems could offer quicker and more precise forecasts of market trends, climatic shifts, or disease outbreaks by utilizing quantum capabilities. However, overcoming difficulties like qubit stability, error correction, and quantizing conventional time series analytic methods is essential for a successful deployment. Quantum time series analysis shows potential for deciphering complicated temporal correlations and assisting in better forecasts and making decisions across a range of time-dependent phenomena as quantum technologies advance [19].

12.2.16 QUANTUM GENERATIVE ADVERSARIAL NETWORKS (QGANS)

With a chance to revolutionize data synthesis and the production of creative material, QGANs represent an intriguing nexus of generative modeling and quantum computing. Quantum parallelism and entanglement are used by QGANs, an extension of conventional generative adversarial networks (GANs), to provide more varied and accurate data samples. Quantum generators and discriminators work together in QGANs to create data distributions that mirror real-world data. Quantum generators alter quantum states, and discriminators evaluate the validity of the created samples. QGANs aspire to outperform classical GANs in the generation of detailed and complicated data patterns, from visuals and music to scientific simulations, by utilizing quantum characteristics. By creating innovative and distinctive content with an unparalleled level of complexity and depth, quantum GANs have the potential to completely transform the creative sectors such as art, entertainment, and design. They could also speed up the creation of high-quality synthetic data for ML model training in cases where real data is limited or privacy-sensitive. However, in order to fully utilize QGANs, issues with qubit stability, error correction, and training strong QNNs must be resolved. QGANs possess the potential to usher in an entirely novel age of creative content generation and data augmentation, with far-reaching ramifications across multiple areas, as quantum computing develops [20].

12.3 CONCLUSION

A new era of computational potential is ushering in with the convergence of quantum computing and ML. The mutually beneficial interaction between these two disciplines offers exciting possibilities for resolving complicated issues that were previously thought to be beyond the scope of conventional approaches. The ability of quantum computing to refine algorithms and reveal complex data patterns opens up a promising new path for ML research. Researchers and practitioners are on the verge of a revolutionary age as the quantum computing landscape develops and technologies advance. Unlocking the full potential of this synergy will depend on continued innovation and collaboration between experts in ML and quantum physics. The development of quantum-enhanced ML will expand our capacity to decipher the intricacies of the world around us as well as change the limits of computation. In essence, the potential and intrigue of ML combined with quantum computing are exciting. It requires an ongoing investigation of potential, a dedication to overcoming obstacles, and a shared vision of utilizing quantum capabilities to open the door for a new generation of intelligent systems that are capable of taking on the most difficult problems. Quantum computing holds the possibility of altering decision-making paradigms and transforming industries through its potential applications in ML, which range from enhancing feature spaces to expediting optimization procedures. However, there are many obstacles in the way of fully realizing this promise, including the requirement for more durable quantum hardware and error-correcting systems.

KEYWORDS

- **machine learning**
- **quantum image**
- **quantum neural network**
- **quantum singular value decomposition**
- **quantum time series analysis**
- **reinforcement learning**
- **video analysis**

REFERENCES

1. Ramezani, S. B., Sommers, A., Manchukonda, H. K., Rahimi, S., & Amirlatifi, A. (2020, July). Machine learning algorithms in quantum computing: A survey. In *2020 International Joint Conference on Neural Networks (IJCNN)*. IEEE, pp. 1–8.
2. Hassija, V., Chamola, V., Goyal, A., Kanhere, S. S., & Guizani, N. (2020). Forthcoming applications of quantum computing: Peeking into the future. *IET Quantum Communication*, *1*(2), 35–41.
3. Schuld, M., Sinayskiy, I., & Petruccione, F. (2015). An introduction to quantum machine learning. *Contemporary Physics*, *56*(2), 172–185.
4. Sajwan, P., & Jayapandian, N. (2019, December). Challenges and opportunities: Quantum computing in machine learning. In *2019 Third International Conference on I-SMAC (IoT in Social, Mobile, Analytics and Cloud)(I-SMAC)*. IEEE, pp. 598–602.
5. Bausch, J. (2020). Recurrent quantum neural networks. *Advances in Neural Information Processing Systems*, *33*, 1368–1379.
6. Kavitha, S. S., & Kaulgud, N. (2022). Quantum machine learning for support vector machine classification. *Evolutionary Intelligence*, *17*, 1–10.

7. Abohashima, Z., Elhosen, M., Houssein, E. H., & Mohamed, W. M. (2020). Classification with quantum machine learning: A survey. arXiv preprint *arXiv:2006.12270*.
8. Cai, X. D., Wu, D., Su, Z. E., Chen, M. C., Wang, X. L., Li, L., Liu, N.-L., Lu, C.-Y., & Pan, J. W. (2015). Entanglement-based machine learning on a quantum computer. *Physical Review Letters*, *114*(11), 110504.
9. Crawford, D., Levit, A., Ghadermarzy, N., Oberoi, J. S., & Ronagh, P. (2016). Reinforcement learning using quantum Boltzmann machines. arXiv preprint *arXiv:1612.05695*.
10. Zahorodko, P. V., Modlo, Y. O., Kalinichenko, O. O., Selivanova, T. V., & Semerikov, S. (2021). Quantum enhanced machine learning: An overview. In *CEUR Workshop Proceedings*.
11. Shaikh, T. A., & Ali, R. (2016, December). Quantum computing in big data analytics: A survey. In *2016 IEEE International Conference on Computer and Information Technology (CIT)*. IEEE, pp. 112–115.
12. Kunczik, L. (2022). Quantum reinforcement learning—Connecting reinforcement learning and quantum computing. In *Reinforcement Learning with Hybrid Quantum Approximation in the NISQ Context*, pp. 41–48.
13. Pandey, S., Basisth, N. J., Sachan, T., Kumari, N., & Pakray, P. (2023). Quantum machine learning for natural language processing application. *Physica A: Statistical Mechanics and its Applications*, *627*, 129123.
14. Tang, E. (2019, June). A quantum-inspired classical algorithm for recommendation systems. In *Proceedings of the 51st Annual ACM SIGACT Symposium on Theory of Computing*. pp. 217–228.
15. Liu, N., & Rebentrost, P. (2018). Quantum machine learning for quantum anomaly detection. *Physical Review A*, *97*(4), 042315.
16. Gao, X., Zhang, Z. Y., & Duan, L. M. (2018). A quantum machine learning algorithm based on generative models. *Science Advances*, *4*(12), eaat9004.
17. Bernal, D. E., Ajagekar, A., Harwood, S. M., Stober, S. T., Trenev, D., & You, F. (2022). Perspectives of quantum computing for chemical engineering. *AIChE Journal*, *68*(6), e17651.
18. Wittek P. (2014). *Quantum Machine Learning: What Quantum Computing Means to Data Mining*. Academic Press.
19. Emmanoulopoulos, D., & Dimoska, S. (2022). Quantum machine learning in finance: Time series forecasting. arXiv preprint *arXiv:2202.00599*.
20. Dallaire-Demers, P. L., & Killoran, N. (2018). Quantum generative adversarial networks. *Physical Review A*, *98*(1), 012324.

Index

E

N

Q

For Product Safety Concerns and Information please contact our EU representative GPSR@taylorandfrancis.com Taylor & Francis Verlag GmbH, Kaufingerstraße 24, 80331 München, Germany